Dive Deeper

DIVE DEEPER

Journeys with *Moby-Dick*

George Cotkin

OXFORD
UNIVERSITY PRESS

OXFORD
UNIVERSITY PRESS

Oxford University Press is a department of the University of Oxford.
It furthers the University's objective of excellence in research,
scholarship, and education by publishing worldwide.

Oxford   New York
Auckland   Cape Town   Dar es Salaam   Hong Kong   Karachi
Kuala Lumpur   Madrid   Melbourne   Mexico City   Nairobi
New Delhi   Shanghai   Taipei   Toronto

With offices in
Argentina   Austria   Brazil   Chile   Czech Republic   France   Greece
Guatemala   Hungary   Italy   Japan   Poland   Portugal   Singapore
South Korea   Switzerland   Thailand   Turkey   Ukraine   Vietnam

Published in the United States of America by Oxford University Press
198 Madison Avenue, New York, NY 10016

www.oup.com

Oxford is a registered trade mark of Oxford University Press in the UK and certain other countries.

Library of Congress Cataloging-in-Publication Data
Cotkin, George, 1950–
Dive deeper : journeys with Moby-Dick / George Cotkin.
   p.   cm.
Includes bibliographical references and index.
ISBN 978-0-19-985573-5 (cloth : alk. paper)—ISBN 978-0-19-985575-9 (pbk. : alk. paper)
1. Melville, Herman, 1819-1891. Moby Dick. 2. Sea stories, American—History and criticism.
3. Mass media and literature. I. Title.
PS2384.M62C67   2012
813'.3—dc23   2011045737

9 8 7 6 5 4 3 2 1

Printed in the United States of America
on acid-free paper

For great friends and scholars:
Casey Blake
Jim Hoopes
Nelson Lichtenstein
Kevin Mattson
Robert Rydell
Ann Schofield

TABLE OF CONTENTS

A NOTE TO READERS

"Have ye seen the White Whale?" This query fixes Ahab's attention whenever his ship has a chance encounter with other vessels on the high seas. Today such a question strikes us as silly. After all, *Moby-Dick* is anchored in the canon of great literature and afloat in the oceans of popular culture. It is perhaps America's greatest novel.

Moby-Dick is *our* book because of its formidable themes. "To produce a mighty book," Melville realized, "you must choose a mighty theme." And you must approach such themes with guts and gusto. Melville dared to use "Vesuvius as an ink stand" as he rattled off pages that confront the meaning of existence and possibility of God. Indeed, Melville wanted in *Moby-Dick* to dive deeper into these issues. Contemporary readers, too, can dive into the novel in order to ruminate about issues such as totalitarianism and terror, race, gender, sexuality, class, colonialism, and the value of friendship.

Since the early twentieth century, poets and philosophers, writers and artists, ad men and cartoonists, filmmakers and composers, playwrights and comedians have turned to *Moby-Dick* for inspiration and material. Such encounters with the book, brilliant and bemused, enduring and ephemeral, insightful and muddled, are all part of the biography of a book and its readers. This is the subject matter of *Dive Deeper*.

Today, when imperial hubris and a cocky sureness reign, we need *Moby-Dick* more than ever. It is a book that honors its readers by shaking their foundations.

An early reviewer chided Melville for composing a "chowder" of a book. *Moby-Dick* does mix genres, abuse narrative conventions, lose characters, veer into fascinating tangents, and commit other presumed sins. Then again, Melville probably found chowder an appetizing meal, and it works as a method.

Dive Deeper, too, is something of a "chowder" of a book. It respects and mimics Melville's signal contribution to modernist and postmodernist creativity by linking each of its chapters to one in the novel, by dint of phrase, symbol, content, or rhythm. Each chapter herein opens with a brief summary of what is happening in the corresponding chapter of the original volume. It helps to keep in mind that *Moby-Dick* is about a chase, after meaning as much as in pursuit of a whale.

Melville begins *Moby-Dick* with Ishmael in a confessional mode, and I will return the favor. Over the last few decades, I have made it a practice to reread the novel once every five years or so. I have long been attracted to its tragic and rebellious aspects, to its existential undertow. It forces me to think more about the possibilities and pitfalls of life. And it stirs the chowder of my creativity.

In the summer of 2008, along with my wife and in-laws, I went on an Alaskan cruise-ship vacation. What better novel to pack for the trip than *Moby-Dick*? I reread it while whales bounded about and excesses of food and comfort beckoned aboard. It was then that I decided that I must spend more time with *Moby-Dick*. But what could I do with this novel that had already attracted a universe of commentary? In time, I took to heart Melville's imperative to dive deeper, to try for something more creative.

Enough explanation. Let us raise the Blue Peter flag that signals our ship's readiness to embark into the immense sea of meaning, representation, and creativity that is the living legacy of *Moby-Dick*.

Dive Deeper

Etymology

(Supplied by a Late Consumptive Usher to a Grammar School)

The pale Usher—threadbare in coat, heart, body, and brain; I see him now. He was ever dusting his old lexicons and grammars, with a queer handkerchief, mockingly embellished with all the gay flags of all the known nations of the world. He loved to dust his old grammars; it somehow mildly reminded him of his mortality.

> "What the white whale was to Ahab, has been hinted; what, at times, he was to me, as yet remains unsaid."
>
> Ishmael, quoted in *Moby-Dick; or, The Whale* (1851), chapter 42, "The Whiteness of the Whale."

Moby-Dick—name commonly associated with the novel written by Herman Melville. First appeared as, *The Whale*, published in England in October 1851 by Richard Bentley. Published on a cold November day in 1851 in the United States by Harper's, with the full title, *Moby-Dick; or, The Whale*. The American edition, in contrast to the British, included the Epilogue. It, like Ishmael, "escaped to tell thee." 12mo., 635 pages in length.

Moby Dick—without the mysterious hyphen, refers to the White Whale, the leviathan that is the symbol of . . . First well-publicized sighting reported by Jeremiah N. Reynolds in an article titled "Mocha Dick" in the *Knicker-bocker Magazine* in May, 1839. He refers to this leviathan as "an old bull whale, of prodigious size and strength, . . . *white as wool*." It has been reported earlier by Mr. Owen Chase that in November 1820, a "very large spermaceti whale," perhaps eighty-five feet long, "with tenfold fury and vengeance in his aspect" did attack and sink the good ship *Essex*, originating from Nantucket.

"Moby-Dickering"—term coined by Charles Poore in 1952 to refer to endless debates about symbols and meaning of *Moby-Dick*.

Moby-Dick has been published in nearly all the languages of the known world.

Extracts

(Supplied by a Sub-Sub-Librarian)

It will be seen that this mere painstaking burrower and grub-worm of a poor devil of a Sub-Sub appears to have gone through the long library corridors and information highways, picking up whatever random allusions to *Moby-Dick* he could anyways find in any book or digital preserve whatsoever, sacred or profane. Therefore you must not, in every case at least, take the higgledy-piggledy statements, however authentic, in these extracts, for veritable gospel criticism. Far from it. As touching Melville's contemporary critics generally, these extracts are solely valuable or entertaining, as affording a glancing bird's eye view of what has been promiscuously said, thought, fancied, and sung of *Moby-Dick*, by many nations and generations, including our own.

EXTRACTS

"I love men who *dive*."
   Melville (1849)

"[H]e who has never felt, momentarily, what madness is has but a mouthful of brains."
   Melville (1849)

"[A] strange sort of book, tho', I fear; blubber is blubber you know, tho' you may get oil out of it."
   Melville (1850)

"[A] book in a man's brain is better off than a book bound in calf—at any rate it is safer from criticism."

Melville (1850)

"Let any clergyman try to preach the Truth from its very stronghold, the pulpit, and they would ride him out of his church."

Melville (1851)

"Though I wrote the Gospels in this century, I should die in the gutter."
Melville (1851)

"Dollars damn me; and the malicious Devil is forever grinning upon me, holding the door ajar."

Melville (1851)

"[A]ll my books are botches."
Melville (1851)

"I stand for the heart. To the dogs with the head!"
Melville (1851)

"Think of it! To go down to posterity is bad enough, any way; but to go down as a 'man who lived among the cannibals'!"

Melville (1851)

"This is the book's motto (the secret one),—Ego non baptizo te in nomine—but make out the rest yourself."

Melville (1851)

"A Polar wind blows through it, & birds of prey hover over it."
Melville (1851)

"I have written a wicked book, and feel spotless as a lamb."
Melville (1851)

"Leviathan is not the biggest fish;—I have heard of Krakens."
Melville (1851)

"[R]ising to the verge of sublime."
London *Morning Advertiser* (October 24, 1851)

"[A]n ill-compounded mixture of romance and matter-of-fact."

London *Athenaeum* (October 25, 1851)

"Who would have looked for philosophy in whales, or for poetry in blubber."

London *John Bull* (October 25, 1851)

"[A] bulky, queer looking volume, in some respects, 'very like a whale' even in outward appearance."

New Bedford *Daily Mercury* (November 18, 1851)

"[N]ot worth the money."

Boston Post (November 20, 1851)

"This volume of Moby Dick may be pronounced a most remarkable sea-dish—an intellectual chowder of romance, philosophy, natural history, fine writing, good feeling, bad sayings."

Evert Duyckinck, New York *Literary World* (November 22, 1851)

"No one can tire of this volume."

Philadelphia *Saturday Courier* (November 22, 1851)

"We regret to see that Mr. Melville is guilty of sneering at the truths of revealed religion."

New York *Commercial Advertiser* (November 28, 1851)

"'Moby Dick, or the Whale,' is all whale."

New York *Spirit of the Times* (December 6, 1851)

"[U]nfit for general circulation."

New York *Methodist Quarterly Review* (January, 1852)

"Who is this madman" [?]

New York *Christian Intelligencer* (January 22, 1857)

"[A] trick of metaphysical and morbid meditations until he has almost perverted his fine mind from its healthy, productive tendencies."

Fitz-James O'Brien (1857)

"[I]t is a medley of noble impassioned thoughts born of the deep."

W. Clark Russell (1884)

"[W]hat a queer yarn it is."
    Boston Post (October 2, 1891)

"[A] turbulent and misty spray."
    Donald G. Mitchell (1899)

"Not in his subject alone, but in his style is Melville distinctly American."
                    Archibald MacMechan (1899)

"[A] rather strained rhapsody with whaling for a subject and not a single sincere line."
                    Joseph Conrad (1907)

"[R]eads like a great opium dream."
    Raymond C. Weaver (1919)

"[A]n extraordinary work in morals."
    Frank Jewett Mather Jr. (1919)

"[The whale's] whiteness is both the sign and veil of his mystery."
                    E. L. Grant Watson (1920)

"[I]t is not everybody's book."
    Frank Swinnerton (1921)

"He is fate, this Moby Dick, and the terrible old Captain Ahab is the tragic will of man which defies it and tracks it down, only to be overwhelmed and to perish by it."
                    Van Wyck Brooks (1921)

"[I]f it captures you, then you are unafraid of great art."
                    H. M. Tomlinson (1921)

"Of course he is a symbol. Of what? I doubt if even Melville knew exactly. That's the best of it."
                    D. H. Lawrence (1922)

"What then is Moby Dick?—He is the deepest blood-being of the white race."
                    D. H. Lawrence (1922)

"Of Captain Ahab I should never stop talking if I once began."

Van Wyck Brooks (1923)

"Of rimless floods, unfettered leewardings"

Hart Crane (c. 1924)

"Monody shall not wake the mariner.
This fabulous shadow only the sea keeps."
Hart Crane (1925)

"a most solemn, mystic work"

Rockwell Kent (1926)

"May the shade of Herman Melville therefore forgive me the liberty I have taken."

A. E. W. Blake, abridger (1926)

A "prophetic song, flows athwart the action and the surface morality like an undercurrent. It lies outside words."

E. M. Forster (1927)

"I wish I had written" it.
William Faulkner (1927)

Moby-Dick has "the kind of truth few men are able to put in words."

Archibald MacLeish (1929)

"Each age, one may predict, will find its own symbols in *Moby-Dick*."

Lewis Mumford (1929)

"a labyrinth, and that labyrinth is the universe."

Lewis Mumford (1929)

"The whale is a metaphysical image of the Universe."

Hart Crane (1932)

"the great poem, the epic of Puritan civilization, and to have marked a turning-point in its evolution, if not quite its end."

Conrad Aiken (1937)

"kept me in a state of almost continuous excitement."
C. L. R. James (1944)

"This captain, Ahab by name, knew space. He rode it across seven seas."
Charles Olson (1947)

"Like Ahab, American, one aim: lordship over nature."
Charles Olson (1947)

"a symbolic smash-up of the American world."
Richard Chase (1949)

"harpoons, lances, cutting-spades."
Newton Arvin (1950)

"a book about dictatorship"
Donald Weeks (1950)

"boring!"
Press Survey of Students (1950)

"not a neat book"
Gordon H. Mills (1950)

"The White Whale is the disguised form of the hermaphroditic mystery."
Harry Slochower (1950)

"Beethoven's *Eroica* in words."
Henry A. Murray (1951)

"Why didn't the men revolt?"
C. L. R. James (1952)

"ablaze with anger"
R. W. B. Lewis (1955)

Ishmael "embodies for us man as a thinker"
Alfred Kazin (1956)

"not a mystery . . . it is a book about a mystery."
Harry Levin (1958)

"Ishmael has a story too, but it is chiefly left to our imaginations."
Granville Hicks (1958)

"[A] love story . . . cast in the peculiar American form of innocent homosexuality."
Leslie Fiedler (1960)

"Ahab's pursuit of the whale . . . is both a search for significant evil and for his own identity."
Lowry Nelson, Jr. (1962)

"a Doomsday book about water"
Edward Dahlberg (1962)

"[Ahab] dared, and made that murderous death-white whale kill him . . . He permitted suicide."
Edwin S. Shneidman (1963)

"Melville is not a novelist: he is an annotator and labeler."
Brigid Brophy et. al. (1967)

"[The doubloon is] a fit symbol of symbols."
Paul Royster (1986)

"Like a classic hysteric, Ahab has presented himself rhetorically as a flaming queen."
David Leverenz (1989)

"[*Moby-Dick* is Melville's] quest to give masculinity cosmic force."
Camille Paglia (1991)

"One question underlies all of *Moby-Dick*: 'So what's eating you?'"
K. L. Evans (2003)

"in Melville that part of what makes him great is his immense ambition."
Tony Kushner (2005)

"Modern American literature . . . begins with *Moby-Dick*."

E. L. Doctorow (2006)

"Each time I reread it, it is as if I am reading it for the first time."

Philip Hoare (2008)

"[*Moby-Dick*] is the sea we swim in."

Greil Marcus (2009)

"I propose to live like Melville."

Anthony Caleshu (2010)

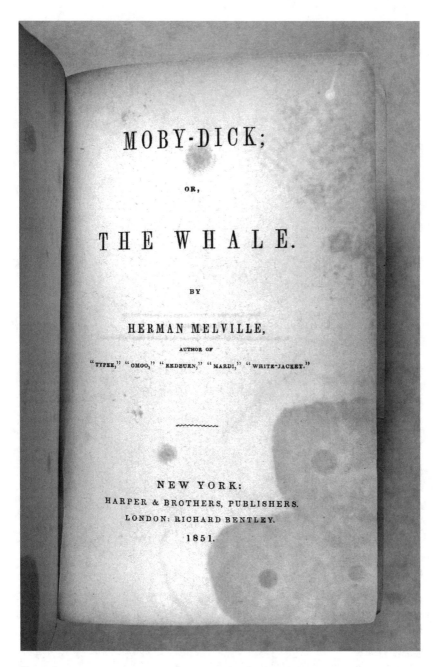

Figure 1.
Rare first edition of *Moby-Dick*, owned by Samuel Willard, killed in the Civil War.

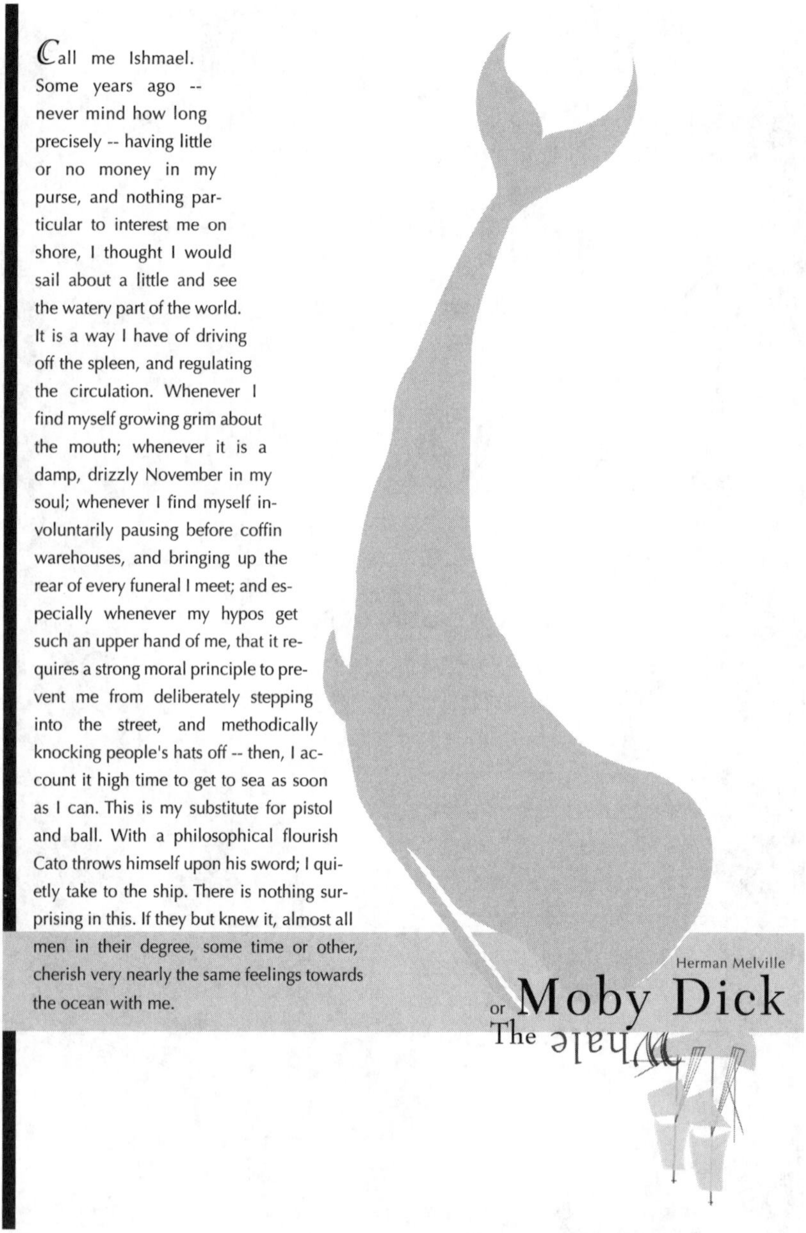

Call me Ishmael. Some years ago -- never mind how long precisely -- having little or no money in my purse, and nothing particular to interest me on shore, I thought I would sail about a little and see the watery part of the world. It is a way I have of driving off the spleen, and regulating the circulation. Whenever I find myself growing grim about the mouth; whenever it is a damp, drizzly November in my soul; whenever I find myself involuntarily pausing before coffin warehouses, and bringing up the rear of every funeral I meet; and especially whenever my hypos get such an upper hand of me, that it requires a strong moral principle to prevent me from deliberately stepping into the street, and methodically knocking people's hats off -- then, I account it high time to get to sea as soon as I can. This is my substitute for pistol and ball. With a philosophical flourish Cato throws himself upon his sword; I quietly take to the ship. There is nothing surprising in this. If they but knew it, almost all men in their degree, some time or other, cherish very nearly the same feelings towards the ocean with me.

Herman Melville

or Moby Dick

The Whale

Figure 2.
"From a Whale's Point of View." Illustration by Andrea Bryant, 2008.

CHAPTER 1

Loomings

ISHMAEL EXPLAINS WHY HE GOES WHALING

"Call Me Ishmael"—hands down the most famous opening line in American literature. These three words are as striking and clear as an old church bell ringing in the noon hour. They are friendly, beckoning words that alert readers to the symbolism and mystery that power the novel.

Two contemporary cartoons capture the allure of these three magical words. Gary Larson plays with the opening line in one cartoon. A writer is huddled over his desk, around him are discarded pieces of paper. They read, variously, "Call me Larry," "Call Me Warren," "Call Me Al." Ishmael has yet to emerge victorious. Or, in a *New Yorker* magazine cartoon a man says to a woman at a bar, "You'll probably think this is just some opening line, but . . . Call Me Ishmael."

The Book of Genesis tells us that Ishmael was the son of Hagar, by way of aged Abraham. But Sarah, Abraham's wife, grew jealous. Ishmael was exiled, fated to wander the earth. He became the father of princes who would unite one day to found a nation. As narrator of Melville's novel, Ishmael, in his own manner, brings forth a mighty new continent of the mind.

Ishmael looms in "Loomings" as credulous, drawn to tall tales, and open to possibilities. His story about the immense stature and power of the White Whale and Captain Ahab makes Godzilla and Paul Bunyan seem diminutive in comparison.

On the first page of *Moby-Dick* we learn that Ishmael harbors thoughts of suicide, especially when he feels that "damp, drizzly November" in his afflicted soul, and he is overly prone to self-examination. Instead of "pistol and ball," he opts for the sea, for adventure and paycheck. While he considers the sea palliative for a storm-tossed soul, he maintains that "meditation and water are wedded for ever." If so, then this bodes to be a rocky marriage.

The irony, of course, is that in casting off to sea, Ishmael has signed onto a vessel bound for a suicidal reckoning with the White Whale of meaning.

French writer Albert Camus famously opened his book *The Myth of Sisyphus* (1942) by remarking: "There is only one really serious philosophical question, and that is suicide. Deciding whether or not life is worth living is to answer the fundamental question in philosophy. All other questions follow from that."

Camus decided against suicide, although he trembled at its compelling logic. He had known crushing poverty as a child. Much of his adult life was spent chained to his tuberculosis—"my secret anguish," he called it. Chills and sweats, weakness and coughing fits wracked his body. His yen for cigarettes could be seen as a suicidal wish. For Camus it was more of a protest—affirmation of pleasure over prudence. He embraced life, in all of its sensual pleasures and horrendous realities, its cherished dreams and chaotic contingencies. He recognized the absurd nature of existence—the deep distance between our desires and the tricks played upon them by an indifferent reality. Resignation he considered a form of suicide. Camus's story of the demigod Sisyphus, punished to roll a boulder up a hill for eternity, always to find it tumbling down anew, was not a resounding tragedy. Sisyphus had chosen life. Even with the backbreaking labor of his toil, Camus concludes that "one must imagine Sisyphus happy."

Camus found Melville's writing, especially *Moby-Dick*, "bursting with health, strength, upsurges of humour, and human laughter." All in the matter of a chase that fate had decreed must end with Ahab's demise—for Captain Ahab is a man "driven mad by grief and loneliness" and no small amount of hubris. Camus thrilled to Ahab's willingness to question the essential nature of creation. But in directing his metaphysical anger with such fanaticism, Ahab succumbed to the urge for domination, the totalitarian principle that had darkened a decade of Camus's life and devastated most of the European continent.

Rebellion, rather than resignation, against the scourge of totalitarianism became Camus's credo. Unlike Ahab, he was attracted to sweet reasonableness; he aspired to be neither victim nor executioner. Moderation—exemplified by Starbuck, the first mate aboard the *Pequod*—has its allures. But one imagines that Camus, unlike Starbuck, would not have buckled to Ahab's will.

Ishmael and Camus are fellow voyagers. Ishmael, by chance or by divine intervention, survives the ordeal; he lives to tell his story. He celebrates the plurality of life and chafes against the will to dominate. Camus lived long enough—though he died at the age of forty-six—to create his own stories and essays that remain instructive about how we can engage the world without reducing it to our own self-indulgent desires. The world plays tricks upon us; existence is an ironic tome. Yet we struggle to persevere.

CHAPTER 2
The Carpet-Bag

ISHMAEL HUNTS FOR LODGING IN NEW BEDFORD

Wandering the wintry, "dreary" streets of New Bedford on a cold Saturday night, Ishmael searches for a warm place to sleep. One establishment's front door appears welcoming but upon opening a second door, he finds himself an object of attention, both for the color of his skin and for the ruckus he has caused by tripping over an "ash box." He has chanced upon a black church and the one hundred or so parishioners who are "weeping and wailing and teeth-gnashing" as they listen to a sermon on the blackness of blackness. Presumably, they are being serenaded by a sermon about the horrors of hell.

Regaining his composure, Ishmael flees, soon ending up at the Spouter Inn. Will the Spouter Inn be any brighter than the blackness of blackness foretold in the church?

On a cold December evening in 1840, Melville perambulated through New Bedford's streets, anticipating shipping out on a whaler. At that moment another young man, Frederick Douglass, was in the town. Only a few years earlier, he had escaped from Baltimore and life as a slave. New Bedford, with its large population of antislavery Quakers and free and runaway African-Americans, was a comfortable place for Douglass to live with his wife, Anna, and their two children. Comfortable but hardly ideal. Churches remained segregated by race, as did employment possibilities.

Douglass had hoped to ply his trade as a ship's caulker, but many whites resented working side-by-side with a black man. He was forced to labor for less pay by hauling supplies on and off ships. Within a few years, however, Douglass emerged as a great orator, preaching for the abolition of slavery and authoring one of the classics of American literature, a narrative of his life as a slave, published in 1845.

Is it entirely fanciful to imagine that the black minister quickly glimpsed presiding over "the great Black Parliament" in the New Bedford church, mentioned in this chapter, was Frederick Douglass? By 1841, Douglass was an "exhorter" in the church ministered by Thomas James, himself an escaped slave. There, Douglass honed his oratorical skills on his favored topic: the abolition of slavery. When Douglass spoke about the blackness of hell, he was referring to the institution of slavery. By the time Melville sailed on the *Acushnet*, Douglass was a force in antislavery circles, someone who could testify personally to the evils of the institution, to the fire its horrible whip left upon the flesh.

Douglass and Melville were two giants of nineteenth-century American culture. Even if they missed one another that winter in New Bedford, both were riveted to the central questions of their era: could America exist as a nation half-slave and half-free and are there essential differences between the races?

Melville tended to keep his political cards close to his vest. In his better moments, he embraced a genuinely democratic and humane attitude about slavery and race. At other times, his ideal of Unionism undermined his take on slavery. But concerns with slavery are sprinkled throughout *Moby-Dick*. While he was writing his tome, the Fugitive Slave Act of 1850 had been passed. His father-in-law, Judge Lemuel Shaw, had ruled that, in accordance with the law, an escaped slave named Thomas Sims must be wrenched from freedom in Boston and returned to servitude in the South.

Are the crossracial friendship between Ishmael and Queequeg and the musing about the whiteness of the whale commentaries on the vexing question of race? Is Ahab leading the ship of the American state into uncharted, dangerous seas?

Perhaps the most astute comments about politics of *Moby-Dick* came from a contemporary of Melville. James McCune Smith, an African-American polymath (abolitionist, physician, essayist, and educator) dropped a reference to *Moby-Dick* in a piece, "Horoscope," which appeared in the abolitionist sheets of *Frederick Douglass' Paper* in March 1856. Smith had, in all probability, also read Melville's *Typee*. He may well have been responsible for a "Literary Notice" about publication of *Moby-Dick* in *Douglass' Paper* that was recorded in an earlier issue. Smith deplored the divisions and lack of leadership among African-Americans. All too often, he announced, blacks felt "repulsion" towards other blacks, preferring for instance to shop at a white-owned rather than a black-run grocery store. Blacks, he claimed, were less supportive than whites in the north (by a margin of 10 to 1!) of the "manly resistance" of a Frederick Douglass against oppression.

"Horoscope" also found the antislavery leadership of William Seward and Horace Greeley inadequate, not "morally fitted to advance the cause of Human Freedom." Smith wrote that they reminded him of Stubb ("a boat-steerer"), the third in command on the *Pequod*, who in the final chase after *Moby-Dick* tells his rowing men to "start her [their craft] like thunderclaps," while also warning them "Don't hurry yourselves; take plenty of time." Such contradictory messages, coming from Stubb—echoed by Seward and Greeley—boded ill for realizing what Smith held most dear: true "HUMAN BROTHERHOOD" [as between Ishmael and Queequeg]. What was needed, averred Smith, were leaders "seized and possessed in the innermost fibers of their being with a full and cordial belief that all men are by nature *free* and *equal*."

Ahab possesses the iron backbone of a John Brown. And he is willing to go through the gates of hell in pursuit of the White Whale. But he is a fanatic and a tyrant—and that is invariably a devastating combination.

Figure 3.
Would Ishmael have fared better here? "Moby Dick Inn," Photograph by Chad Perry.

CHAPTER 3

The Spouter-Inn

ISHMAEL FINDS A PLACE FOR THE NIGHT AND AN UNANTICIPATED BEDMATE

Moby-Dick is about seeing. From the masthead of the *Pequod* a sailor scans the ocean for the telltale spouting of whales. Whenever Ahab comes across another ship, he enquires: "Have ye seen a White Whale?"

Sight is limited, sometimes by our monomania, which allows us to see only what we desire to see. Sometimes the images and their meaning pile one upon another, as if a camel's hump had been transposed upon the back of a whale.

Ishmael's manner of viewing the world is of the latter variety. His disposition is to take it all in, to see plurality where others see singularity. His vision, however, is often compromised by a surrounding darkness. Adequate light is to seeing as sufficient air is to breathing.

When he enters the Spouter-Inn, Ishmael encounters a large painting. He tries to discern its shapes but is stymied at first by the "dim light." Strange but compelling "masses of shades and shadows" slowly emerge. He opens a window to gain additional illumination and quickly realizes that the "black mass of something hovering in the centre of the picture" could be many things, from the "Black Sea in a midnight gale" to the "breaking of the icebound stream of Time" or, most apt for the story that follows, "the great Leviathan itself."

Loitering around the painting, and after consulting with "aged" connoisseurs of the image, Ishmael concludes that his first impression was correct: the painting depicts nothing less than "chaos bewitched"—a ship is sinking off Cape Horn, its masts alone above water. Most inexplicably, "an exasperated whale" is apparently in the act of leaping above the ship, "in the enormous act of impaling himself upon three masts."

Such a reading, of course, sparkles with anticipation, with foreboding of Ishmael's forthcoming voyage. But he fails to comprehend the premonition. This is reminiscent of Ishmael's contemporary Elizabeth Peabody, who after walking into a tree exclaimed: "I saw it but I did not realize it."

Later in the chapter, after much back and forth with Mr. Coffin, proprietor of the Spouter-Inn, Ishmael finally settles into a large bed for the night. He knows that he will be sharing it with a harpooner, rumored to have been walking the local streets peddling a shrunken head. When Queequeg finally enters the dark chamber, Ishmael is again forced to rely upon his limited powers of observation. He discerns tattoos covering the body of his roommate, but only haltingly does he see that Queequeg is, in the parlance of the time, a savage—moreover, a savage who takes himself to bed with tomahawk in hand.

Ishmael soon realizes that Queequeg is a rather fine fellow. The problem with vision at first glance, or the formation of judgments based upon prejudice, is that "Ignorance is the parent of fear." Once his ignorance has been sated, Ishmael gathers that however different Queequeg's skin coloration and markings, the odd idol that he worships, or the strange garments he wears, Queequeg is a "human being just as I am." Thus, it is "Better to sleep with a sober cannibal than a drunken Christian." Not surprisingly, Ishmael awakens to find himself having "never slept better."

Figure 4.
Ishmael and Queequeg sleep together, Woodcut by Rockwell Kent.

CHAPTER 4

The Counterpane

A "SAVAGE" SPENDS THE NIGHT WITH ISHMAEL

Ishmael arises to find bedmate Queequeg's arm "thrown over me in the most loving and affectionate manner. You had almost thought I had been his wife." The homoerotic intonation of the relationship between Ishmael and Queequeg has long been obvious to discerning readers. Newton Arvin was, perhaps, the first scholar to call attention to it.

Arvin was happiest in the late 1940s when he was composing his biography of Herman Melville and waking up in the morning with his arm around his own partner, the youthful, immensely talented writer, Truman Capote. A respected literary critic with a tenured position at Smith College in Northampton, Massachusetts, Arvin had been married to a former student, but it did nothing to dampen his homosexuality. By the early 1940s, he had slumped into middle age and suffered a nervous breakdown, spending time in an asylum. His life was at loose ends, with a future that appeared to be written in dark ink.

Events took a fortuitous turn when Arvin arrived at the Yaddo Writer's Community in Saratoga, New York, in June 1946. Forty-five years of age, he met the fetching twenty-one-year-old Capote. Almost immediately, they were smitten with one another. The relationship proved to be invaluable for both men. Capote found Arvin a wonderful mentor and father figure. At Arvin's behest, Capote reread American classics, including *Moby-Dick*, and he listened to Arvin recite passages from his work-in-progress on Melville. In turn, Capote opened Arvin up to a world of unrestrained gay sexuality.

Initially, Arvin was aglow with love. He socialized with Capote and his uncloseted gay pals, and he even delighted in showing off his young lover. A young colleague remembered Arvin was like "a bridegroom . . . introducing his bride." While Arvin hankered to escape from the closet, he was horrified about any harm that might be caused to his academic reputation. Writing to Capote, he admitted, "I am an impostor. Won't I some time be caught and exposed?"

He had good reason for his fears. The postwar years trembled with extreme anxiety about male sexuality. Public leaders and writers worried loudly if men had been reduced by their wives and mothers to effeminate wimps. Such anxiety, moreover, fed into Red Scare fears and resulted in gays being dismissed in huge numbers as "security risks" from government positions. Publication of Alfred Kinsey's *Sexual Behavior in the Human Male* (1948) steamed readers up with its findings that at least one-third of adult males had engaged in some form of homosexual activity. At this moment of heated discussion about male sexuality—the Kinsey report was on the *New York Times* bestseller list for twenty-seven weeks—Arvin published his analysis of Melville's sexuality and homosocial themes in *Moby-Dick*.

Arvin must have identified with Ishmael's suicidal thoughts, desire to escape, and embrace with Queequeg. In Arvin's view, Ishmael (via Melville) carried lots of baggage, harboring his own Freudian *thanatos* or death wish. This arose, in part, because of his failure to achieve human connection—note that Ishmael is the prototypical outcast or orphan. And, as Ishmael relates in this chapter, his stepmother was cold and unloving.

Eros, the psychic need for love and fellowship, thankfully intervenes, sweeping Thanatos aside. Ishmael falls in love with his newfound friend. Alas, Ahab, with his own will to self-destruction, undermines any full, long-term working-out of their erotic attachment. But the power of love endures, at least in a metaphorical manner. The ship goes down and all seems to be lost; Ishmael is on the verge of being swallowed up by the sea. At this moment, he latches onto the sole remaining manifestation of Queequeg's goodwill—his wooden coffin which has been refashioned into a life buoy. Ishmael is rescued by the good ship *Rachel*, allowed to survive and tell his story of Ahab and the White Whale.

Arvin finds a perfect postwar parable in the love that passes between Ishmael and Queequeg. At a time when critics derided homosexuality and the effeminacy of modern American males, Arvin introduces us to figures of power and determination that are comfortable in their homoeroticism. In contrast, Ahab the bellowing heterosexual character—with wife and child awaiting his return to Nantucket—is sexually crippled (gone is his "capacity for heterosexual love"). He is a chaste monster of desire, focused only on revenge against Moby Dick. Arvin also brings to the surface Melville's own ambivalent relations with his parents, his devastation at the loss of his father, his antagonism and desire for his mother, and his need to find love and affection, with both men and women.

While Arvin had briefly discovered Eros and companionship with Capote, the relationship was doomed for many reasons: differences in age and experience, Arvin's contradictory desires for scholarly solitude and boisterous affection. By the 1950s, alone and with his literary fame unable to sustain his sense of self, Arvin plunged back into a depressive, suicidal state.

He now sought sexual satisfaction with rough trade in rundown bus stations. In 1960, his small, secure world came crashing down when police raided his Northampton apartment, confiscating various magazines and photographs that they deemed to be homosexual and pornographic. Arvin faced his worst nightmare—a public trial, knowledge on the part of friends and colleagues about his homosexuality, and the end of his teaching career. Under pressure, he provided the police with the names of two fellow homosexuals, paid a fine, and received a suspended jail term. Soon he was back in hospital and sanitarium, riddled with thoughts of suicide as the easiest means of escape. Some surcease was found in a biographical study of Henry Wadsworth Longfellow. Upon concluding his final book, Arvin suddenly began having excruciating stomach pain that was diagnosed as incurable pancreatic cancer. He died in March 1963.

CHAPTER 5

Breakfast

QUEEQUEG AND ISHMAEL BREAKFAST

Humor is the ballast that keeps afloat Melville's ship of tragedy. Ishmael notes that "a good laugh is a mighty good thing, and rather too scarce a good thing." The jokes directed at Ishmael by Peter Coffin, the proprietor of the Spouter-Inn, are good-natured. Yet, in directing barbs at others, one

Figure 5.
A tragic novel generates humor: "Moby Dick Meets Mr. and Mrs. Avocado," Photograph by Kim Weston.

should never confuse appearance with reality. Beneath surface affection or tomfoolery may be something deeper, something more substantive.

Irony, satire, puns, and jokes—all are part of Melville's arsenal. Melville sails the traditional waters of American humor with its emphasis on the tall tale, the frontier setting (the vast sea replaces the open wilderness), myth, and fantasy. American humor is central to the American character— defining it and also mocking its pretensions. Also in the tradition of American humor, as Melville well recognized, is a sardonic, "ultimate secret" that is to be revealed.

A critic once observed that there is a good deal of "cheerful nihilism" in the pages of *Moby-Dick*. Melville was consciously following the path blazed by such masters of eviscerating wit as Rabelais, Bayle, Jonson, Sterne, De Quincey, and, of course, Shakespeare. Comedic and satirical elements in *Moby-Dick* allowed Melville some impunity when he tossed his harpoon into the cherished presumptions of his era. Well before Freud, Melville sensed that jokes are rarely benign. They bubble up from the deepest levels of our fears and anxieties in what appear to be an acceptable, even jovial form.

The vast cultural divide between Ishmael and Queequeg allows Melville to skewer, with "corrosive whimsy" in the words of John Bryant, Christian professions of superiority and morality. What could be more absurd—in both comedic and tragic terms—than to have Ahab pushing himself and crew across oceans in mad pursuit of a mysterious whale? How but through the humor filling the chapters on the "science" of cetology and on the nature of the whale's whiteness, could Melville aim his barbs at both science and theology?

The cosmic joke that hits hard in *Moby-Dick* is not about whether there is a God. It is about why such a God should be so distant or mean-spirited. Does this deity take perverse pleasure in joking with the lives of so many poor souls? This may be the "ultimate secret" that Melville's humor seeks to reveal. Or, maybe the point is that the joke is on us?

CHAPTER 6

The Street

ISHMAEL WANDERS THE STREETS OF NEW BEDFORD

The polyglot town of New Bedford astonishes and delights Ishmael. Rather than being pegged as "outlandish" in this town, his pal Queequeg is merely one of many odd-looking and oddly named specimens of humanity from around the globe. "Feegeeans, Tongatabooans, Erromanggoans, Pannangians, and Brighggians" bustle about with "green Vermonters and New Hampshire men, all athirst for gain and glory in the fishery." As Ishmael ambles about, he pauses to admire the rosy bloom on New Bedford's young women. He marvels, too, at the stately mansions erected upon the foundation of a business based in blubber.

Ishmael wandered the streets of New Bedford at the end of the great age of whaling. By the late 1830s, more whaling ships sailed from its port than from all the others in the world. Ten thousand men were employed in the New Bedford business of whaling.

These numbers soon began to droop. In 1859, discovery of petroleum in Pennsylvania undermined the necessity for whale oil to banish the darkness of night. New Bedford rode out this decline, in part, by building a plant to process this new oil source. Whaling continued but in more straitened circumstances. In 1871, ice claimed twenty-two whaling ships from New Bedford off the coast of Alaska. By 1925, the age of whaling in New Bedford had ended.

The city proved to be resilient, soon becoming a major textile-manufacturing center—at least until the 1970s when that industry deserted for warmer climes and cheaper, non-union labor. New Bedford's attention, however, never drifted away from the sea. The city remains today a key fishing port, with over 250 ships trolling, mostly for scallops. Cargo from around the world passes through its docks, and even some gargantuan cruise ships make it a port of call. It is also home to a great whaling museum, a must-see for all fans of *Moby-Dick*.

Alas, New Bedford is a grim city. With the decline of the textile mills and an epidemic of drug use, the city became a haven for crime and poverty. One-fifth of its population lives below the poverty line. Crime abounds. In 1983, a young woman named Cheryl Araujo was gang-raped in Big Dan's bar—an incident made famous by the film *The Accused*, starring Jodie Foster. In 2001, a drug bust netted over 600 pounds of cocaine—a white-powdered fantasy pursued by many, generations after Ahab.

CHAPTER 7

The Chapel

ISHMAEL ENTERS THE WHALEMAN'S CHAPEL FOR SUNDAY SERVICE

Cold marble tablets on the walls of the Whaleman's Chapel in New Bedford speak to the grim reality of the whaling profession. It is nearly a suicidal enterprise, stinking of death.

Concerns of death and immortality, suicide and hope haunted poet Hart Crane's life and work. When he was twenty-three years old, and feeling sulky at finding himself back in provincial Cleveland after living a bohemian life in New York City, he discovered *Moby-Dick*. He read it alongside other monuments of modernism, T. S. Eliot's *The Waste Land* and James Joyce's *Ulysses* (smuggled into the United States by a friend). The homosexual Crane rhapsodized about how *Moby-Dick* offered "half-exciting erotic suggestions of dear Queequeg." Crane would read the novel three or four times over the next decade; a handful of months before he took his own life in 1932, Crane saluted *Moby-Dick* as "tremendous and tragic."

Crane was perhaps the first American artist to gulp down *Moby-Dick* and funnel its themes, atmosphere, and prose into his own work. In October 1925, Crane penned "At Melville's Tomb," a monody resonant with his own artistic concerts about the sea, love, and hope. The poem, a centerpiece of American modernism, made Harriet Monroe, editor of the journal *Poetry*, gag with disbelief at his swooping metaphors, verbal juxtapositions, and muddled meanings. It seemed to her—as one of Melville's friends had said of *Moby-Dick*—to be some confused "intellectual chowder."

"At Melville's Tomb" is Crane's fullest and most explicit encounter with Melville. Significantly, Melville had also composed a poem "Monody," which reads in part,

> To have known him, to have loved him
> After loneness long;
> And then to be estranged in life,
> And neither in the wrong;
> And now for death to set his seal—
> Ease me, a little ease, my song!

Scholars are unsure if Melville's funeral oration was intended for his friend Nathaniel Hawthorne or his son Malcolm. Melville composed the poem after Malcolm's suicide in 1867. Malcolm was buried in Woodlawn Cemetery in the Bronx, New York. Melville followed him there twenty-four years later.

The precise meaning of Crane's poem is famously elusive. The poem's language is sometimes so obscure that it has become emblematic of the vicissitudes of certain modernist works. Even on the level of fact, the poem surprises, since Melville is buried not in a tomb but in the ground, with a gravestone on top. Consider the opening stanza:

> Often beneath the wave, wide from this ledge
> The dice of drowned men's bones he saw bequeath
> An embassy. Their numbers as he watched,
> Beat on the dusty shore and were obscured.

Upon reading the poem, exasperated editor Monroe inquired of Crane: "Take me for a hard-boiled unpoetic reader, and tell me how *dice* can *bequeath an embassy* (or anything else); and how a *calyx* (of *death's bounty* or anything else) can give back a *scattered chapter*, *livid hieroglyph*, and how, if it does, such a *portent* can be *wound in corridors* (or shells or anything else)." Yet, for all of these and more concerns, Monroe kindly admitted that Crane's "ideas and rhythms interest me." But "by what process of reasoning would you justify this poem's succession of champion mixed metaphors?"

Never at a loss for words, Crane responded with an exuberant letter designed to clarify his seemingly "elliptical and actually obscure" choices. While respectful in his letter to Monroe, in private he was dismissive, calling her "the woozy old spinster" of American poetic taste. In another letter he denounced Monroe as the sort of person who might rush up to Isaac Newton to wonder if the genius mathematician was, perhaps, "a little bit too mathematical." Or, perhaps she was like those nineteenth-century readers who failed to appreciate how Melville in *Moby-Dick* was after a grand theme in a grand manner.

Crane did, more or less successfully, abandon his abstract discussion of the "logic of metaphor" to a specific explanation of the metaphors he employed in "At Melville's Tomb." The bones of drowned sailors, over many years, were ground by the action of the sea and salt into "little cubes," which could resemble dice. Since they could be tossed around, the metaphor of dice, with its suggestion of contingency, was further related to the unanticipated end of voyages begun with high expectations. He never explained, however, how dice might "bequeath / An embassy."

CHAPTER 8

The Pulpit

FATHER MAPPLE'S PULPIT IS DESCRIBED

The formidable presence in this chapter of Father Mapple, a "very great favorite" among seamen and their families, was based perhaps upon the Methodist minister Edward Thompson Taylor.*

Many of the worthies of the era—from Ralph Waldo Emerson to Charles Dickens, from Jenny Lind, the Swedish nightingale, to Harriet Martineau— flocked to hear Taylor preach at the Seaman's Bethel Church in Boston. Martineau was awed by Taylor's eloquence, proclaiming him one "of the last class of originals."

*Some scholars consider Enoch Mudge, a Methodist minister who employed poetic language in his sermons, to have been the model.

Taylor was born in Richmond, Virginia on Christmas day 1793. Few joyful presents came his way in his early years. At the raw age of seven, he went to sea as a sailor. Drawn to the solid shore of religion, he was licensed to preach the gospel at the age of twenty-one. Five years later, he was ordained a minister in the Methodist church. By the time Melville might have heard him preach, Taylor was in his middle years, sturdy of jaw, solidly built, and beaming with goodwill, although he was more than capable of

Figure 6.
Orson Welles as Father Mapple in the 1956 film version of *Moby-Dick*, directed by John Huston. Photograph by Bob Penn.

cutting sarcasm when the situation warranted it. He came of age theologically when old-school Calvinist doctrines of predestination, sin, and damnation were withering on the vine. Taylor never denied sin—he was, after all, an old salt who had lived aboard ship with all sorts of desperadoes and had prowled ports bursting with illicit pleasure palaces. He was repelled, however, by images of an angry, unkind God, a deity parsimonious with the gift of grace. The notion of infant damnation—the old Calvinist saw that a child not predestined for salvation who expired after a single breath was headed for hell—struck Taylor as horrific and implausible. Nor did he warm to Reverend Wigglesworth's sweet assurances that such a poor child would at least occupy one of the nicer rooms in hell!

When Taylor preached—from his prow-like pulpit high above the congregation—he mesmerized with a voice modulating between loud and soft tones, sometimes, as Martineau described it, "melting into a tenderness like that of a mother's wooing of her infant." He delighted in Christian charity, love, and companionship. He reminded his congregants that though they might spend a "season" in the arms of sin, they could—by desire, faith, and effort—gain God's grace for an eternity in Heaven.

Taylor peppered his sermons with images drawn from his years at sea:

Aloft . . . That's where you are going—with a fair wind—all taught and trim, steering direct for Heaven in its glory, where there are no storms or fowl weather . . . A blessed harbor, still water there, in all charges of the winds and tides; no diving ashore upon the rocks, or slipping your cables and running out to sea, there: Peace—Peace—Peace—all peace!

Would Melville have taken comfort in such tender theological tidings? If he had, he could not have composed *Moby-Dick*.

In the 1956 film version of the novel, Orson Welles sizzled in the role of Father Mapple. Welles had long been fascinated by the novel. His ego was sufficiently immense to have no qualms about revising the sermon for the film. Director John Huston responded in his hoarse knife of a voice, "That's very good, very good indeed, but now try it as written in the script." Thirty years later, Gregory Peck, who had played Ahab in the film, appeared as Father Mapple in a television version of the novel. He was far superior as Mapple than he had been as Ahab.

CHAPTER 9
The Sermon

FATHER MAPPLE DELIVERS HIS SERMON ON JONAH
AND THE WHALE

God is a rather nice, reasonable fellow, according to Father Mapple. In his magnificently rendered sermon, Mapple finds that despite Jonah's refusal to follow God's commandment to go to Nineveh, he is let off the hook and freed from the belly of the beast. Sure, God's storm has rocked Jonah's ship to and fro and has thrown a scare into his shipmates. Yet the upshot of the tale is positive. God is forgiveness and love. In the sermon that Ishmael, along with sailors and their families, hears at church that day, Mapple barely hints at the fire and brimstone theology that had sounded in the Presbyterian pews of Melville's youth.

The story of Jonah in the Bible is an odd one, and it differs markedly from Mapple's rendering. Mapple views Jonah as shaken to his foundations by the storm while aboard ship and by God's anger with him. In the Bible, however, Jonah sleeps soundly in the midst of the terrible storm while everyone else is "terror-stricken." Rather than beseech God's forgiveness, Jonah spends three days and three nights in the giant fish before he offers a prayer, one that is less a testament to repentance than a mere recognition of God's power. Nonetheless, the prayer works and Jonah is "vomited" up on land. As earlier commanded, Jonah goes to Nineveh to tell the people there that they have sinned greatly and that they must repent, lest God destroy them. The people of Nineveh are no fools, and they immediately give up their "wicked ways" and enter into a period of fasting and repentance.

It turns out that the reason why Jonah had initially refused God's order to go to Nineveh was that he was convinced of God's overly merciful nature. When Jonah learns that God has allowed the people of the city to survive, his reaction is described as "greatly displeased." Why he should be so pissed off at God's humanitarianism is never hinted at. Perhaps Jonah feels that an angry God is the best God, and if God is not going to play such a role, then Jonah wants no part in the proceedings. Jonah sits under a tree and sulks. God asks him: "Are you right to be angry?" Jonah remains upset that his God is "a gracious and compassionate God, long-suffering, ever constant, always ready to relent and not inflict punishment."

In effect, Jonah's anger with God's contradictions and contrariness resembles Ahab's stance. If the White Whale is a representation of God, then its taking of his leg and blankness of meaning stoke the fires of Ahab's rage.

Why did Melville choose this story for Mapple's sermon rather than another Biblical tale, for instance the story of King Ahab? Like his namesake, Ahab is a rebel against God. Of course, the description of Jonah in the commodious belly of a whale is a perfect vehicle for the sea-laced metaphors that Mapple employs. The comparison between Jonah and Ahab as fellow-travelers in defiance of the Lord, however, seems strained. Jonah's frustration is based, as far as the story reveals, in his sense that God lacks a will to punish. Ahab, in contrast, sees only a God that is hell-bent on causing suffering, misunderstanding, and death.

Mapple's sermon, then, represents a vision of God as loving and forgiving. It may also be framed as absurd in content and in presentation, issuing forth from a ship's bow and flavored with the salty language of sailors in a church that sweats with bloody deaths. Melville might listen to this sermon and consider it a grand illusion, a sop to those living in a world that is apparently meaningless and obviously horrific.

CHAPTER 10

A Bosom Friend

ISHMAEL AND QUEEQUEG ARE UNITED BY GIFTS AND A SMOKE

Ishmael and Queequeg have already physically bonded. Now it is time for their relationship to progress to a more spiritual level. Ishmael observes that behind Queequeg's savage mien, customs, and tattoos lurks a very good man, "You cannot hide the soul." Ishmael thoughtfully concludes that Queequeg is "George Washington cannibalistically developed."

To celebrate their friendship, a smoke on Queequeg's tomahawk "wild pipe" is proposed. After their "genial smoke," Queequeg presses Ishmael close to him and pronounces them "married" to one another.

In the mid-1980s, beginning in urban ghettoes, a different substance was smoked in pipes—crack cocaine. Derived from that white dream-substance cocaine, crack was relatively inexpensive and offered an explosive high. It was also supremely addictive and dangerous. Many squandered their lives to procure these magical rocks that offered them escape from the mundane world.

What possible relation can exist between cocaine (in its white form or crack derivative) and the White Whale? Well, in the 1990s, Ricardo Pitts-Wiley, director of the Mixed Magic Theater, developed a way of contemporizing *Moby-Dick*. But he refused to alter the essential outlines of the classic story. He came up with an ingenious solution, a play titled: *Moby-Dick: Then and Now*.

A stage version of the play is enacted on the top of scaffolding, with Ahab, Ishmael, Queequeg, and company undertaking their doomed quest for the White Whale of meaning and fantasy. On stage-level below, a different but related story unfolds, with at-risk youngsters playing the roles. Alba leads a gang called "The One." Her brother Pip, who is fascinated with cetology, is killed in a drive-by shooting. Alba seeks revenge against his presumed killer—White Thing. It is unclear whether White Thing is a male or female, fiction or reality—perhaps White Thing is the exemplification of the wonder and waste of cocaine. Alba, along with her posse of Que, Stu, Daj, and Tasha, navigate the violent streets of the cocaine trade and all of its dangerous offshoots.

Thus we encounter two worlds, united by puffs on a pipe and a mysterious white entity; two worlds, each bringing death in its wake.

CHAPTER 11

Nightgown

QUEEQUEG AND ISHMAEL GET COZY

A snug and cuddly opening to the chapter, as Ishmael and Queequeg enjoy the warmth of their shared bed at the Spouter-Inn. Only a few paragraphs in length, the chapter is a bridge, showing the now "married" couple in comfort before they embark on their fateful adventure at sea.

The closeness of Ishmael and Queequeg, along with passing but pressing references to darkness, may be suggestive of the friendship then in full flower between Melville and Nathaniel Hawthorne.

In the summer of 1850, Melville was living in Pittsfield. Not far away resided Hawthorne. On Monday morning, August 5, the two writers finally met. A large party, consisting of literary figures David Dudley Field, James T. Fields, Evert Duyckinck, Cornelius Mathews, and Oliver Wendell Holmes, and including Hawthorne and Melville, frolicked up Monument Mountain, carrying food and drink with them. Melville, then just past thirty, reportedly bounded about, demonstrating his agility and energy. Later, the group reconvened for dinner and more libations.

By the end of the evening, Hawthorne had invited Melville to visit him at home. According to his biographer Brenda Wineapple, Hawthorne admired the "bearded and bronzed" Melville, a man who, unlike him, had traveled the world and returned with a trunk full of experiences. Melville, in turn, considered Hawthorne a literary genius. Over the next fifteen months, their friendship waxed and waned; Melville's exuberance some-times made the shy Hawthorne beat a retreat.

The influence of Hawthorne upon Melville and *Moby-Dick* is obvious. Melville dedicated the volume to his friend but more importantly, Haw-thorne inspired Melville: made him want to dive deeper, to recognize that his mighty powers had previously been insufficiently tapped. Writing a review of Hawthorne's recently published *Mosses from an Old Manse*, Melville sounded a new theme in his life: "it is better to fail in originality, than to succeed in imitation." This admonition fueled his fevered work on the new novel in the months that followed.

Might a glimmer of this relationship between Melville and Hawthorne be reflected in the camaraderie that unfolds between Ishmael and Queequeg? Obviously, Hawthorne was no "savage," and he was unadorned by any tat-toos (although he had, in effect, placed something like one upon the chest of Hester Prynne in *The Scarlet Letter*). Hawthorne could be, like Queequeg, aloof and self-contained, but also capable of warmth and fellowship.

Melville fell for Hawthorne as hard as Ishmael swooned for Queequeg. As Melville wrote in his gushy review of *Mosses*, Hawthorne was a giant of American letters; if not the equal of Shakespeare, then at least his kissing cousin. Melville's language about Hawthorne's work is over-the-top with emotion and innuendo. Melville announces himself (writing anonymously as "a Virginian Spending July in Vermont") bewitched by "Hawthorne's spell" and "soft ravishment." Rather than pulling back from such terms, after a day's reflection, Melville announced further that "Hawthorne has dropped germanous seeds into my soul . . . and further, shoots his strong New England roots into the hot soil of my Southern soul."

In the review, Melville nicely dissected the nature of Hawthorne's mind and soul. There is, he announces, a "black conceit [that] pervades him through and through," "blackness ten times black" that coexists with his "Indian-summer sunlight." Hawthorne is a man of parts, a man of depths.

Melville casts lightness and darkness, affection and foreboding over this chapter. Ishmael remarks that no one can grasp the depths of their personal identity without, as it were, closing their eyes tightly, forcing out the light. Although we prefer to dwell in the brighter, "more congenial layers" of existence, it is only in the depths of darkness, in acknowledgment of the power of evil, that we gain full measure of ourselves and others.

Of course, Captain Ahab, who looms as the hulking, unannounced presence in the early chapters of the book, is a figure that traffics fully with the "power of blackness"; it makes for his tragedy but also for his greatness.

Under the spell of Hawthorne the man and writer, Melville opted for new possibilities, charting a course away from composing another pleasant novel of adventure in favor of one sunk into the depths of monstrous metaphysics and monomania. He had come to the realization that "You must have plenty of sea-room to tell the Truth in."

CHAPTER 12

Biographical

QUEEQUEG'S HISTORY IS REVEALED TO ISHMAEL

Queequeg and Melville have at least one thing in common. Both of them escaped from Eden, and both of them probably regretted it.

Melville was twenty-one years old when he jumped ship with his mate Toby at Nuku Hiva Harbor in the South Sea Marquesas Islands. He found himself with an injured leg among the Typee tribe that he presumed to be cannibals. He was neither eaten nor nibbled. A few years later in his first book, *Typee* (1846), he recounted that the tribe's members were a handsome and overall kind group of "savages." He marveled at their customs and enjoyed the uninhibited charms of a young woman. Yet Melville was no

Rousseau, enamored of the state of nature. The natives were indolent; thanks to their lush surroundings, they effortlessly plucked breadfruit for sustenance from trees. After more than a month with the natives, Melville fled because his concerns about cannibalism continued to stew and because boredom had set in.

Although Melville at times praised Christian missionaries among natives of the South Sea Islands as engaged "in truth a just and happy cause," he could also be scathing. In both *Typee* and his next book, *Omoo* (1847), the deleterious effects of Christian missionary work are noted. Too often, he wrote, natives were forced to drop their "light-hearted joyousness" to be "civilised into draught horses and evangelised into beasts of burden." In bold strokes, Melville lectured his readers that, "Among the islands of Polynesia, no sooner are the images overturned, the temples demolished, and the idolators converted into *nominal* Christians than disease, vice, and premature death make their appearance."

We learn in this chapter that, in his youth, Queequeg longed for his own fanciful Eden of Christianity. The son of a king, with royal blood flowing in his veins, Queequeg could have ascended to the throne but he wanted out of this Eden. He was convinced that by living in Christendom he could learn various useful things and then return home to make his people even happier.

To achieve such noble ends, Queequeg cleverly managed to board a Sag Harbor vessel leaving the island. In a battle of wills that he was sure to win, he forced the captain to allow him to stay aboard. Since that moment, Queequeg had traveled the world as a sailor and harpooner on whaleships, living among Christians, walking the corridors of Christian cities, and observing lives as different from his own earlier years as that which Melville had encountered in the valley of the Typee.

Queequeg fails, however, to find much of value, concluding that "even Christians could be both miserable and wicked; infinitely more so than all his father's heathens." Born a pagan, Queequeg resolves to die a pagan.

Both Queequeg and Melville, then, fled from Eden, or something close to it. Queequeg frets that his years among Christians have "unfitted him for ascending the pure and undefiled throne" that was his ancestral right to occupy. Now he must continue as a harpooner until the time comes when he feels "himself baptized again" in a *summa superior* of savagery.

Within a few years of his South Sea idyll of sorts, Melville had settled into the hard ground of a new life of marriage, family, and trying to earn sufficient monies to keep all in bourgeois comfort. Greater than normal tensions blackened the hallways of the Melville home, and one can easily imagine Herman—when he was not preoccupied in splattering ink as he composed his novels at breakneck speed—fondly recalling the easy sexuality and unanchored freedom of his early days among the "savages."

CHAPTER 13

Wheelbarrow

ISHMAEL AND QUEEQUEG HEAD FOR NANTUCKET TO FIND A WHALING SHIP

Some travel about the world without ever leaving home; they carry with them bags full of stale preconceptions. Other travelers like Melville and Ishmael, gad more lightly, ready to unfurl their rug sack in another culture.

As Ishmael and Queequeg stroll about New Bedford they draw stares and derision from some of its inhabitants. Islanders like Queequeg are not especially strange sights in the environs, but the easy camaraderie between Ishmael and Queequeg disconcerts some in the town. Folks talk easily, in the abstract, about the greatness of human fellowship, but when they see it in action, especially across a racial divide, they are shocked because of their own narrow set of prejudices.

Once aboard the packet schooner bound for Nantucket, Queequeg notes a bumpkin unkindly mimicking him. He trounces the fellow fiercely. Moments later, "the tremendous boom . . . now flying from side to side" knocks the fellow overboard. Queequeg dives into the storm-tossed waters to save the fool's life. Cultural divisions, at least for the moment, stop boiling and Queequeg is hailed as a jolly fellow.

The great German sociologist Max Weber once defined culture, later appropriated by American anthropologist Clifford Geertz, like this: "man is an animal suspended in webs of significance he himself has spun." Queequeg, a wise man, tells two stories that reveal how we are entrapped in such cultural webs of significance.

He first offers a comic tale that recalls his own cultural ignorance. He was once given a wheelbarrow to haul his heavy travel chest from one spot to another. Never having encountered a wheelbarrow, Queequeg does not know what to do with it. Finally, he secures his chest in the barrow, picks it up and carries it to his destination.

Not only savages partake of such cultural mishaps. Queequeg relates how a "very stately punctilious captain" misbehaved at his sister's wedding ceremony. As per custom, a great priest places his fingers in a "large stained calabash like a punchbowl." It is an ancient ceremony whereby the priest consecrates the liquid and, after its consumption, the marriage. When the bowl passes immediately to the captain, and considering himself the equal to the priest, the ignorant westerner proceeds to wash his hands thoroughly in what he understands to be nothing more than "a huge finger-glass." Suffice it to say, this cultural faux pas makes the wedding guests explode with laughter.

No culture is without its webs of significance and laughter, Queequeg teaches us that long before Weber and Geertz.

CHAPTER 14

Nantucket

A DISCUSSION OF NANTUCKET AND ITS PROUD WHALING HERITAGE

Odd that Melville chose to have the *Pequod* depart from Nantucket rather than New Bedford. When composing *Moby-Dick*, Melville had yet to set foot on the island. He gathered his information about Nantucket from two books, both published in 1835: Obed Macy's *The History of Nantucket* and Joseph C. Hart's novel *Miriam Coffin, or The Whale-Fisherman*.

Both works are rich portraits of an island that had long been synonymous with whaling, from the late seventeenth until the early nineteenth centuries. Melville perused these volumes for a sense of the island's "accidental" history—Captain Bartholomew Gosnold happened upon it in 1602 while on his way to Virginia. Soon after settlement in the mid-seventeenth century, a "scragg" whale wandered into the harbor; locals rapidly developed a harpoon to dispatch it. Since precious few whales entered the harbor, enterprising Nantucket men went to sea to hunt them down. Around 1712, Christopher Hussey, while on lookout for Right whales, claimed the first sperm whale for Nantucket's seamen. Nantucket was soon agog with all the activities associated with whaling.

J. Hector St. John Crevecoeur, who had visited Nantucket late in the eighteenth century, lavished praise upon the town. The people were hardy and industrious, neat and courageous. Only one aspect of the island haunted him. A most "disagreeable smell" emanated from the large amounts of whale oil stored on the island.

By the 1840s, the grand days of Nantucket as a whaling center had passed. Deep-water, land-connected nearby New Bedford rose to prominence. By the end of the decade, 75 whaleships departed from Nantucket while 254 such vessels sailed from New Bedford.

Melville scholar Howard P. Vincent concluded that Melville wanted Nantucket as port of departure for Ishmael and Queequeg because it had symbolized for a century the "whaling genius" of Americans. Melville admits as much in this chapter: "poor old Nantucket is now much behind" New Bedford in the whaling industry, but she was once the "great original—the Tyre of this Carthage."

The symbolic weight of Nantucket derives from more than mere nostalgia and history. It also serves as a metaphor for the voyage of the *Pequod* that casts away from its wharf. The ship is doomed, perhaps because of its captain's monomania about a white whale, or perhaps because it is intended to represent the ship of the American state going down in a sea of political and racial turmoil.

Fate plays tricks on individuals as well as upon confident nations. Once, no doubt, the Nantucket descendents of Ahab, Peleg, Bildad, and Starbuck (not to mention innkeeper Coffin) held it as gospel truth that their industry and faith would reap continued rewards for them. As Macy phrased it, "The wide ocean is the source of their livelihood, and they breast its waves and grapple with its monsters in every latitude between the polar ices." As the nineteenth century trudged forward, the reek of whale oil remained but the profits and powers of the industry—and the way of life that it had fostered—had departed from Nantucket.

CHAPTER 15

Chowder

ISHMAEL AND QUEEQUEG DINE—ONLY CHOWDER IS SERVED

Melville studs his text with inside jokes, fanciful allusions, and arcane references. All of the above season this chapter called "Chowder."

Ostensibly, the chapter amusingly relates the culinary adventures of Ishmael and Queequeg at the Nantucket eatery presided over by Mrs. Hosea Hussey. At the Try Pot, she offers them the choice of clam or cod. Ishmael cannot imagine a meal sufficiently constituted by a single clam. He is soon enlightened by Mrs. Hussey; she serves only chowder, this evening's fare being made with either clam or cod. After finishing what Ishmael calls a "smoking chowder" of clams, he and Queequeg delight in one made with cod. Satisfied, they take to their suite for the night.

More is cooking in the inn's pots than chowder. The very name of the place, The Try Pot, anticipates the large vats for the onship chore of extracting oil from the whale's blubber. The images of the wooden pots used to make the chowder at the inn are darkened by their likeness to gallows. The hanging of the pots and the hanging of men blend together.

In July 1840, in the *Knickerbocker Magazine*, Henry Cary (writing under the penname John Waters) published an essay, "Discursive Thoughts on Chowder." He metaphorically engaged the emergent split between the literary communities of New England and New York City. The Boston literary scene was dominated by Emerson and transcendentalism, with its metaphysical flights and studied emphasis on nature. The New York literati, in contrast, eschewed the trappings of German-endowed philosophy in favor of a literature of carefully constructed form and heady doses of realism. The metaphor of chowder, then, was particularly apt, given New England's taste for chowder cooked in a white base while New Yorkers preferred a red tincture to the dish.

Although Melville may not have read the chowder essay when it was first published, he would no doubt have been aware of the metaphor. His friend Evert Duyckinck had had a piece appear in the same issue of *The Knickerbocker* as Cary's. Three years Melville's elder, Duyckinck was from deep Dutch roots, well educated (Columbia College, 1835), and a thorough cosmopolitan. After gaining admittance to the bar in 1837, he toured Europe for two years before marrying in 1840 and settling into his home. By 1848, Melville had come into his orbit—as had Poe earlier—sharing drinks and camaraderie, and merrily borrowing books from his friend's ample library. Duyckinck, in his role as a critic and publisher, did what he could to promote Melville's career.

Duyckinck and Melville had many affinities without being a perfect fit. Both men cherished the ideal of an American literary community unlinked to European literary fashions. They devoted themselves to a high-quality American literary nationalism. But Duyckinck's desire to "cultivate taste" in Jackson-era America was based upon stern presumptions. He rejected the mixing of genres and waved away any hints of blasphemy (he was a devout Episcopalian), and he hated departures from the terra firma of realism. This is not to say that Duyckinck was a prude—along with Melville, he delighted in Rabelaisian humor, enjoyed his drink, and disdained idle puffery. But Melville's *Moby-Dick*, which he reviewed in his journal *Literary World* on November 22, 1851, a week after it was published in the United States, forced him to weigh his distaste for much in the novel against his friendship with Melville.

The novel was "an intellectual chowder," wrote Duyckinck. And he found it unappetizing, berating Melville's "practical running down of creeds and opinions" of religions, linking it to "the conceited indifferentianism of Emerson." By this he meant that as Emerson's expansive oneness of vision could embrace all creeds, Melville's rapier wit was equally at home in attacking all creeds. Melville stood condemned, as well, for employing the "run-a-muck style" of Emerson's comrade Thomas Carlyle.

While a "remarkable sea-dish," *Moby-Dick* was "an intellectual chowder of romance, philosophy, natural history, fine writing, good feeling, bad sayings." In sum, by tossing too many disparate styles, forms, and thoughts into his chowder of a book, Melville had produced something less than palatable to Duyckinck's refined tastes.

CHAPTER 16

The Ship

ISHMAEL SIGNS ON FOR THE *PEQUOD*

As Ishmael signs up for duty aboard the *Pequod*, his imagination is aflutter about the identity of Captain Ahab. He does not, however, inquire about the rather odd name of the ship. He simply takes a look at the vessel and decides, fatefully, that it will suffice for him and Queequeg.

Melville certainly had reasons for naming his ship after a tribe of Indians, the Pequots, who had been annihilated by forces from Massachusetts Bay Colony in the 1630s.

The circumstances leading up to the Pequot War are confusing. One account proceeds as follows: a trader named John Gallop was on his small boat, just off Block Island, when he espied fellow trader John Oldham's boat, with a group of Indians on her deck. He knew that something was amiss, so he shot at them and rammed the smaller vessel with his larger one. Most of the Indians went overboard and those remaining on the vessel were killed by Gallop. He then located the body of John Oldham, his head cleaved by an axe and his legs nearly cut off. As one chronicler of the event put it, "The blood of the innocent called for revenge."

What a perfect name for the ship that Ahab steers with burning revenge. Like Oldham, Ahab has an axe of sorts in his own mind, one that was cut with painful memories of his first encounter with Moby Dick. And one of his legs has been slashed by the powerful jaws of the White Whale.

The Pequot War, which began in earnest in August of 1636, was a particularly bloody episode in the history of New England. Led by Captain John Endicott, an army of about forty white soldiers and two Indians attacked Block Island, a main refuge of the Indians. Endicott's victory was quick and total. His forces continued to search the area, killing Pequots as they found them. The Pequots, for their part, denied any role in the murder of Oldham. The colonists rejected this view and waged war upon the Pequots, whom they considered "Satan's children" or the "devil's instruments." Such instruments of the devil had to be exorcised. Colonists destroyed Pequot villages and burned their crops, and tracked down Pequot men, women, and children in the swamps where they hid. Once found, they were, as John Winthrop put it, "all gotten."

The Pequot War was the first major war of extermination against Native Americans. It helped, as one historian put it, in the building of the American nation state.

Might Melville have had this in mind when he named his ship after this Indian tribe? Its crew is varied in terms of race, including an Indian named Tashtego who is one of its harpooners. Certainly we are giving nothing away in noting that the *Pequod* will sink, taking down almost the entire crew with it. Is this a statement on Melville's part about the thirst of America and its desire for pure whiteness? Or did Melville choose the name simply because it appealed to his sense of the perverse, to the earlier dismasting of John Oldham?

CHAPTER 17

The Ramadan

QUEEQUEG PRAYS AND FASTS IN HIS ROOM, WHICH ALARMS ISHMAEL

Did Melville discover his model for Queequeg within the pages of a *Narrative of the United States Exploring Expedition* (five volumes, published in 1845)? The expedition was led by Charles Wilkes (see chapter 124).

Resourceful scholar David Jaffé finds an engraving from the second volume, on page 396, of Ko-Towatowa, a New Zealand chief, lording over the area of Kororarika. He greatly resembles Queequeg. Melville tells us that Queequeg hailed from Kokovoko, which does have phonetic similarities with Kororarika. The image of Ko-Towatowa shows his regal quality, with a long nose and mien that summons forth the famous description of Queequeg as "George Washington cannibalistically developed." Intricate tattoos grace the face of Ko-Towatowa. He wears the same type of blanket worn by Queequeg, as described by Melville. Jaffé is hardly fazed by the full head of hair that Ko-Towatowa sports in contrast to the shaven Queequeg. After all, Melville borrows and appropriates without undue concern, as well he should.

To drive home his argument, Jaffé finds that, according to Wilkes's narrative, natives such as Ko-Towatowa engaged in a lively trade of shrunken heads, worshiped a carved wooden figure, and fasted in the way that Melville describes in this chapter "The Ramadan."

If Melville was less than true to this model for Queequeg, then consider the liberties that John Huston took when casting Queequeg for his film

Figure 7.
Ko-Towatowa, a possible model for Queequeg? From *Narrative of the U.S. Exploring Expedition.*

version of the novel. Huston was friends with Friedrich Ledebur, a tall and imposing Austrian aristocrat, who was as distant from a Pacific Islander as possible. Yet, with his almost Indian-nickel profile and aristocratic bearing, there was some logic to him portraying Queequeg. But Ledebur had to be transformed. As Huston told his pal, "Now Friedrich, I don't want you to be worried but we're just going to do a little thing to your hair." Moments later Ledebur's flowing mane had been completely shorn, his body shaved, and temporary tattoos placed all over him. He did not protest. One suspects that Ko-Towatowa would have reacted differently.

Figure 8.
Richard Basehart as Ishmael explains a book to Friedrich von Ledebur as Queequeg in John Huston's 1956 film version of *Moby-Dick*. Photograph by Ernst Haas.

CHAPTER 18

His Mark

CAPTAINS PELEG AND BILDAD QUESTION QUEEQUEG'S RELIGIOUS CREDENTIALS BUT MARVEL AT HIS HARPOONING SKILLS

A pair of Quakers are the principal owners of the *Pequod*. Both have braved storm and sea for most of their lives in search of whales. Whaling is as integral to them as fog to New Bedford. These "fighting Quakers" sprinkle their speech with "Thous" and "Thees." Yet they are a study in contrasts. Captain Peleg is "brown and brawny," his eyes wrinkled by years of squinting into gales; he is full of his own Nantucket-anchored brand of bluster and humor, softened with a humane edge. Captain Bildad is tightly wound, strict, and pious, his body long and gaunt, as if an unnecessary pound constituted a sin against worldly propriety and godly design. "This world pays dividends," according to Bildad, and he seeks them as vigorously as he does the keys to heaven.

Ishmael has learned in chapter 16 that Bildad is a stingy man who drives a hard bargain. He has offered the inexperienced Ishmael the 777th lay—that percentage to be realized from any profits the voyage accrues. It is a paltry amount, hardly worth the effort. Peleg leaps to defend Ishmael's interests, and he engages in a robust clash of will and wit with his partner. Finally, it is decided to grant Ishmael the 300th lay.

Peleg and Bildad reappear in this chapter, when Ishmael introduces them to his newly discovered soul-mate Queequeg, whom he wants them to hire as a harpooner on the *Pequod*. Their pious Quaker hearts tremble at the sight of this apparent savage. The owners demand proof that Queequeg is a Christian, in good standing. This offers Ishmael a chance to have some fun with these Quaker captains. He claims that not only is Queequeg a member of the First Congregational Church, but a deacon in said church. Peleg and Bildad—who insist on calling Queequeg variously "Quohog" and "Hedgehog"—have sufficient sentience to imagine that Ishmael is pulling their respective legs.

All of their theological concerns vanish, however, once Queequeg demonstrates his expertise in tossing his harpoon into a minuscule, far-away target. Queequeg is hired immediately, earning a generous ninetieth lay. Peleg then remarks that "Pious harpooners never make good voyagers—it takes the shark out of 'em."

The clash of personalities and perspectives of Captains Peleg and Bildad is humorous, sometimes even raucous. Their interchanges bring to mind another oddly mismatched team, the comic duo of Bud Abbott and Lou Costello. Abbott was tall and thin, wily and lazy. Costello was short and dumpy, ill educated and energetic. In the heyday of their radio fame, in the 1930s and 1940s, they had a routine called, of all things, Moby Dick.

The skit opens with Costello telling what he calls a bedtime story about a whale named Moby Dick. Abbott solemnly promises not to interrupt his partner's palaver. No sooner has Costello begun than Abbott questions Costello's notion that a whale can have a nose. Not a nose, says Abbott, a whale has a spout. Costello replies, with his richly inflected speech, "It's spout time you keep your mouth shut." The wordplay continues hot and heavy, as Abbott lectures Costello that a clam is an abalone. You mean to say, replies Costello, that a clam is a baloney? On and on it goes, with Gershwin's opera rendered as "Porgy and Bass" and a line floats by about a Captain Epsom, who is an "old salt." Ouch.

No mention is made in the five-minute routine of Captain Ahab or Ishmael. The point is not to retell the story; their listeners know its general outlines and cultural significance. The humor arises from how well Costello can mangle the language and solemnity of a classic tale.

Peleg and Bildad provide humor before the storms of the *Pequod*'s voyage. Abbott and Costello delivered their jokes during the depression and Second World War. Melville, one imagines, would have appreciated their humor, for in his own life, the darkness of economic collapse had engulfed him.

CHAPTER 19

The Prophet

A BEDRAGGLED STRANGER CONFRONTS ISHMAEL AND QUEEQUEG

Melville may have had his own particular quarrel with God, but he was certainly God-besotted, choosing Biblical names and associations for many of his characters, including Ishmael and Ahab. Perhaps no character in the novel plays closer to type than the prophet Elijah in this chapter.

Elijah confronts Ishmael and Queequeg on the Nantucket dock, moments after they have hooked their destinies to the voyage of the *Pequod*. His queries cut to the bone. He asks Ishmael if on the just-signed contract there is any stipulation regarding their souls. Elijah is a finger pointer, sending forth waves of gibberish, information, and prophecy. He knows that Ahab's blasphemous plan is doomed, sure to take all down with him. Alas, Ishmael shuns Elijah's prophecy, proclaiming him "humbug."

In the Bible, Elijah is a prophet, an agent of God tasked with bringing King Ahab and Queen Jezebel to ruin. He flits in and out of the text, often looking to God for the power to confront these enemies and for reassurance concerning his own safety. The land of Ahab, where the God of the Hebrews is now compromised by worship of Baal, has been punished by constant rain, bringing starvation and death. After a particularly dastardly deed undertaken by Ahab and Jezebel against an innocent neighbor, a prophecy comes that dogs will lick Ahab's own blood. Ahab falls to the ground and begs forgiveness for his mountain of sins. God, through Elijah, allows Ahab to live, but a pox is sent down upon his son and descendents. When Elijah speaks, one should listen.

Melville is doing more than parading his Biblical knowledge and playing with themes that will inform his novel. Through the character of Elijah he is reenacting an American tradition named after another prophet, Jeremiah. Perfected in the seventeenth century, the jeremiad took the form of a sermon that chided parishioners for having drifted from the strict faith and actions of an earlier generation, thereby threatening to topple the Puritan City upon the Hill. The point of the jeremiad was not simply to induce guilt. It was also meant to alert the people that ruin was in the offing if they did not return to the fold and take up the challenge of renewal.

By Melville's time, the jeremiad had been secularized, expressed in political speeches and editorials as a fear that Americans no longer hewed to the principles of the republic's original, lofty goals. Instead, they were seeking to satiate themselves with profits, slaves, and imperial conquests.

In this sense, the *Pequod* is symbolic of the American ship of state at a perilous moment in the nation's history. Melville wrote when a political compromise had been struck for the preservation of the union at the cost of its soul. Not only would the institution of slavery have a chance to expand in some new territories wrenched from the Mexican War, but the ugly arm of the "peculiar institution" now reached into provinces of freedom. Fugitive slaves, according to the compromise, could be returned to their "legal" owners and thus back into a life of enslavement. Melville chilled at this reality—brought about when his father-in-law, Lemuel Shaw, ruled to uphold the provision in a famous case—and may well have imagined that doom was on the horizon for the nation if she did not set her sails upon a new, righteous course.

A fanatic like Ahab could not recognize the evils of his ways. He must bring Elijah's prophecy to fruition. Elijah might have been speaking directly to Ishmael, but, through Melville's politics and prophecy, he was addressing a much wider audience.

CHAPTER 20

All Astir

AUNT CHARITY HELPS TO PROVISION THE *PEQUOD*

It is hard to imagine anyone more unlike Aunt Charity than actress Renée O'Connor, who first gained fame portraying Gabrielle, sidekick to Xena, the warrior princess, on the television series of that name. But now she appears, in the opening scene of the film *2010 Moby-Dick*, clad in a bikini, as Michelle Herman ("M. H.", get it?) who is a specialist in whales. Before she knows it, she is a member of the submarine crew on the *Pequod* in search of the high-flying and death-bringing white whale.

The women of Nantucket did not, in general, go hunting for whales, but no less than its men, they lived and breathed whaling. Aunt Charity, sister of Captain Bildad, is part-owner of the *Pequod* and active in helping it prepare to cast off. She is "a lean old lady of a most determined and indefatigable spirit." She is "kind-hearted," working to ensure that all the needs of the crew will be satisfied once they are at sea. She bears a "jar of pickles," quills for the chief mate, and a "roll of flannel for the small of some one's rheumatic back." She is an angel of comity and compassion, and she is sure to make a profit from a successful voyage.

By the nineteenth century, it was common for whaling expeditions to stretch out over three years. The wives, sisters, and relatives of whaling men thus attained a certain sphere of independence. While they remained connected to the rhythms of domesticity, they also entered more fully into the world of commerce. With their husbands at sea, women kept hearth and home together. They raised children, balanced books, managed businesses, and earned income with piecework from sewing or from taking in boarders. One section of Nantucket was known as "Petticoat Row," for its shops run by females. Based upon their Quaker religious beliefs and circumstances, the women of Nantucket were an educated and hearty lot, with the feminist leader Lucretia Coffin Mott and the scientist Maria Mitchell among their most noted members.

Some men disdained the stature and power that Nantucket women presumably wielded. In the novel *Miriam Coffin*, Joseph Hart wrote of women gone wild when their husbands were at sea. The wife of a whaler secures power-of-attorney from her husband (which was unusual) and thus begins to seethe with ambition, spending wildly and seeking to make a fortune. Alas, her plans go awry, and she squanders their wealth. When the man of the house finally returns from his years at sea, he berates his wife, banishing her from the world of men to the confines of the kitchen.

CHAPTER 21

Going Aboard

ISHMAEL AND QUEEQUEG BOARD THE *PEQUOD*

In his initial conception of *Moby-Dick*, Melville imagined the relationship between Queequeg and Ishmael as the story's centerpiece. That explains why in the first two dozen chapters so much attention is devoted to Queequeg. Melville intended to team Queequeg up with a fellow named Bulkington as the dynamic duo (a version of James Fenimore Cooper's Natty Bumppo and Uncas in *The Last of the Mohicans*) fighting against the White Whale. Ishmael would suffice as their admiring chronicler.

Queequeg manages to make himself comfortable and dignified in his given environment. As he and Ishmael board the *Pequod*, they come upon a sailor deep in sleep. Queequeg sits down upon the sailor, transforming him into a comfortable cushion. Ishmael is shocked at this behavior until Queequeg explains that in his homeland it is common to purchase slaves and to fatten them up, not for better eating in this case, but to serve as portable cushions. Thus if one comes upon a lovely spot and wishes to rest, then the fattened servant will be a cushion—portable to a high degree.

While the pair shares a smoke from Queequeg's tomahawk pipe, Ishmael notices that whenever it is passed over the sleeping sailor's body, the sharpened side faces down. Queequeg remarks to Ishmael, "Perry easy, kill-e; oh! perry easy!"

Raymond Chandler, in his classic essay "The Simple Art of Murder" (1950), opined that "It is not funny that a man should be killed, but it is sometimes funny that he should be killed for so little, and that his death should be the coin of what we call civilization."

Yes, it is pretty easy to kill a man and it is not funny. Sometimes out of necessity, sometimes for pure pleasure men are killed. Captain Ahab is at this moment "visibly enshrined within his cabin." He will, by his mania, charisma, and power of command, claim the lives of Queequeg and his sleeping cushion. Is it better to die questing after an illusion, to confront questions for which there may be no answers, or to live in comfort without higher ideals?

CHAPTER 22

Merry Christmas

THE SHIP PREPARES TO LAUNCH ON "A SHORT, COLD CHRISTMAS" DAY

In the hushed confines of the Northwestern University Rare Books room rests a first edition of *Moby-Dick*. Two inches thick, its heft is as obvious as its musty odor. The initial pages of the volume are stained purplish by age. The interior pages, however, are appealingly clean and crisp.

On the inside cover in neat handwriting appear the words: "Sidney Willard, Jr., Dec. 24, 1851, Harvard." Was the book his Christmas present? From whom?

Willard's father was a staunchly religious man, a professor of Hebrew literature at Harvard, no doubt aware of Melville's blasphemous reputation. As a leader in the movement for the propagation of Christianity, the senior Willard would have bristled at Melville's earlier attacks against missionaries. Perhaps it came from another family member or friend. It remains unknown if Willard ever read the novel, given to him a month after its publication in the United States. The pages lack marginalia or underlining.

It is known, however, that Sidney Willard Jr. was slaughtered, along with over 1,200 of his comrades, at the Battle of Fredericksburg in the War Between the States, almost exactly eleven years after he had inscribed this volume.

CHAPTER 23

The Lee Shore

AT THE HELM OF THE SHIP IS BULKINGTON, A MAN OF SUBSTANTIAL PARTS

By chapter twenty-three, Bulkington has appeared twice in the novel. We first met him at the Spouter-Inn. He is respected by the raucous sailors but he stands apart from the crowd. Six feet tall, "with noble shoulders and a chest like a coffer-dam," Bulkington is a Southerner by birth, for whom "in the deep shadows of his eyes floated some reminiscences that did not seem to give him much joy." We learn that he has just touched land after a four-year voyage on a whaling ship, yet he is already signed up to sail on the *Pequod*. With Ahab exiled to his cabin, it is Bulkington who on Christmas day steers the ship "into the cold malicious waves" that inaugurate its voyage. Bulkington is James Fenimore Cooper's Natty Bumppo aboard ship.

No sooner have we encountered this monument of a man than he disappears from the book. All we can be certain of is that he shares the same briny fate with the rest of the crew, with the exception of Ishmael. What happened?

Melville did not keep a journal and early drafts of *Moby-Dick* do not exist, so scholars can only speculate about Bulkington. The best explanation suggests that he was to be the heroic center of the book in its early conception, an exemplar for Ishmael. Bulkington would hunt down the White Whale, less for revenge than because of the challenge that it presented. After all, men of Bulkington's stature and standing are presumed to be adventurous. And interesting, too. Such men hold a secret in the recesses of their souls that makes them—in the American adventure story—take to the wilderness or sea. They were, when Melville was writing, American archetypes.

But at some point in his writing, Melville shifted direction. He veered away from the placid waters of anticipated archetypes. Thus Ahab replaces Bulkington as the pursuer of Moby Dick and Queequeg pushes Bulkington aside as bosom friend and protector for Ishmael. This, too, primes the story by opening up friendship across a cultural divide while affording Melville more opportunities to skewer Christianity over presumed savages. Otherwise, how could Ishmael wonder if Queequeg is thinking that "We cannibals must help these Christians"?

One question remains. Why didn't Melville excise the paltry four paragraphs in the book where Bulkington is present? No one knows, but it may be that Melville simply liked the writing or perhaps he wanted to maintain the vestiges of his initial conception. If *Moby-Dick* had been a success he might return to Bulkington, assaying for readers the mysterious background of this promising character. It is also possible that he wanted to erase from view the ideal of the heroic, white-pioneer American. Maybe by the conclusion of his labors he was simply too exhausted to notice or care.

Little attention over the years has been paid by scholars to Bulkington, other than to wonder about his odd presence in the text. In the late 1940s, however, Richard Chase, a young, politically conscious college professor, sought to pump meaning into Bulkington.

Chase was drawn to Bulkington as a "true Promethean hero," the "heroic American." He represented the mythos of American power and independence, capable of charting a course that would lead to growth rather than destruction. Bulkington has the raiment of heroism in his physical power and in the tragedy that he keeps covered in his heart. Reading Chase, you can almost feel him regretting that Ahab superseded Bulkington!

Chase wrote his account of Bulkington at a heady historical moment. In the late 1940s, some liberals sought to distance themselves from previous associations with Communists, without dropping support for social reform. Liberals like Chase wanted a passionate and realistic engagement with the menace of the Soviet Union. This was, after all, the dawning of the Cold War period. Chase and other intellectuals were drawn to Melville because they viewed him as an ally in developing a tragic sense of life.

Liberals opposed utopian schemes, such as Communism. They thought it naïve and dangerous to believe that the state could create a perfect society in the name of higher ideals. For them, Bulkington was the sort of fellow who should have remained at the helm of the *Pequod*, leading it homeward to the relative safety of the leeward shore. But that would have been a very different story.

CHAPTER 24

The Advocate

ISHMAEL WAXES ABOUT THE PROFESSION OF WHALING AND ITS HISTORY

All honor to the underappreciated whalemen of the world! Even if they be "butchers of the bloodiest badge," declares Ishmael, the havoc they cause is but little compared with the "unspeakable carrion" strewn upon heroic battlefields. Moreover, whalers spill blood for a worthy cause—to light the world. They have also long supplied another form of illumination, thanks to their exploration and mapping of the world while searching afar for their quarry. With mounting enthusiasm, Ishmael tells us that whaling has a noble history, reaching far back into the past: it "may well be regarded as that Egyptian mother, who bore off-spring themselves pregnant from her womb."

The history of whaling in North America commenced, no doubt as it did elsewhere, when a beached whale offered itself up for dissection to the native population. Since whales made themselves available in this manner infrequently, connoisseurs of their meat and blubber ventured out farther into the sea in search of them. In 1605, Captain George Waymouth observed Native Americans off the New England coast going out in small boats after a whale, which they called "powdawe." They fired volleys of arrows into the beast until it spouted no more. After towing it to land: "they call all their chief lords together, and sing a song of joy," before they divide up the shares.

In 1614, Captain John Smith went a-whaling off the coast of Maine. After his famous adventures with the Jamestown colony, Smith had gone back to England. Yet he longed to return to the New World. Since the Virginia colony was off limits to him, he signed up to lead an expedition to more northern climes. His mission was for profit—"to take Whales and make tryalls of a Myre of Gold and Copper." In many ways, Smith was an Ahab-like figure—proud and conceited, restless and impetuous, adventurous and imperious, stern and relentless.

Smith failed to conquer a single whale. As he put it in *A Description of New England* (1616), "we found this Whale-fishing a costly condition: we saw many, and spent much time in chasing them; but could not kill any." Smith filled up his ship with copious amounts of dried fish (mostly cod), along with bear and other skins from hunting expeditions ashore. Unlike Ahab, Smith would return safely to merry old England, there to compose his books and die peacefully at age fifty-one.

CHAPTER 25

Postscript

MORE ABOUT THE GREATNESS OF WHALING

Ishmael continues to wax in this brief chapter about the benefits of whaling and its by-products. He concludes, "Think of that, ye loyal Britons! we whalemen supply your kings and queens with coronation stuff!"

One Briton returned the favor, more or less.

John Bonham scintillated as drummer for the British rock group Led Zeppelin, which reigned from the late 1960s to the 1970s. The group's name originated from a phrase that Keith Moon, the drummer for The Who, sometimes used: "going down like a lead balloon." Doodling around with that phrase, band manager Peter Grant came up with Lead Zeppelin.

He then decided that Led "looked a lot simpler—and it was all that light and heavy irony."

The group was built from the remnants of The Yardbirds, with guitarist Jimmy Page as its guiding force. Their repertoire was heavily blues-based, although the group was open to various styles. Bonham was a great fan of classic and vigorous jazz drummers Gene Krupa and Buddy Rich.

Led Zeppelin worked hard to draw fans into the music, exuding an almost preternatural energy. Page played his guitar with a violin bow while Robert Plant sang with touching urgency.

Excessive sexual, drink, and drug exploits also defined the band. It was not unusual for Bonham to snort cocaine while drumming, then after the show to "wind down" by drinking a bottle or more of Jack Daniels, or whatever other alcohol might be available. At such times, he became violent—picking fights, destroying hotel rooms, and falling into a stupor until roused for his next performance.

Bonham's most famous drum solo—perhaps the best known in rock music*—is in a song called "Moby Dick." It began as bits and pieces that Page put together for a recording. In such a form it is uninspired; it was originally called, "Pat's Delight," after Bonham's wife. How and why it was called "Moby Dick" is unclear. As the drum solo grew lengthier and wilder, it possibly evoked for Page, an inveterate reader, an association with the bulky novel. Perhaps, too, Page imagined Bonham as an Ahab figure, searching for the perfect syncopation that would transcend the moment.

The drum solo is preceded by powerful guitar riffs. Bonham then takes center stage with his exploration into drum improvisation—his own journey deeper into the nature of his instrument and his own demons. Depending on his mood, the drum solo could last for a few minutes although sometimes it was elongated to forty-five minutes of nonstop drumming.

Rumor had it that fellow band members took advantage of the break to have sex with groupies backstage before returning to conclude the set with fevered guitar riffs.

Bonham's drumming shifted between the use of sticks and bare hands. In either mode, he achieved not only rhythmic intensity but also a heightened power of sound. As he sweats profusely—the longer versions of this

---

*Rock musicians have often turned to *Moby-Dick*. Consider heavy metal group Mastodon and their superinfused recording "Leviathan." In another vein, Moby (real name Richard Melville Hall, descended from Melville) began as a punk rocker before transforming himself into a techno composer–musician and spokesman for vegetarianism. There is also a technopunk band called Captain Ahab.

number are escapades in endurance—he is as relentless as Ahab, a rush of drum waves pounds the shore as the audience is lifted into a state of rapture. It is a great moment in rock history.

Alas, neither Ahab nor Bonham was able to vanquish the demons that haunted them. In Bonham's case, his end came in 1980. According to the East Berkshire Coroner's Court report, Bonham was an "accidental suicide" or a case of "death by misadventure" (a fitting description for Ahab) caused by the consumption of immense amounts of alcohol.

CHAPTER 26

Knights and Squires

STARBUCK IS DESCRIBED AND SOME WORDS ARE OFFERED ABOUT WORKING MEN AND DEMOCRACY

F. O. Matthiessen, professor of literature at Harvard University, helped to establish the greatness of *Moby-Dick* in his book *American Renaissance* (1941). While he also addressed the writings of Emerson, Whitman, and Thoreau, Matthiessen devoted over 140 of the 650 pages of *American Renaissance* to *Moby-Dick*.

Matthiessen especially loved one passage in "Knights and Squires" chapter. His Harvard students recall him intoning it in classes:

> But this august dignity I treat of, is not the dignity of kings and robes, but that abounding dignity which has no robed investiture. Thou shalt see it shining in the arm that wields a pick or drives a spike; that democratic dignity which, on all hands, radiates without end from God; Himself! The great God absolute! The centre and circumference of all democracy! His omnipresence, our divine equality!
>
> If, then, to meanest mariners, and renegades and castaways, I shall hereafter ascribe high qualities, through dark; weave round them tragic graces; if even the most mournful, perchance the most abased, among them all, shall at times lift himself to the exalted mounts; if I shall touch that workman's arm with some ethereal light; if I shall spread a rainbow over his disastrous set of sun; then against all mortal critics bear me out in it, thou just Spirit of Equality, which hast spread one royal mantle of humanity over all my kind! Bear me out in it, thou great democratic God! who didst not refuse to the swart convict, Bunyan,

the pale, poetic pearl; Thou who didst clothe with doubly hammered leaves of finest gold, the stumped and paupered arm of old Cervantes; Thou who didst pick up Andrew Jackson from the pebbles; who didst hurl him upon a war-horse; who didst thunder him higher than a throne! Thou who, in all Thy mighty, earthly marchings, ever cullest Thy selectest champions from the kingly commons; bear me out in it, O God!

A type of transcendent equality reigns over this passage. Of course, in the everyday hurdy-gurdy of life, inequality rules, on the ship as much as in the counting-house, factory, or faculty meeting. But, as Melville suggests and Matthiessen applauds, God is a democrat who anoints, as it were, the poor and forsaken. Even outside the realm of the purely divine, a democratic ethos and creativity are to be found.

Melville announces his allegiance to the Democratic Party of his era by praising former President Andrew Jackson. While this might smack of unsavory nationalism and racism, since Jackson was a fanatical foe of Native Americans, a slaveholder and nationalist, such an undertone in the passage is assuaged somewhat—in Matthiessen's view—by Melville's sympathetic depictions of Queequeg and other people of color in the book. He offers us a holy trinity to worship—the skilled sailor, the dreamy seeker, and the defiant hero. Even Christians, after all, can learn much from savages and sailors.

As a student at Yale in the 1920s, Matthiessen had tutored Hungarian immigrants in English to help them to pass their citizenship examination. It was a highpoint in his life, as these men shared with him their prohibition-era homemade wine and friendship. As he returned one evening to his Yale quarters, Matthiessen was aglow "in the natural and hearty comradeship of these men." He remarked years later, "It was the kind of comradeship that I wanted never to lose." It is the type of solidarity or comradeship that is apparent among the "mariners, mystics and renegades" that Melville depicts in *Moby-Dick*. The work-centered fellowship of the men on the ship was for Matthiessen the essence of Christian love and devotion.

As a mostly closeted gay man—"damn it! I hate to have to hide when what I thrive on is absolute directness"—Matthiessen thrilled to one line in this passage—"if I shall touch that workman's arm with some ethereal light." It evoked for him an experience that had occurred in 1925. Visiting a chapel in England, he ogled "a workman—husky, broad-shouldered . . . the perfect Chaucerian yeoman." Later, he recalled fondly, "We stood there talking about a quarter of a minute, and as he went on I deliberately let my elbow rub against his belly. That was all. . . .

I didn't want anything more. I was simply attracted by him." Such attraction, abstracted to a love of common humanity, although not bereft of a certain sexual *frisson*, added to Matthiessen's appreciation for this passage in *Moby-Dick*.

CHAPTER 27

Knights and Squires

ISHMAEL CONTINUES TO DESCRIBE THE CREW

Another scholar, C.L.R. James, quite different from Matthiessen, also exulted in *Moby-Dick*. Battered by a duodenal ulcer, surrounded by Stalinist political enemies, and under threat of imminent expulsion from the United States, James composed *Mariners, Renegades, and Castaways*. He worked on it twelve hours a day while being held in detention at Ellis Island in the summer of 1952. Although he had legally entered the United States in 1938, coming as a lecturer under the auspices of the left-wing Workers Party, once his visitor's visa had expired, he chose to live a somewhat below-the-radar existence. Finally, FBI agents intruded on his idyll and sent him to Ellis Island.

During the bleak four months of his imprisonment, and an easier time at a hospital on Staten Island, James no doubt wandered down the corridors of his memory to the time when he had read *Moby-Dick* in full during the summer of 1944. He was then recovering from an operation on the troublesome ulcer. One day he took a stroll away from the monotony of being housebound, stopping to browse at some books for sale in a used furniture store. For twenty-five cents he bought a copy of *Moby-Dick*. Twenty years earlier, while still living in his native Trinidad, James had started the novel but quickly tossed it aside. His reaction this time was markedly different: *Moby-Dick* has "kept me in a state of almost continuous excitement."

A political radical, James was part of a small Marxist group that in the early 1940s was opposed to both Stalin and Trotsky. The moment seemed ripe, according to James, for the working class to hook up with African-Americans in the United States to push for revolution. There had been a riot in Harlem in 1943. Congress of Industrial Organizations unions were growing more militant and in various industries workers were striking despite their leaders' demands that they toe the line in support of Second World War industrial peace. The major powers were battling and decimating one another in an Armageddon of combat. In the midst of this hubbub, James predicted that workers were coming to "class consciousness."

At this same moment, James was in love with Constance Webb, a beautiful and bright young actress with radical political views. No wonder he was expansive in his dreams.

Born in 1901 to a lower middle-class family in Trinidad, James was a remarkable man. A well-educated scholarship lad, in 1932 he lit out for the mother country. In England, he quickly established himself as a popular writer on cricket, and he also immersed himself in radical politics. He could chat knowledgably on almost any topic, from sports to film to philosophy. A voracious reader, he was blessed with near total recall and grand intellectual energy. At six feet tall, with sinewy build, jaunty with cigarette hanging from his lips, James cut a handsome figure. Many were drawn to him, both for his ideas and for his charisma. Prior to coming to the United States, he had written *The Black Jacobins* (1938), an invaluable study of Toussaint L'Ouverture and the San Domingo Revolution. The work captured his confidence in the revolutionary potential of the black masses. If slaves had been able to rise up, organize, and cast off the domination of the French Empire, then surely so might the African-American and white working class.

A simple question befuddled James as he read "Knights and Squires," with its talk of heroic and dignified sailors: "Why didn't the men revolt" when faced with Ahab's fatal madness? The question, and his weak response, indicates that he was troubled by this problem. Melville had recognized, from his own years laboring as a seaman, "how men rationalized their subservience to tyranny." This would fit well with the Marxist view that workers fail to revolt because they have internalized the values of the capitalist society rather than coming to consciousness of their own power to change it.

James also pointed out the problem with leadership aboard the *Pequod*. Starbuck harbors a will to rebellion (even if not in the name of working-class revolution), but he is an example of the ineffectual liberal, easily pushed aside by the more powerful will of Ahab. The best answer that James supplies is as follows: the working class in the mid-nineteenth century is unready for revolution. Going after the White Whale is symbolic of the destructiveness at the heart of the industrial civilization. Hence, if Melville had shifted his focus and written about the crew in revolt, he would have blunted his criticism of the overall system, then in its ascendency.

This seems inadequate. Rebellion need not be a simple matter of absolute success or failure at a particular historical moment. It can be a piece in the puzzle of emerging revolutionary consciousness. The revolt in San Domingo that James had documented earlier was successful on some levels, and it certainly represented a model of potential solidarity among the oppressed. Melville shied away from this model—as he did in his later story "Benito Cereno" (see chapter 115). In the tale, slaves take over a slave ship and they come close to succeeding in their rebellion. But they fail when their plot is discovered and repressed by the stumbling intervention of an American captain.

If Melville does, as James avers, present class solidarity among the crew of the *Pequod*, it is marked by "technical skill, endurance and determination" more than by revolutionary solidarity. And these qualities can be, and are, harnessed by the totalitarian Ahab for his nefarious ends. James concludes that the crew opted for "false" solidarity through the fanatical will and heated vision of Ahab. They are not so different from the Germans who flocked to Hitler or the Americans who were rallying under the banner of Senator Joseph McCarthy at the time James entered into full dialogue with Melville's novel.

Figure 9.
Moby Dick in all of his glory, Woodcut by Rockwell Kent.

CHAPTER 28

Ahab

AHAB—"LIKE A MAN CUT AWAY FROM THE STAKE"

Rockwell Kent seemed destined to illustrate *Moby-Dick*. From a well-rooted American family, much like the Melvilles, Kent was an artist, writer, and energetic voyager. Trained as a painter by some members of the Ash Can School of art, he exhibited four of his works in the famous New York Armory Show of 1913, a key moment for the introduction of modernism into America. While always beholden to representation over abstraction, Kent's modernism was stylish and accessible, weighted with emotion and symbolic meaning.

Kent knew the sea with a wary intimacy, having undertaken various voyages, including one to Greenland. In 1929, he and his mates were shipwrecked off the Greenland coast, and he underwent a harrowing three-day mountain climb to find help. In another adventure, he took his eight-year-old son with him to live on Fox Island, twelve miles away from Seward, Alaska. Here he struggled with harsh nature, worked on his art, and read, among other works, Nietzsche's *Thus Spake Zarathustra*. However appealing in theory, Nietzsche's superman was rendered problematic by his isolation from others.

A hearty and energetic individualist, drawn to hardscrabble climes, Kent was committed to a version of Theodore Roosevelt's ideal of the strenuous life. Despite Kent's embrace of a self-reliant, Emersonian individualism, he identified himself as a committed socialist, believing that individualism and socialism were essential to a just society and a good life.

In 1926, Kent began working on his woodcut illustrations for the Lakeside Press edition of *Moby-Dick*. He wrote to the editor that he considered "Moby Dick . . . a most solemn, mystic work." The storyline, full of adventure, was intended as "the medium for Melville's profound and poetic philosophy." The proper approach for the illustration and typography for *Moby-Dick*, he imagined, must be dark: "the midnight darkness enveloping human existence, the darkness of the human soul, the abyss, such is the mood of Moby Dick." Kent brilliantly captured such a mood.

His publishers concurred. They found his initial set of drawings stunning, when he submitted them in 1927. "Your great genius as a thinker, painter, and draughtsman," wrote Kent's editor at Lakeside Press, "was never more successfully demonstrated." The press agreed with Kent that a three-volume edition would best serve the novel, and they also doubled his fee for the illustrations to two thousand dollars. Kent worked on the drawings for four years, interrupted by various adventures and sea travels and other commissions (he was also doing illustrations for a Random House edition of Voltaire's *Candide*). He finally finished them in Denmark in 1929, and they appeared in the beautiful edition of 1930.

CHAPTER 29

Enter Ahab; To Him, Stubb

AHAB DISTURBS STUBB'S SLEEP

Ahab may be a democrat of the spirit—at least to the degree that he acknowledges that all men are equally damned by fate. Aboard his ship he reigns supreme, and all must submit to his vision and plan. Only twice on the long journey of the *Pequod* is Ahab questioned. The first instance comes from the most unlikely of sources, Mr. Stubb, the second mate. Or it may be a case of Stubb simply dreaming of insubordination and Ahab's retribution.

Ahab broods and paces the quarterdeck, his ivory leg resonating loudly on those hunkered below. Stubb's sleep is disturbed, so he ventures out of his bunk to request that Ahab meditate elsewhere. Suffice it to say, Ahab is unsympathetic. He curses out Stubb, calling him a "dog." Stubb also imagines that Ahab has given him a stiff kick in the rear.

In a burst of anger and surprise, it is conceivable that Ahab may have denounced Stubb as a "dog." But it is unlikely that he kicked him. It would have required some very deft maneuvering on the part of a man with one pegged leg. Besides, Ahab forces men to quake simply by the power that emanates from him. No need to kick those of lesser rank. Ahab's powers of persuasion are sufficient to gather mild Ishmael into the clutch of his fanatical vision (see chapter 36).

Melville was more than intimate with the administration of discipline aboard American ships in the 1840s. While Melville may never have smarted under the lash, he certainly witnessed and recounted the practice in his novel *White-Jacket* (1850). There, in the chapter "A Flogging," he describes how the crew is called to the deck to witness the punishment of four sailors for fighting and insubordination: "All hands witness punishment, ahoy!" As Melville relates, "To the sensitive seaman," among whom we must include Melville as one of their number, "that summons sounds like a doom."

The captain orders the prisoners brought up to the deck. The ritual and the penalty for their fight a day earlier is clear. The boatswain takes out four cats-o'-nine-tails—the whips that will be used to strike each of the bare-backed sailors. With the lift of the captain's finger, the punishment begins. Twelve lashes to the tender, exposed skin.

Each man reacts differently to the blows; one shrugs them off with bravado. Another mutters about revenge while another only feels the pain of insult. The fourth sailor, "the missen-top lad" offers up "weeping entreaties and vows of contrition," but they are ignored by the captain who responds—in an echo of words that Ahab will later utter—"I would not forgive God Almighty!"

Melville followed up the chapter on flogging with chapters offering explicit condemnation of the act. It was, he wrote, an evil—and an unnecessary one at that. He stated this at a time when the specter of flogging was well known on the American homeland, in the institution of slavery. While Melville did not directly confront the analogy between the flogging of sailors and the whipping of the slaves, he did, as Andrew Delbanco points out, make it clear that flogging ran counter to the American dream of equality and justice fought. Congress agreed, abolishing the practice not long after Melville's *White-Jacket* had been published.

Alas, we live in an era when new forms of torture have been inflicted in the name of democratic ideals. Maybe we need a Melville to puncture such pretensions.

CHAPTER 30

The Pipe

AHAB DECIDES TO JETTISON HIS BELOVED PIPE

Ahab's mission is clear—to find and kill Moby Dick. To achieve revenge, he recognizes that he must sacrifice pleasure, so he forsakes his treasured pipe, with its allure of serenity. With a hiss, the pipe hits the water. Like an ascetic monk in search of oneness with God through flagellation and deprivation, Ahab embraces denial of pleasure for a greater quest.

What might Sigmund Freud make of this? Born five years after *Moby-Dick* set sail, Freud posited that repression of sexual desire and anarchic tendencies was necessary to bring forth civilization. He recognized, however, that the foundations of civilization—predicated upon repression—are molten. They bubble forth in collective neurosis and mania, threatening at any moment to topple civilization. This intermingling of civilization and destruction, of control and release, has been since Freud's time a mainstay of our thinking. In the 1940s, Walter Benjamin stated with sad recognition, as he sought to escape from the Nazis: "There is no document of civilization which is not at the same time a document of barbarism."

Ahab represents civilization against nature. But the equation is complicated a bit because the White Whale may also be viewed as exemplary of sexual desire. Moby Dick is, after all, a sperm whale that might easily be visualized as a phallic figure of immense proportions, endlessly spouting. Ahab, then, is the paradox of civilization, exerting maniacal control over himself and his desires in order both to conjoin with and to vanquish the whale. His deepest need, dare we say, is to stick his harpoon deep into Moby Dick, an act fraught with Freudian symbolism and stacked with a delirious deck of death imagery.

CHAPTER 31

Queen Mab

STUBB TELLS FLASK HIS DREAM ABOUT AHAB

Dreams, according to Freud and Carl Jung, are the royal road to the unconscious. Stubb, in relating his "dream" about being kicked by Ahab, travels along that thoroughfare.

As he relates it to Flask in this chapter, "You know the old man's ivory leg, well I dreamed he kicked me with it; and when I tried to kick back, upon my soul, my little man, I kicked my leg right off! Ahab seemed a pyramid, and I, like a blazing fool, kept kicking at it."

Edward F. Edinger, a Jungian therapist, spent a good deal of time thinking about Stubb's dream. According to Edinger, Ahab is kicking with all his might against the bare facts of nature while Stubb is kicking at Ahab, whom he imagines as a pyramid.

The pyramid is a recurring image in Melville's work, a reminder of the origins of Mosaic monotheism. In a poem that he later composed, "The Great Pyramid," Melville drove home the point, and he directly associated the pyramids with a species of whale. The solid outside of a pyramid masks its many secret passages and caves. Thus, the pyramid, like Moby Dick, is more than it seems—at once marvelous and massive, mysterious and mystical.

Dreams go beyond mere wish-fulfillments; they are indices of anxiety. Clearly Stubb's dream is a presentiment of hard times in the offing. He announces that his dream has "made a wise man of me." In what manner? Here Stubb is less than proactive. He simply decides that it is best to avoid Ahab, a man who is "bloody on his mind." But silence in the face of fanaticism, surrender to the power of Ahab's vision, is ultimately akin to signing one's own death certificate.

CHAPTER 32

Cetology

ISHMAEL PONDERS THE "UNWRITTEN LIFE" OF WHALES

Nowadays we all know that whales are mammals—science and sentiment attest to this fact.

However, the question was contested in the early nineteenth century. Although scientific taxonomy increasingly placed whales in the mammalian category, popular opinion weighed heavily toward viewing the whale as a fish. Ishmael devotes a good deal of time to this question. His conclusion is clear: "I take the good old fashioned ground that the whale is a fish, and call upon holy Jonah to back me." Perhaps Melville was being ironic here, but whether fish or mammal, the White Whale was to be an estimable enemy for Ishmael and the crew of the *Pequod*.

The issue of the nature of the whale proved to be a lively one during the case of James Maurice versus Samuel Judd, heard in a New York City courtroom in December 1818. As brilliantly narrated by historian D. Graham Burnett, a New York State statute required that all casks of "fish oil" be inspected, with fees applied. But businessman Judd declined to pay Maurice's inspection fee on the basis that the oil inspected had been "spermaceti oil," that is, whale oil. Since whales were mammals, according to

Judd, they did not fall under the statute. This obviously put a crimp in the pocket of Mr. Maurice, who collected a fee from each cask of fish oil that he inspected. He brought suit against Judd on the basis that whales had always been considered to be fish; moreover, they remained fish!

One witness for the defendant was deliciously named Captain Preserved Fish. With thirty years in the business of whaling and hailing from New Bedford, Captain Fish maintained that whales were mammals since they "must breathe the atmospheric air." Dr. Samuel Latham Mitchell, a physician and scientist of great note, testified on the basis of comparative anatomy that whales were mammals. But even with his scientific credentials, Mitchell was unwilling to jettison his faith in the Bible (as he interpreted it), his notion of a Great Chain of Being, and his faith in democratic opinion. On the latter score, one of the trial lawyers, Henry Meigs, commented plainly: the public "don't care a pin whether his blood be cold or hot; mammalian or *Magnolia*, he swims & lives in the sea and they swear he is a fish."

The science of classification did, by this period, firmly place whales among mammals, based on what lay beneath the surface—internal anatomy, the structure of the jaws, formation of lungs, and so on. In this sense, following the tradition first set by the Frenchman Georges Cuvier in the late eighteenth century, dissection—cutting away the pasteboard mask of skin—allowed the anatomist to dive deeper into the mysteries of species.

But, as the plaintiff's lawyer made clear in his expert questioning, not all wanted to dive so deeply into such mysteries. They preferred to stand upon tradition and the common sense of public opinion; like Starbuck, they saw danger in manic pursuit into the nature of things. Whales were sources of wealth, nothing beyond that mattered much. If whale men were pressed to render an opinion on the critical manner of whether whales be fish or mammal, most of them would have opted, as Burnett iterates, for the former designation.

John Anthon, speaking for the plaintiff in a closing statement, took issue with Mitchell's claim that whales were not fish, "and that whale oil is, consequently, not fish oil." Such a view, he proclaimed, would mean that "we should be bound to surrender our common sense." While this might be common practice for folks in New England, it was not a view readily embraced by New Yorkers (recall here Evert Duyckinck's *Knickerbocker* animus against Emersonians).

The jury deliberated for only fifteen minutes, and they returned with a verdict in favor of Mr. Maurice, the plaintiff—he would get his dollars for each cask and he could state with the same confidence as Ishmael, that "the whale is a fish."

It should be noted that the New York State legislature amended the statute in question less than a month following the verdict, exempting whale oil from inspection. Maurice claimed his seventy-five dollars and court fees. With the emergence of professional science, the Darwinian revolution, and the decline of Biblical fundamentalism in the second half of the nineteenth century, the controversial fires burning around whether the whale was mammal or fish had cooled; the whale was a mammal, albeit one that retained its own peculiar mystery and majesty. But, then, Melville always knew that.

CHAPTER 33

The Specksynder

MORE INSIGHTS INTO HIERARCHY ABOARD SHIP

Norman Mailer was nothing if not an ambitious novelist. Keenly aware of literary rank, he aimed to be at the top of his game by writing the Great American Novel. In a notorious piece, "Evaluations: Quick and Expensive Comments on the Talent in the Room," Mailer opined that James Jones was the only contemporary novelist with more natural talent than him. However, while Jones once possessed "the beer-guts of a broken-glass brawl," he had sold out and "handcuffed the rebel in him." Mailer alone, it was presumed, had the gumption and talent to bring about "a revolution in the consciousness of our time."

Mailer had long wanted to write the next Great American Novel. He graduated Harvard in 1943 and soon was a member of the armed forces, seeing action in the Philippines. A studious, self-described, nice Jewish boy from Brooklyn, he drew partly from his own war experiences in his novel *The Naked and the Dead*, published in 1948. Mailer later admitted that, in terms of overall design, *Moby-Dick* had been the biggest influence on his first novel: "I was sure everyone would know. I had Ahab in it, and I suppose the mountain was Moby Dick."

In Mailer's immensely successful first novel, a few characters evoke those in *Moby-Dick*. General Cummings exudes power. He is a modern, bureaucratic fascist—capable of manipulation and thrilled with the exercise of his authority. He acknowledges his own desire to "achieve God." Cummings is like Ahab, "bleak and alone, commanding the heights." The Starbuck that opposes Cummings is Lieutenant Hearn, a man of fine sensibilities and education. Cummings takes sadistic pleasure—unlike Ahab—in crushing and humiliating Hearn. At one point, Cummings commands Hearn to stoop down and pick up a discarded cigarette, an implicit surrender to Cummings's ultimate power over him and the soldiers in his command.

Sergeant Croft also has aspects of Ahab (and Queequeg) to him. Strong and wary, capable of immense exertion—natural man personified—Croft can, through his innate will to dominate, triumph over Hearn. But he is no match for General Cummings, who can bend men to his own will. Within his own frame of reference, Croft exerts power over the men in his command and against the challenges that nature and war throw in his path—he is a superman of sorts, an Ahab on a quest for victory and for self-annihilation.

Croft must lead his platoon on a dangerous trek up Mount Anaka to observe Japanese troop formations and bring back information to help plan for a major attack. The physical monumentality of the mountain is daunting. It is, as Mailer later suggested, a Moby Dick that Croft and his men must vanquish. For Croft the mountain is a welcome opponent: "He had the mountain in his teeth . . . He was continually eager to press on to the next rise, anxious to see what was beyond. The sheer mass of the mountain inflamed him." Croft alone thrills at the task: "He was going to climb it; he swore to himself." It becomes his White Whale and it cannot vanquish him. Despite how the "mountain seemed eternally to rear" above him, Croft sees it as "an iron warp in his mind. He could have turned back no more easily than he could have killed himself." He is Ahabian will, pure and simple.

The mountain is as massive and ubiquitous in the lives of the men as Moby Dick was for Ahab and the crew of the *Pequod*. Mailer notes "the huge body of the mountain glowing oddly in the darkness like a vast monument illumined by spotlights." The mountain is an object of great danger, its shadows hiding natural and human booby traps. Yet it exerts "fascination"—it becomes "alive." Its expanse knows no boundaries—one soldier lying on his back finds that he is unable to see its top.

Croft and the men climb and climb, but their exertions prove to be absurd, not just because the mountain resists them. Their mission is beside the point; military command has, unbeknown to them, decided to launch an attack without their reconnaissance information. They climb but they are forgotten. A nice touch of the absurd.

The platoon nears the summit but they must undertake dangerous leaps—leaps of faith. A soldier named Roth fails and becomes a "little man, tumbling through space." The next morning the remainder of the squad continue, only two or three hours more of climbing remain until they reach the uppermost ridge. They want to turn back but Croft crushes any rebellion. As they continue upward, they become compelled to climb because they now hate the mountain, "with more fervor that they could ever have hated a human being. The stairway became alive, personalized; it seemed to mock and deceive them at every step, resist them with every malign rock."

The absurd intrudes anew. Near the mountain's uppermost ridge, Croft accidentally upends "a light-tan nest shaped something like a football." It is a hornet's nest and their peace has been disturbed. The "furious" hornets, as if emissaries from hell, unleash their attack, stinging Croft and the platoon relentlessly. In a pained panic, the men cease their climb and scurry as quickly as they can back to the base of the mountain, without incident, without accomplishment, without honor.

Unlike Ahab, who learned nothing from his skirmish with Moby Dick, Croft matures. He feels relief, even if temporary, in his inability to scale the mountain. He "was rested by the unadmitted knowledge that he had found a limit to his hunger." No small accomplishment, one that would have betokened a longer life for Ahab had he come to such a realization.

CHAPTER 34

The Cabin-Table

THE OFFICERS, FOLLOWED BY THE HARPOONERS, TAKE THEIR MEAL

Slavery and race relations are resounding themes in *Moby-Dick*. Indeed, some interpreters have found the essence of the novel to be an elaborate examination of racial politics in mid-nineteenth-century America. Writing the book while the Compromise of 1850 was being hammered out and finishing it as his father-in-law, Lemuel Shaw, was enforcing one of its edicts by exiling a fugitive slave named Thomas Sims back to bondage in the South—how could race not be on the mind of Herman Melville?

While Melville was certainly prone to stereotyping blacks, he much preferred to reject racial hierarchies—to challenge the ethnological or scientific racist notions of his era. Various ethnologists and apologists for slavery, during Melville's time, trotted out theories "proving" the innate superiority of the white race against all other groupings. In contrast,

Melville found nobility aplenty among presumed savages and cannibals; he refused in his earlier books to bow down in appreciation of the character and habits of Christian missionaries. He was also particularly attentive to how existing hierarchies were unfair, with how power inhered in the hands of the inferior; it is a common theme in all of his works, as we shall see in the *Town-Ho* story (see chapter 54).

Melville, as Carolyn Karcher explains, had lived among savages and had worked with other races while a youthful sailor. He found good and bad aspects rather evenly distributed among various races. He had as a sailor seen power abused and had felt it himself. He was, by temperament, an egalitarian and a democrat. Melville went beyond many abolitionists in his appreciation for the humanity of African-Americans.

The racial messages in *Moby-Dick* thus point in the direction of racial enlightenment. Although we are told at the outset that Queequeg is from the South Sea Islands, his racial identity is complex—he worships a "Congo idol" and he is often described as black. He is always regal and proud, as is the giant African harpooner Daggoo. Ishmael comes to realize that Queequeg is nature's nobleman, a firm friend, protector, and man of high moral stature. Racial and cultural distinctions melt away, as the two become friends and perhaps lovers, their fates married in so many ways, capturing the ways in which the races in America are intertwined.

Thus, the final accounting with Ishmael surviving, thanks to the coffin-cum-lifesaver built at the behest of Queequeg, becomes a parable of sacrifice. Queequeg goes down with the ship, but his legacy allows Ishmael to live to tell his story and to cherish his memory by imagining a world where racial distinctions and hierarchies are greater fictions than the White Whale.

Melville drives this theme home in this chapter as well. There is a hierarchy at the captain's dining table. Once the officers have consumed their meal (with Ahab defining the pace of eating and demanding silence), the harpooners enter to eat. These men of color "dined like lords" and they expect the very white and not very bright Dough-Boy to serve them with alacrity. Sometimes, to make him move more quickly, Tashtego sticks his fork against Dough-Boy's back. In absolute contrast to racial hierarchy, the deeply black Daggoo once—humorously we are told—snatched Dough-Boy up and placed "his head in a great empty wooden trencher" on the table while Tashtego with "knife in hand, began laying out the circle preliminary to scalping him." Not surprisingly, Dough-Boy is a nervous little fellow in the face of such racially tinged shenanigans from "these three savages" as well as from the stern visage of "the black terrific Ahab." As soon as he has satisfied the wants of the harpooners, Dough-Boy retreats to his pantry, his lip quivering as he no doubt contemplates a racially topsy-turvy world.

Surprisingly, the handful of white Southern reviewers of *Moby-Dick* did not take offense at Melville's barely concealed racial jibes. Perhaps they were less than careful readers. More probably, their ideological armor was so well-wrought that even Daggoo's harpoon could not pierce it. Hence, although Melville prayed for national reconciliation and brotherhood to resolve the issue of slavery, he sensed that the probable outcome would be a bloody trial by fire.

CHAPTER 35

The Mast-Head

ISHMAEL PONDERS FROM UP HIGH

Atop the vertigo-inducing masthead, Ishmael is supposed to scan the sea for whales, with a keen eye fixed for the White Whale in particular. He is a poor lookout, rather prone to long spells of philosophical reverie. He thinks about modern Platonists, followers of Ralph Waldo Emerson and the Concord school of Philosophy. These "absent-minded youth" hustle and bustle about in search of transcendence, for a "blending cadence of waves with thoughts." The upshot of this magical moment is presumed to bring forth a mystical loss of identity, when an individual "takes the mystic ocean at his feet for the visible image of that deep, blue, bottomless soul."

This sounds like a moment of transcendental hogwash. It echoes the famous lines in Emerson's essay "Nature" (1836), when he revs up his prose to imagine "my head bathed by the blithe air, and uplifted into infinite space,—all mean egotism vanishes. I become a transparent eye-ball. I am nothing. I see all. The currents of the Universal Being circulate through me . . . In the tranquil landscape, and especially in the distant line of the horizon, man beholds somewhat as beautiful as his own nature."

If Ishmael, with his head near the clouds, is experiencing this Emersonian moment, then Melville is certain to burst its bubble. Such transcendence to Melville is silly—and dangerous. We are earthbound, the weight of gravity certain to pull us back—sometimes disastrously—to lower soundings. There is danger in such metaphysical high jinks. Ishmael could easily, in the space of a moment, make a misstep on the masthead that will cost him his life—"with one half-throttled shriek you drop through that transparent air into the summer sea, no more to rise forever. Heed it well, ye Pantheists!"

While Melville disdained the empty-headed, soaring metaphysics of transcendentalists, he did respect Emerson. Indeed, in 1849, he had attended a lecture by the sage of Concord. "To my surprise," he wrote, there was much to admire in Emerson, even if some of what he said sounded more like the babble of a "fool [rather] than a wise man," Melville thrilled that Emerson was one of those "men who *dive*" into the waters of thought. Perhaps speaking for himself and his own emerging desires—and significantly employing the whale as a metaphor—Melville continued: "Any fish can swim near the surface, but it takes a great whale to go down stairs five miles or more." Melville, up to this point, had not taken any of his books as deep down as he would soon with *Moby-Dick*.

This was a period when American authors and thinkers were diving deeper and swimming farther from comfortable shores. Emerson's various volumes—most famously his *Essays* (1841) and *Nature*—demanded from Americans a new engagement with the world, one marked by creativity over tradition, by exploration rather than comfort, ideals more than cash value. As he put it famously in his 1837 address "The American Scholar," readers must free themselves from slavish devotion to earlier masters. Genius must be unshackled from the past so that it can create. Such creativity, in Emerson's philosophy, was the sparkle of man's divinity.

Melville proudly cast his lot with this historical moment that saw the rise of American literature, but he distanced himself from the philosophical content embraced by some of these great minds.

CHAPTER 36

The Quarter-Deck

AHAB ADDRESSES THE CREW ABOUT THE WHITE WHALE

In the 1930s, Hitler provoked intense fascination and concern about the power of leaders to seduce the masses. Hitler and Ahab seem to be cut from the same cloth of cruelty and fanaticism.

Each man was, after all, monomaniacal—driven to achieve his peculiar ends by the force of an iron will and without regard to cost or logic. For Hitler, extermination of the Jews was an obsession, to the point of diverting resources necessary for the prosecution of the war. He heaped upon the Jews all of the ills that afflicted humanity, no matter how paradoxical or absurd his claim that Jews were at once rapacious capitalists and grubby Marxists. In his blood-tinctured vision, the Aryan race was pure, and the need to protect it from the virus of Jews was a mission that could only succeed once the specter and reality of Jews had been wiped from the face of the earth. Hitler was secure in this conviction; it fired his hatred, warped his perceptions, and helped to bring an abrupt end to his vision of a thousand-year reich.

During his rise to power and initial period of rule, beginning in 1933, Hitler was a mesmerizing speaker—addressing massive throngs of followers in carefully staged events. His vision encompassed a mythical past and a fervent future that whipped up the enthusiasm of his followers to march with him through the fires of hell—if need be. He became synonymous with the modern notion of a demagogue.

Ahab appears as a fictional precursor of Hitler. There is the obvious shared monomania, with Ahab's desire for revenge and his willingness to plop all of the wrongs of existence upon the back of the White Whale. This is Ahab's private vision, one that ensnarls his heart, mind, and soul. The problem that he faces as captain of the *Pequod* is how to snare the crew of the ship in his plan. While his power as captain is immense, it is not absolute—mutinies do occur when the captain of a ship proves he is incompetent or overbearing, and when his greed for revenge trumps profits. The problem for Ahab—as for any modern demagogue—is how to transform a private goal into a public vision, assented to with fervor and conviction.

Upon the quarterdeck, Ahab assembles the crew and begins with a call and response—a technique of address common in evangelical church services (or in a kindergarten class). With theatricality and pacing of presentation, Ahab "vehemently" inquires of the crew: "What do ye do when ye see a whale, men?" "Sing out for him!" the crew responds. Ahab wends his way forward, building up the intensity of responses and sealing the deal by dramatically nailing a doubloon, a "Spanish ounce of gold" to the mainmast. It is the reward for the first sailor to cry out that he has sighted "a white-headed whale with a wrinkled brow and a crooked jaw." And soon the name of that whale is uttered with dread apprehension, Moby Dick.

Starbuck identifies, in contrast, with land-based concerns; he has no truck with airy ideals or morbid fantasies that stand in the way of assured profits. His is a voice of reason—"How many barrels will thy vengeance yield thee even if though gettest it . . . it will not fetch thee much in our

Nantucket market." Logic, alas, is a rubbery cudgel against the iron will of fanaticism. Starbuck's further retort that "To be enraged with a dumb thing, Captain Ahab, seems blasphemous," too, falls short.

Ahab is a visionary, for "All visible objects," he lectures Starbuck, "are but as pasteboard masks." And the mystery of the whale—the mystery and meaning of life—must be pierced by Ahab's harpoon. "Talk not to me of blasphemy, man; I'd strike the sun if it insulted me. . . . Who's over me? Truth hath no confines." While Ahab is fixed in direction, unwavering in will, the problem of gaining the enthusiasm of his crew remains unbidden. For this, more than a bit of demagogy, the reward of a doubloon and a draught of rum are required.

With theatrical flair and a nod towards ancient and blasphemous rituals, Ahab commands the harpooners join their lances. Ahab touches the axis, at its crossed center. He then fixes his intense stare upon the visages of his underlings—Starbuck, Stubb, and Flask. As Melville puts it, "It seemed as though, by some nameless, interior volition, he would fain have shocked into them the same fiery emotion accumulated within the Leyden jar of his own magnetic life. The three mates quailed before his strong, sustained, and mystic aspect."

He unites these specimens of white America with their "pagan kinsmen" (Queequeg, Tashtego, and Daggoo). All of them drink from the "goblet end" of their harpoons a toast to the task before them and they (with the presumed exception of Starbuck) cry out (as does the rest of the crew, Ishmael included), "Death to Moby Dick! God hunt us all, if we do not hunt Moby Dick to his death!" With the crew in a tizzy of emotion, Ahab dismisses them and returns to his cabin to chart their now intertwined fates.

CHAPTER 37

Sunset

IN HIS CABIN, AHAB RUMINATES ABOUT MOBY DICK

Revenge,* as Melville well understood, has always been an insistent theme in literature, from the Greek tragedies, then the Bible, and much of Shakespeare. It remains a constant: in *The Godfather*, the Corleone family is involved in

*On forgiveness, the flip-side of revenge, see chapter 100.

vendettas to settle accounts with various rivals. As Mario Puzo noted in the book, "Accidents don't happen to people who take accidents as a personal insult." Ahab is such a person.

Intent upon revenge against the White Whale that has dismembered him and, in all probability, contributed to a loss of his sexual potency, Ahab does not for a second consider himself a madman, although he is willing to pronounce himself "madness maddened" or a "demoniac." In his own mind, he seeks to "dismember my dismemberer." Here Ahab is following the injunction in the book of Exodus about an "eye for an eye."

But how do you dismember a whale, since it is, in effect, without limbs? Must the scales of justice, then, be balanced only by the death of Moby Dick? Or is the desire for retribution against a beast such as Moby, as Starbuck has just remarked, a dangerous conceit, a form of madness in and of itself? After all, the point of vengeance is to direct it against a responsible party. Can a beast be held responsible?

While there is surely tension between revenge and justice, the latter is a system for taking revenge out of the hands of the individual and ceding it to the authority of the state, with assured punishments. The "talion" is predicated upon the notion that a value can be put upon various actions. Hence, in the time of King Aethelberht in Kent, from 590 to 616, compensation for a lost eye was fixed at 10 shillings; while a big toe brought the same amount, the loss of an entire foot was worth 50 shillings. Justice, even when a price is not affixed to a lost appendage, is premised upon commensurability. Punishment is expected to bear some relation to the severity of the crime.

From Ahab's perspective, the crime that Moby Dick has committed against him is of the highest order—it goes beyond a simple case of dismasting, it leaps into a metaphysical assault upon the very state of his being. It is a cleaver from the hand of God that has revealed the world as riven by chaos and contingency, ill-will and evil. In this sense, Moby Dick is responsible since he either exemplifies the chaos of the universe or serves as a weapon in the hand of a God that has chosen to smite Ahab. Against this "reality," Ahab demands vengeance, even at the cost of his life and that of his cowed crew.

Today we tend to think revenge a sloppy vestige of savagery existing against the totem of advanced civilization. In Melville's time, however, a culture of revenge was central. Indeed, some have suggested that the culture of honor that reigned among the white planters in the South helped lead to the Civil War. Southern Ahabs, known as Fire-eaters, spouted states' rights doctrines, defended the institution of slavery, and sanctioned secession from the Union. Their tempers flared easily and they were quick to take umbrage at any hint of a slur upon their honor. Most famously, six years after the publication of *Moby-Dick*, Congressman Preston Brooks from South Carolina severely beat Charles Sumner, the antislavery Senator from Massachusetts, with a cane, while he was huddled at his senate desk. Apparently, in Brooks's mind, Sumner had demeaned the honor of his cousin, Senator Andrew Butler, by comparing him with Don Quixote. Perhaps a comparison with Captain Ahab would have been equally apt had Sumner read *Moby-Dick*.

CHAPTER 38

Dusk

STARBUCK REALIZES HE CANNOT DEFY AHAB

Aspects of Herman Melville can readily be seen in the characters of Ahab and Ishmael. But might there be a current of Melville and his situation in Starbuck as well?

Starbuck admits to himself that his "soul is more than matched; she's overmanned; and by a madman!" He has failed in his initial attempt to dissuade Ahab from his reckoning with Moby Dick. Starbuck lacks neither bravery nor ability. He is simply wedded to his family and to the reasonable notion that one faces dangers when earning a living. Beyond these ideals, his ambition stalls.

With a family consisting of two baby boys and a wife to support, a farm near Pittsfield purchased thanks to a loan from his father-in-law, and two less-than-successful novels (*Mardi* and *Redburn*) recently published, Melville was a man burdened. In a letter from the period during composition of *Moby-Dick*, he writes, "Dollars damn me; and the malicious Devil is forever grinning in upon me, holding the door ajar. . . . What I feel most moved to write, that is banned,—it will not pay."

But Melville exuded ambition, especially after its wood had been kindled by his meeting Hawthorne and imagining writing the Great American Novel. As he shifted from composing *Moby-Dick* as a standard, money-begetting adventure tale to something deeper, he may have felt like Starbuck that he had signed on for a mad and dangerous voyage. He desperately wanted to escape from his reputation as the "man who lived among the cannibals!" and only wrote about them.

Akin to Starbuck, Melville is constantly aware that his responsibilities extend beyond his own borders to include his family and daily responsibilities to them. Yet, like Ahab, an inner voice steers him steadily forward into the deepest waters of his own creativity and onto the dangerous shoals of potential literary failure. Thankfully, he chose this course and, as a result we have *Moby-Dick*.

CHAPTER 39

First Night-Watch

STUBB CONCLUDES THAT LAUGHTER IS THE BEST RESPONSE TO CALAMITY

Hundreds of cartoons have poked fun at the story of Moby Dick and Ahab. Almost all of them presume that anyone of reasonable intelligence and education is familiar with the general story. Although the seas of life are often tragic, as Stubb notes, they benefit from humor—"a laugh's the wisest, easiest answer to all that's queer." But life sometimes demands more than laughter.

Stubb is a neglected character in the novel. He is a capable harpooner, cracking wise in the face of danger. Might Melville be suggesting through Stubb that there is as much wisdom in laughter as there is in woe? Such jocular wisdom allows Stubb to endure the affronts of nature *and* Ahab, that force of nature. But it is, in the end, insufficient unless interspersed with a well-honed tragic sensibility. Stubb also helps to mix his tragic tale with bursts of humor. It might help to take some of the sting out of Melville's more outrageous views, especially concerning religion.

Charles Schultz in his "Peanuts" strip played with the famous first line of *Moby-Dick*. Atop his doghouse, Snoopy is composing what he anticipates will be a great novel. Charlie Brown says that the novel "starts too slowly—you need a more powerful beginning." After pondering a better opening, Snoopy pens, "Call me Ishmael." A *New Yorker* magazine cartoon shows an adult whale reading a bedtime tale to a baby whale. The baby whale says, "'Moby-Dick'? Again?"

Finally, in a Gahan Wilson cartoon for the *New Yorker* magazine, Moby Dick says to another whale, "Now that I've wiped him out, I kind of miss the little peg-legged bastard."

CHAPTER 40

Midnight, Forecastle

SOME OF THE CREW DANCE AND SING ON DECK

No chapter in *Moby-Dick* exhibits more movement and song than "Midnight, Forecastle." Sailors dance and sing with abandon. A jig is called for and one sailor commands Pip, the African-American cabin boy, to accompany them on his tambourine. Pip demurs. A French sailor tells him to "Beat thy belly, then, wag thy ears." A sailor from the Azores locates Pip's tambourine. As Pip plays, sailors merrily dance.

Enjoying his pipe near the action, Tashtego remarks about the dancing French sailor: "That's a white man; he calls that fun: humph! I save my sweat." A few moments later, more racial messages fly. The Old Manx sailor says "Our captain has his birth-mark; look yonder, boys, there's another in the sky—lurid-like, ye see, all else pitch black." To which the African harpooner Daggoo responds, "What of that? Who's afraid of black's afraid of me! I'm quarried out of it!" A Spanish sailor tells Daggoo: "harpooner, thy race is the undeniable dark side of mankind—devilish dark at that. No offence."

But Daggoo takes deep offence when the Spanish sailor further states that lightning in the sky is nothing more than "Daggoo showing his teeth." Daggoo springs towards the Spanish sailor, growling "Swallow thine, mannikin! White skin, white liver!" Just as a potentially fatal row is about to happen, a squall scatters the men on the deck, and Pip closes the chapter with his refrain: "Oh, thou big white God aloft there somewhere in yon darkness, have mercy on this small black boy down here; preserve him from all men that have no bowels to feel fear!"

What are we to make of this dancing and shouting, tinged with racial clues and conflict? According to scholar Sterling Stuckey, the sailors on deck are engaging in the ring shout dance, a traditional religious-mystical African dance practiced by slaves. Melville, in Stuckey's view, had encountered versions of this dance while growing up in New York City and later in Albany, both cities with large African-American communities in the early nineteenth century. He proposes that Melville saw performances of the ring shout in the famous Pinkster Day parades of free blacks. He might also have procured a further glimpse into the ring shout dance from Charles Dickens's observations of one contained in his well-known *American Notes*, published in 1842.

What these white sailors are doing, however, does not fit historian Lawrence Levine's description of a slave ring shout and dance: the slaves form a circle moving counterclockwise, chanting a story, usually one that is religious in orientation, invariably with strong hints of salvation in the offing. The ring dance and shout generally continued for many hours, with a building sense of the ecstatic, mingled with exhaustion, until some of the participants have a vision—"Dere's room enough, room enough in de heaven, my Lord / Room enough, room enough, I can't stay behind."

Even if the dance aboard the *Pequod* that blustery night is not the ring dance and shout, the chapter remains laden with racial innuendo. The white sailors may be viewed as engaged in a blackface performance, hence the unwillingness of the sailors of color—Tashtego, Daggoo, and Pip—to participate. As we saw in chapter 34, Melville may once again be making a comment about racial issues. Here he is showing the racial division among the crew members which is designed to parallel the racial divisions in the United States and around the world.

More likely, the chapter fuses racism with prophecy. The fate of the entire crew, whatever their racial divisions, is joined by their allegiance to Ahab, with his "birth-mark" of doom. The chanting is a form of the blues—an acknowledgment of the pain and suffering that the sailors will experience—tinged with a hint of transcendence, if not ultimate, then at least in the moment of the dance and singing. Pip, beguilingly a voice of sanity—even when he is driven mad later in the novel—rightfully has the final comment in this chapter. It comes just before we learn more about Moby Dick.

Pip connects the force of nature's "white squalls" with the White Whale. The two terms make him "jingle all over," like his tambourine, in fear and trembling. Pip realizes that the crew has been sworn to chase after Moby Dick, and he also knows that in their fanaticism, they are willing to sacrifice poor Pip to their "higher" designs. Perhaps, then, the *Pequod* is representative of the madness of a nation that had recently ordained a compromise designed to allow Pip and his black brethren to be subjugated, even when they had found quiet waters in free states. Pip's shout is the authentic voice of the slave praying for salvation and preservation from mad white men.

CHAPTER 41

Moby Dick

ISHMAEL SPEAKS OF HIMSELF AND THE WHITE WHALE

Ishmael opens this chapter by referring to himself as "I, Ishmael," the only time he does so in the novel. He is in a self-revelatory mood, admitting that—as much as anyone else on board—he has taken an oath to pursue Moby Dick. He did it out of the "dread in my soul," no doubt referring back to his admission in the first chapter that he was prone to dark, suicidal thoughts. But he was roused by "wild, mystical, sympathetical feeling," and he felt at one with Ahab and the crew. He has now learned about this voyage of revenge—about the whiteness and ferociousness of the whale and its initial cutting encounter with Ahab. Moby Dick, in his massive whiteness, is now regarded as simply "the deadliest ill."

Ishmael will soon vanish from the center of the text, as Melville focuses on Ahab and the frantic chase after the whale. We seem, by this point in the tale, to have all the information that we require concerning Ishmael, both as a participant and narrator.

But do we really *see* Ishmael? Might we, by our own protocols of reading and recognition, have failed to alight upon a truth that further drives home Melville's fascination with racial issues?

Why, asks Fred V. Bernard, do we presume that Ishmael—and Ahab, for that matter—is white? There is nary a place in the text where Ishmael's race is described. His rhetoric throughout the novel is concerned with racial images, with plenty of sympathy and admiration shown for those of other races, such as Queequeg, Pip, and Daggoo. Within the context of his time, were he a white man, Ishmael's racial attitudes would have been unusually exemplary in their liberality. The confusing qualities of race are often on display in the novel, as at one point Queequeg, with his odd clothing, is thought to be a fugitive slave. And Ishmael is often the butt of jibes that would be commonly directed against a person of color in that time period.

Ishmael remarks at one point, "Who ain't a slave?" He is frightened above all by the whiteness of the whale, which threatens his very existence. He works menial jobs (a digger of ditches, canals, and wells), positions that were often occupied by men of color. Yes, he has also been a teacher, before he has put his hand in a "tar pot." Ishmael is most comfortable among the multiracial and multinational crew. In addition, the Biblical Ishmael's mother is described as a "bondservant" in the book of Genesis, and Ishmael was, on occasion, a name that slaves possessed.

And what of Ahab? Might he, too, be either black or of mixed race?

Ahab's skin color is described by Melville as "solid bronze" and his face is "tawny." Ishmael, at one point, refers to the "black terrific Ahab." Are these descriptions more than simply metaphorical, as Bernard suggests?

Does an understanding of Ahab as black or "mixed blood" account in some way for his obsessive quest after the White Whale? What are we to make, in this context, of the remark in the novel that Ahab "piled upon the whale's white hump the sum of all the general rage and hate felt by his whole race from Adam down." Is Ahab at war with himself, with his racial miscegenation as he attempts to harpoon the ultimate symbol of power and whiteness? The only pity or fellow feeling he demonstrates is aroused by Pip, the black cabin boy.

From Bernard's lively perspective, a mulatto Ahab stirs the racial cauldron of *Moby-Dick*. It also helps to explain Ishmael's fascination with Ahab, since they would then share a racial profile. Might the novel be read as a parable of attempted racial revenge? Whales are, as Ishmael points out, normally black in their color; Moby Dick alone is white. Might Ahab and Ishmael be engaged in a reverse form of racial cleansing, attempting to return to the blackness that is in man and nature?

There was, after all, a man named Paul Cuffe, a well-known black whaler captain who, like Ahab, worked for Quakers. But this, along with the evidence marshaled above and imaginatively assayed gold pieces of interpretation, does not sufficiently make the case. It does, once again, bring forth appreciation for the subtle cunning and imaginative spaces that Melville has afforded his readers. It hammers home how much his novel defied racial categories of his era.

CHAPTER 42

The Whiteness of the Whale

ISHMAEL PONDERS THE MANY MEANINGS OF THE TERM WHITE

Melville likes to play with, almost to flaunt, the symbol of whiteness. In this chapter, he riffs on the variety of associations that the color white has possessed throughout history. It is a color of dualisms—connoting purity as well as blankness. Thus it merges well with the sublime, with something that is at once awesomely beautiful and achingly horrific. At sea, in the most northern and southern climes, whiteness can represent a danger to ships, in the presence of icebergs. On and on Melville muses, telling us at one point that "Though in many of its aspects this visible world seems formed in love, the invisible spheres were formed in fright." White captures, then, both the love and the fright.

Moby Dick, the albino whale, is symbolic of all these associations and more—he is the burden of Ahab's dreams and the fantasy of Ishmael's reflections. Perhaps, too, as with the color white, the White Whale "calls up the peculiar apparition to the soul."

Writing a century after Melville, William Gass has an extended meditation on a color, at once immensely learned, frolicsome, and lewd. But his concerns the color blue. Like Melville, he wonders about the metaphysical as well as physical manifestations of a color. He finds that blue (along with green) has the most "emotional range." Blue, of course, often refers to the sky but it is also indicative of heaven—think here of the song "My Blue Heaven." It commonly connotes the sea—and can hint at a place of peace, as in the "blue lagoon."

The deepest association of blue is with a feeling of being depressed and with a form of music. The term "blue devils of nada," as Albert Murray tells us, refers to that existential moment when an individual rubs against the nothingness of existence. The abyss of meaning or the humdrum nature of labor can propel one into the blues feeling, a deep, lowdown, lonesome feeling. For Murray and Ralph Ellison, this condition is spiritual and material, part of the rhythms of African-American life but not confined to it alone. When the blues intrude, the best solution is to play with the feeling, to sweat it out in dancing, shouting, singing, and drinking. Out of the blues arises that most elemental of emotions, an epiphany of liberation, no matter how fleeting.

Melville is a prose blues musician of the highest order. Indeed, his tale about the White Whale might easily have been subtitled, "A Study in Blue." As already noted, Ishmael sings the blues; that is why he takes to the sea— to sail on the greatest expanse of blue, the expanse that makes up most of the surface of our planet. The Blue Peter is the signal for the *Pequod* to cast off on its adventure, and it is only after the voyage has begun, that Ahab emerges from his blue isolation to address the crew.

Ahab is, without doubt, bedeviled by the blue devils of nada. He wants to punch through the mask of appearances to find out if they are behind the veil of life. He also suffers from them as a result of his earlier confrontation with Moby Dick. Because of his dismasting, he is unable to dance those blues away. It would have been better for Ahab to have danced wildly as best he could than to have undertaken his voyage of vengeance.

CHAPTER 43

Hark!

STRANGE, OMINOUS NOISES ARE HEARD BELOW DECK

Angels in America, Tony Kushner's Pulitzer Prize-winning play, was composed when the AIDS epidemic began to ravage the gay community. At first, the disease was met with silence. The election of Ronald Reagan as president coincided with the onslaught of AIDS, and his administration refused to address this modern plague. Kushner's play dissected the American psyche as it teetered on the edge of the millennium; he wanted to sound a loud "hark" about this terrible disease and the American political climate. By 1990, when the play was first performed, close to 19,000 had died from AIDS. The death toll was soon to explode.

Angels in America consists of two linked plays, both of them teeming with characters, drenched with symbolism, and etched with innovative staging. When Kushner refers to the play as a "gay fantasia," he hits the mark. The ambition of the work is staggering and it is here especially that Kushner's spiritual and intellectual link with Melville and *Moby-Dick* looms large.

Kushner acknowledges that Melville is his "favorite American writer." *Angels in America* shares with *Moby-Dick* an immense "ambition and size"; as Kushner notes, when artists attempt such "large gestures" they flirt with hitting "inflated, even hysterical chords on occasion." Listen to Kushner register his admiration for Melville's willingness to dive deeply into himself, his art, and his culture:

> Failure and the wild embrace of failure; the recognition that the pursuit of success in art as well as in whale-hunting or in love is also the pursuit of failure; an openhearted passion for the doom that trails all human enterprise; the freedom to try to seize the entire world, to apprehend the unapprehendable; the madness to attempt such a comprehensive apprehension, to attempt to stuff the cosmos into the confines of a book . . . these are aspects of what draws a person to "Melvilleland." It's an apt phrase. Melville *is* a land, it lies outside over there. It's an alternative, a cause, and a cult object as much as a genius.

Are there echoes of *Moby-Dick* in *Angels in America*? Certainly the presentation of lawyer and influence-peddler Roy Cohn, with his larger-than-life personality, has affinities with Ahab. He is a man driven by dark forces;

he shows no guilt or concern that his actions—and his immense contradictions—have caused death and suffering. He is the captain of his own ship, able to bark orders and have people readily obey him. He is oddly loyal to his ideals and vicious in pursuit of them. His passion is his hatred, and he directs it with a dangerous accuracy: "I save my hate for what counts." He has chased his entire life the White Whale of disloyalty to American ideals, as he narrowly defines it. Like Ahab, he has his own mad "clarity" about his nemesis, and he has been "unafraid to look deep into the miasma at the heart of the world, what a pit, what a nightmare is there—*I have looked, I have searched all my life for absolute bottom, and I found it, believe me.*" Life, Cohn concludes, before AIDS takes him away, is "tragic, brutal and short." In his mad quest, Cohn avers, "I never wavered."

At the heart of the Kushner's play is a character named Prior Walter. Wracked by the AIDS virus, abandoned by his lover, on the verge of death—Prior survives with his humanity intact, as does Ishmael. Prior is able, at the conclusion of the play, to find that AIDS "will be the end of many of us, but not nearly all . . . and we are not going away. We won't die secret deaths anymore. The world only spins forward . . . And I bless you: *More Life*. The Great Work Begins."

CHAPTER 44

The Chart

AHAB CHARTS THE MOVEMENTS OF THE WHITE WHALE

Novelists, as we have seen with Norman Mailer and will with other writers in future chapters, have chosen to hunt after the Great American Novel. Not surprisingly, they have viewed *Moby-Dick* as their model, attempting to gauge its strengths and weaknesses so that in their own work they might produce a work that bulges with equal greatness.

The first mention of the term "Great American Novel" appeared in an essay by J. W. De Forest in *The Nation* (1868). In the years immediately following the calamity of the Civil War, he desired a novel that would encompass "the American soul," that would tie its diverse parts together in a vast "tableau." De Forest supported the very ideals that Melville had envisioned nearly two decades earlier when he thought about Hawthorne's work and called for national greatness in American literature. Alas, De Forest showed no knowledge of Melville's entry into the field of great literature.

We live today in a world with unlimited borders. How, in such a spider-world of connections, can we even speak of a novel as American? And what would an American novel have that defines it as peculiarly American? Must it deal with American themes—and are such themes distanced from those common to other lands? Is it simply a designation of geographical proximity, indicative of the fact that the author resides within the confines of the United States? In sum, the concept may well be antiquated, if not absurd.

Nonetheless, many continue to uphold—with zeal akin to Ahab poring over his charts in this chapter—the ideal of the Great American Novel. It translates into a book that is generally bulky (although great American novels such as Mark Twain's *The Adventures of Huckleberry Finn*, F. Scott Fitzgerald's *The Great Gatsby*, and Toni Morrison's *Beloved* are not especially long). The presumption, too, is that the book will be composed with stylistic panache, accessible but daunting, interrogating the American past but bursting with meaning for the present. No small order.

Perhaps that is the point of the notion of the Great American Novel. It is a yardstick (one without precise markers, however) that is designed to push the writer to extend his or her reach, to put onto paper words that will live, if not forever, then at least for a long, long time. There are worse ambitions—ask Ahab.

For some writers, the burden of composing such a novel can be debilitating. To the daily grind of writing creatively is added fear of failure, of not diving deep enough. Word that so and so is writing the Great American Novel creates a buzz of expectation that can rarely be satisfied when the book sees the bright light of publishing day—such as, for instance, Harold Brodkey's *The Runaway Soul* (1991). Others may rest more comfortably in holding onto the potential of writing such a book by keeping it close to the breast, by not letting it out in the world—at least then it retains its potential as a contender for the Great American Novel.

Many writers find the ideal inspiring. Ambition is the lifeblood of American society, as F. Scott Fitzgerald understood. In the realm of the creative intellect, however, it is often viewed as suspect. In a welcome burst of honesty, Maxine Hong Kingston let the cat out of the bag when she stated: "Every American novelist wants to write the Great American Novel." And, if they uphold *Moby-Dick* as their model, what is wrong with that?

Models that inspire are those that present challenges and that defy mimicry. *Moby-Dick*'s greatness for aspiring and established writers lies in its scope, its bravura, its shifts in style and narrative, its lyricism, its experimentation (think of the clever use of the Etymology and Extracts sections), its blurring of the lines between learned tome and adventure story, its breaking of racial and sexual taboos, and in its subtext about the nature of the American experiment. All of this and more in a single novel!

Why not then call it a Great American Novel and attempt, in one's own manner, to write something that might cohabitate with it in the penthouse suite of literature. Melville would expect nothing less.

Philip Roth, in *American Pastoral* (1997), took a good shot at the Great American Novel at the end of the twentieth century as he navigates the fortunes of an upwardly mobile American family and the chaos of the nation as exemplified by their daughter. In an earlier, slighter work about baseball, *The Great American Novel* (1973), he humorously opens with the line: "Call Me Smitty." Others, too, Kurt Vonnegut among them, have succumbed to the same joke; Vonnegut begins *Cat's Cradle* (1963) with: "Call me Jonah." The point of these openings is to poke fun at the notion of a Great American Novel, but also to make a bow in its direction, by admitting that any attempt at something that reaches, that attempts to dive deeper, must acknowledge *Moby-Dick*, that monument that stands today as exemplary of the Great American Novel.

CHAPTER 45

The Affidavit

ISHMAEL RELATES TALES OF THE POWER OF SPERM WHALES

The story of Moby Dick, Ishmael tells us, is no "monstrous fable." The world yields its fair share of fantasies, to be sure. But Ishmael's narrative was intended to be no more "facetious than Moses, when he wrote the history of the plagues of Egypt." As God showed His divine vengeance and power, so did the White Whale demonstrate its own "great power and malice." Listen to the well-documented tale of what happened when a sperm whale rammed the *Essex*.

On August 12, 1819, the whaling ship *Essex* departed Nantucket with grand expectations—in the midst of a depression, one of the few products holding its price was whale oil. The crew of twenty-one manning the 87 foot long ship, had every intention of filling the hold with such a product. The initial year of the voyage was typical: whales were killed, the trying out process began with the cutting in and stripping of the blubber, boiling it down in try-pots, then saving it in casks. The rounding of Cape Horn had been difficult, taking one month. Squawking among the crew over scanty rations stirred tempers and seditious feelings, but the captain, George Pollard Jr., had proven stern. The boat headed to the North Pacific Ocean to continue its hunt until full of whale oil and other whale products.

At a position more than 1,500 miles west of the Galapagos Islands, on November 20, 1820, the crew sighted whales. As whalers had done for centuries, they sent out boats in pursuit. The largest whale in the pack seemed to be acting strangely; its head was marked by scars and its entire bulk—at 85 feet long it was almost the size of the *Essex* and it probably weighed about eighty tons—was headed directly at the ship. It found its mark—butting the ship with tremendous power. First Mate Owen Chase later wrote that he and the sailors, "looked at each other with perfect amazement, deprived almost of the power of speech."

Speechlessness, abject horror, and devout disbelief were reasonable reactions, for never had it been reported that a whale had purposefully rammed a ship. Alas, as the men worked the pumps to bail water from the ship, the whale picked up speed (up to perhaps 6 knots) and rammed the ship anew. This blow caused the *Essex* to list and go down. Crew member Thomas Nickerson recalled, "Here lay our beautiful ship, a floating and dismal wreck." The whale had proven victorious, a victory that Chase decided had been "anything but chance"; it was an act of "decided, calculating mischief" on the part of a sperm whale.

Thenceforth, began an even more harrowing tale. The crew abandoned the *Essex* and took to smaller boats, with whatever provisions they could salvage. In the middle of nowhere, three small boats—one commanded by Pollard, another by Chase, and the third by Matthew Joy, with a total of twenty men—drifted in the middle of nowhere. After spirited discussion, they rejected heading for the closer Marquesas, 1,100 miles away, out of fear of cannibalism there. That concern would prove, in retrospect, ironic. Instead, they lit out for the coast of South America, more than 3,000 (!) miles distant, believing it their best chance at survival.

A narrative of horrors followed, as provisions shrank with each passing day. The sun seared the men's flesh and the coast of South America seemed no closer. Luck was not on their side; no whaleboats were about to rescue them. Only the sad option remained of finding land and sustenance. As the days turned, the men's hunger and thirst grew. They began to satisfy their needs as best they could; they killed the tortoises aboard their boats, drinking their blood and eating their meat, "entrails and all." When the tortoises were gone, the men had to resort to cannibalism to survive. They drew lots and the man with the short stick was singled out for slaughter.

Finally, after some men chose to remain on an island and others continued their deadly sea journey, on February 18, 1821, Chase and his surviving crewmen (who by now were counting their ninetieth day) were rescued when they happened upon a ship at sea. Five days later, Pollard and his small boat were nearing the Chilean coast. Starving, thirsty, raw from the reality of their cannibalism, Pollard and his men were deep into "days of horror and despair." But those days ended abruptly when they saw a nearby ship. Imagine the reaction of the crew of the rescue ship, the *Dauphin*, as they took in the emaciated survivors and glanced at the human bones that filled the small boat.

Thanks to these surviving witnesses—all Ishmael's of a sort—the world would come to know full well "the great power and malice at times of the sperm whale."

CHAPTER 46

Surmises

ISHMAEL EXPLAINS AHAB'S MONOMANIA AND PLAN FOR THE VOYAGE

There is plenty of conceit and bluster in Ishmael's tale, especially when he imagines himself crawling into the private niches of his captain's consciousness. According to Ishmael, Ahab has but one object in his mind—"the ultimate capture of Moby Dick." All other aspects of the voyage are subsidiary to it and Ahab is cunning in his madness. He recognizes that to maintain the loyalty of his crew, he must occasionally allow the mundane rhythms of a whaling voyage (such as killing whales) to play out.

Thus, imagine, if you will, what if the voyage of the *Pequod* had been perfectly normal. This is the scenario Anne Finger presents in her wonderful story "Moby Dick, or, The Leg." She recognizes that Melville's tale is a proper jump-off point for new imaginings, new renditions. Miraculous though it be, according to Finger, Ahab did not get entwined to the death with Moby; the *Pequod* did not tumble into the vortex.

In fact, on a later voyage, Ahab is shipwrecked, washing up on the uncharted shores of an island in the Pacific. By eating a mysterious fruit that grows only on that secret atoll, Ahab has been granted longevity—he has lived a century and a half. He finally returns to New Bedford where, much to his surprise, he finds a well-known volume purporting to tell the tale of a ship, its captain, and a mad chase after a White Whale.

Ahab's memory differs greatly from Ishmael's. To hear Ahab tell it, Ishmael from the start of the voyage was fixed in his attention on Ahab's missing limb. Verily, he could not take his eyes from it, although it was not there, in reality. Ahab did have a white leg, but was its whiteness as White as a white man's skin? These philosophical conundrums apparently vexed the metaphysically minded young Ishmael. Ahab, however, had more important things on his mind; along with Starbuck, he was determined to transform blubber into dollars. He was, it must be remembered, a New Bedford sailing man, born and bred.

One month of a long whaling voyage folds into another month, and a whaling ship's captain, no less than the crew, broods about unattended needs. Lonely and ever practical, Ahab finds himself attracted to the ginger-haired young Ishmael, whom he knows cannot take his eyes off him—or at least that part of him that is not there. In Ahab's view, "My absent leg to [Ishmael] was like the head of old Medusa: it aroused in him a simultaneous dread and desire, a yearning of and hatred for some thing he dared not look on and yet must look on."

Six months into the voyage, Ahab and Ishmael are alone on the deck and they exchange a kiss, that most "democratic device." As Ahab puts it, "I have a mouth, thou has a mouth, she or he has a mouth, ye have mouths—we all have mouths. In this act two bodies connect, not as male and female, not as top and bottom, but in perfect, egalitarian harmony." They later share another moment of furtive intimacy. Ahab finds that he is unable to resist joining Ishmael and others in squeezing the sperm from the blubbery mass. At one point, Ishmael accidentally squeezes Ahab's finger instead of a globule of oil. It is a moment when the two men meld together, but the closeness is shattered immediately as Ishmael's face "became all beclouded" with anxiety.

The object of Ahab's chase is Moby Dick but not for the metaphysical reasons that Ishmael ascribes. Without much ado, Ahab vanquishes Moby Dick as he would any other whale and turns his blubber into serious income. With the rest of the crew, Ahab feasts upon Moby's meat. He returns home with no tale to tell, or no tale out of the ordinary.

Even before the ship has returned to harbor, Ishmael becomes monomaniacal in his need to put pen to paper. As Finger notes, "he wrote and wrote and wrote." And the tale of *Moby-Dick*, in all its magnificence and modification, is his gift to us. It is his "fearsome meaning making" exemplified. However, it is not the story of Captain Ahab, that sane and successful seafarer.

Thanks to Anne Finger, Ahab has managed to tell his tale—and in a short story, no less.

CHAPTER 47

The Mat-Maker

STRANGE SOUNDS AND THE SIGHTING OF WHALES

In the midst of mat-weaving aboard the *Pequod*, a strange sound is heard—"long drawn, and musically wild and unearthly." It comes from Tashtego, who screams out that there is a sperm whale school, two miles off the lee-beam.

Strange sounds readily inhabit the novel, the cry of "There she blows!," the hiss of Fedallah, the roar of the waves, and so much more. *Moby-Dick* lends itself readily to musical renditions.

In 1999, the performance artist Laurie Anderson debuted her work *Songs and Stories from Moby Dick*. A techno-artist of great virtuosity and storytelling ability, Anderson has long sought to interrogate the big, brash, and bedeviled entity that is the United States. Like so many others, Anderson first read *Moby-Dick* in high school. A later encounter had her "in love with the language." She read it five more times, preparing to adapt it to her own purposes. She adored the varied voices that Melville "invented—historian, botanist, dreamer, chemist, librarian." Anderson, the ultimate pastiche artist, "liked the jump-cutting around, and the way he was so free about saying, all right, now I'll tell you a story about these old bones, now I'll tell you a story about a pyramid and now I'll tell you a story about something else. And I thought, 'This is my guy.'"

In the song, "One White Whale," Anderson's electric violin emits strange, long-drawn-out sounds. She also employs an instrument—a "talking stick"—that, according to one listener, resembled nothing so much as a harpoon that makes sounds "musically wild and unearthly." In the course of the performance, with projections and light show accompanying it, Anderson blends various musical styles and sounds. She grooves to the mysteries of the story, to evoke Ahab's quest (she sees him as a delicious, albeit unlikely combination of the cartoon character Popeye and the iconic singer Tom Waits!), the mysteries that Pip encounters, and the inner being of the whale.

Anderson's attempt to bring *Moby-Dick* to music was hardly unprecedented. But the novel does present problems. Composer Benjamin Britten played around with the idea of an opera of *Moby-Dick* before settling for *Billy Budd* instead. Samuel Barber thought, too, of an opera, but he dropped it because "an opera that had a lot of whales and water, but no soprano, had a doubtful future. . . . Too much water for an opera, and too much wind." Or so Barber imagined.

Then what about a cantata, for male chorus, soloists, and orchestra, thought Bernard Herrmann? In the mid-1930s, Herrmann was a composer still in his mid-twenties, trying to resurrect the "fabulous shadow" of Melville's creation. He had first read *Moby-Dick* while a teenager. In the mid-1930s, Herrmann was working for CBS radio on its programming, and he also conducted on-air works for them. He would soon collaborate with Orson Welles and the Mercury Theater, as well as doing the music for films such as *Citizen Kane* and *Vertigo*.

The initial inkling for composing the cantata *Moby Dick* came to Herrmann when he was courting budding novelist Lucille Fletcher. As he accompanied her on long subway rides back to her home in Brooklyn, Fletcher began working on a novel about a New England church organist named Josiah Abbott. Herrmann started to wonder what type of music Abbott might compose. Herrmann had his eureka moment as the BMT subway hurtled forward, exclaiming: "'Golly, that's too good an idea to waste on just a novel. I think I'll write that cantata myself." Eventually the project morphed into his orchestration for *Moby-Dick*.

Once he had tasted the idea, it consumed him. Whenever he could take time away from his normal overload of work, Herrmann searched out information about *Moby-Dick* and its author. He traveled to Nantucket to steal time "wandering about the streets of that ancient whaling town." He spent parts of two summers in Massachusetts, going to old churches so that he might better feel the music that he would compose for Father Mapple's sermon. He visited the New Bedford whaling museum, trying to imagine what it would have felt to be afloat with Ahab and Ishmael. New England poet W. Clark Harrington aided him with the selection and arrangements of the material from *Moby-Dick*. Many of the words used in the libretto were taken verbatim from the novel, others were adapted to fit better with the orchestration.

The tragic sense that informs the novel did not require any leap of the imagination on Herrmann's part. He was in some ways a Captain Ahab personality—a driven man, obsessive and incapable of empathy, always on the verge of self-destruction. If there is one theme recurrent in his art, it is death. Melancholy and outsized romanticism defined his life and musical style—perfect vehicles through which to approach *Moby-Dick* in musical form.

His cantata in some ways fit the 1930s' zest for a usable American past, for identification with those heroic souls who confronted the nastiness of the environment. In the figure of Ahab, moreover, listeners to the cantata might have gained insight into the mania that was driving Hitler and fascism in Germany at that historical moment. As a Jew, Herrmann understood the threat of fascism, and he had shivered while in Paris in the midst of Nazi officers, who he was convinced had been ridiculing him as a Jew. Although he was never an enthusiastic left-winger, he was connected with many of them, ranging from his childhood friend, writer Abraham Polonsky, to composer Aaron Copland. Radicalism was *au courant*, and Herrmann breathed it in. But his sense of the tragic distanced him from the optimism that spewed from poet Carl Sandburg and others. The good ship *Pequod* goes down, the crew perishes, the whale survives. Only Ishmael lives to tell this tale. The cantata was, then, a Popular Front work, but one with a tragic tonality.

Herrmann's cantata *Moby Dick* opened at Carnegie Hall in mid-April, 1940. The New York Philharmonic performed the piece under the direction of Sir John Barbirolli. The cantata form depends, like poetry, upon tones and images, the piercing ability of a few words to express emotions and ideas.

There are moments of musical bravura and narrative sweep in Herrmann's cantata. As to be expected, the bass notes are suggestive of the mystery of the deep and of foreboding. Violins accompany Ishmael as he opens with his tale of woe. The chorus strikes a dirge, as they perform the Jonah Sermon. A single voice from the chorus soars with "I saw the opening maw of hell." When God's name is invoked, drums and cymbals sound, suggesting God's power far more than His mercy. Flutes grant us a sense of the *Pequod* on calm seas, until that is interrupted with Ahab's call and response with the crew. A cacophony of sounds, with drums predominant, accompanies the crew as they scream "Death to Moby Dick!" When Ahab goes into his meditation, the orchestration hums with him, ever so softly. But the calm is broken by a spirited interlude where Pip, the cabin boy, is encouraged to play a tune. As the tempo rises, the chorus rings out with "Hip, hip, hip," repeated nearly twenty times. Ahab's nostalgia for the peace of land is effective, as he imagines his soul rested with death. But the sighting of the White Whale brings back the pounding orchestration, as Ahab and crew—in spite of Starbuck's pleas—take off after Moby. In the midst of the chase, Ahab emits a hint of his madness, as his laughs in the face of disaster. The chorus responds with "The jaw, the jaw." Ahab's final words: each one uttered slowly, until the last word, "spear" is elongated, a last gasp. The chorus screams, then a pause. The climax is signaled by the drums and horn sections, when Ishmael almost in a whisper, says "And I only am escaped to tell thee."

Other composers over the years have decided to "tell thee" in operatic and symphonic versions the story of *Moby-Dick*. Let the following list suffice for those wanting to sail the symphonic waters. Operatic and symphonic versions of *Moby-Dick* have been composed by Peter Mennin, Peter Westergaard, Rinde Eckert, Giorgio Ghedini, and Richard Brooks, Doug Katsaros and Mark St. Germain, and Philip Stainton. The latest is a major opera which opened in Dallas in 2010, by Jake Heggie, who states that the novel is "operatic itself . . . with a lyrical quality that really soars." Perhaps less memorable is *Moby Dick! The Musical.**

*For a hard-rock encounter with Moby, see chapter 25 on Led Zeppelin; for a rap account of Ahab and the whale, see chapter 51 on MC Lars; for Bob Dylan's take on Ahab, see the Epilogue.

CHAPTER 48

The First Lowering

THE MEN GO AFTER A SPERM WHALE

Anticipation accompanies the first lowering of the small whaleboats once a sperm whale is sighted. A heavy sea mist blinds the crew as they seek out their prey. In darkness, the boats are lifted up and dropped down by the churn of the waves. Into the ocean, into the "heart of that almighty forlornness" go Starbuck, Ishmael, Queequeg and others. A single lantern is held aloft by noble Queequeg, who serves as a "sign and symbol of a man without faith . . . hope in the midst of despair."

Moby-Dick had its first lowering into the sea of American fiction on November 14, 1851. Issued by Harper's, the volume was 635 pages in length, with the rather dear price of $1.50, in an initial printing of 2,915 copies. It had already been brought out a few weeks earlier, in a shoddy London edition by Richard Bentley, with a different title, *The Whale*.

The American edition appeared on an icy day in the northeastern United States, betokening the arrival of a cruel winter that somewhat matched the reception of the volume. Henry David Thoreau was in Concord doing some surveying work. He jotted down in his journal that it was the sort of day "in which you must hold onto life by the teeth." Just before daylight in Manhattan, "some evil-designed person" set fire to the cow stables located on 28th Street, near 3rd Avenue, not far from where Melville sometimes worked while in the city. Police discovered the blaze and dowsed it with buckets of water before damage could be done.

The world can be an indifferent or harsh place for books that challenge established categories and expectations. Initial and influential reviews for Melville's "wicked book" came from England. They were not the sort to kindle Melville's joy or to promise coins for his family's scant coffer. It should be noted that the English edition of *Moby-Dick* published by Bentley was marred in a number of unfortunate ways. Passages deemed to be blasphemous or shocking were changed or excised. Even more problematic, the English edition omitted Melville's crucial Epilogue! There Melville recounts how Ishmael survived the wrath of Moby Dick and was rescued by the *Rachel* while floating on the sea, thanks to Queequeg's coffin refashioned into a life raft. Without this concluding page, readers puzzled over how Ishmael could have narrated a story in which it appeared that he had gone down with his fellow sailors! Nor could they find any hint of the potential for redemption suggested by the orphaned Ishmael being rescued and living to tell his tale.

A number of worthy themes jump out from the English reviews. Almost all reviewers were familiar with Melville's earlier books, which they generally admired. This new work, however, frustrated, since it ill fit with the adventure genre that they had expected from Melville. His heated prose and metaphysical flights, interrupted by long and technical discussions of cetology, pushed the book into an entirely new realm which some English reviewers found "phantasmal," "an ill-compounded mixture of romance and matter-of-fact," whose philosophy and "rhapsody" "repels the reader rather instead of attracting him." Readers were warned that they might be further alienated by the grittiness of some of the scenes and the unrefined language employed by the sailors. This was, after all, an age of a genteel reading class that anticipated books marked by purity of mind and language, as well as consistency of style. On all these counts, *Moby-Dick* could be infuriating.

Nevertheless, even among the initial flurry of English reviews some exploded with admiration for *The Whale*. The *London Leader*, while admitting the novel was "a strange, wild, weird book," also acknowledged it was "full of poetry and full of interest." This review praised the novel but was unable to explain Melville's strange mixture of romantic adventure and cetological speculation. Although complaints were lodged against *The Whale* because it "lacked the trim orderliness of an English Park," some reviews recognized it as a novel that sparkled "with the tangled overgrowth and luxuriant vegetation of American forests." Melville was deemed a writer of genius, blessed with inspired prose. One review spoke for many in finding *The Whale* "a most extraordinary work" essentially *sui generis* in its "merit."

In the United States, *Moby-Dick* was not ignored, as was once thought. Rather, it garnered a good deal of attention and mixed reviews. Two of the early and unfavorable reviews of his book were culled from British newspapers with a large following in the United States. These negative responses were reprinted, sometimes verbatim, in the American press and may well have influenced some of *Moby-Dick's* American reviewers to shun the wild book.

As in England, a few reviews took Melville to task for his frothy language and disrespect for religious niceties. One review offered its "decided protest against the querulous and caviling innuendo's" that Melville presumably lodged "against objects that should be shielded from his irreverent wit." The highly influential *North American Review* simply reproduced the unfavorable notice that had already appeared in the London *Athe-naeum*. Another paper ridiculed the book's dialogue as "false and absurd." Despite all of the time that Melville had spent among seamen, this reviewer averred that he had a tin ear for their "lingo." The *Boston Post* chafed at the high cost of the book, concluding that it was not worth the price.

In the main, however, American reviews of *Moby-Dick* greeted Melville and his new book with varying degrees of solicitude but generally without ardor—and that hit Melville hard. Some marveled at Melville's "genius" in producing a book that "displays graphic powers of so rare an order"; Melville "writes with the true gusto of genius," exclaimed another review. The New York *Home Journal* described *Moby-Dick* as "a very racy, spirited, curious and entertaining book which . . . enlists the curiosity, excites the sympathies, and often charms the fancy." Indeed, almost any author, established or otherwise, would thrill to the song of such reviews. The influential *New York Literary World* worried that too many themes and subjects competed for attention in the novel, but it praised "the acuteness of observation" and "the freshness of perception" that defined the work. Other reviews marveled at Melville's deep knowledge of whaling, wit, powers of observation, and more. The New York *Christian Intelligencer* went so far as to predict that *Moby-Dick* would be as successful a work as his earlier novel *Omoo*. In a similar vein, another reviewer imagined that Melville's novel "will match his previous works in the race for popularity."

Alas, *Moby-Dick* quickly faded from the attention of the public. But it would resurface, in time, in time.

CHAPTER 49

The Hyena

ISHMAEL WONDERS ABOUT HIS FATE UNDER AHAB'S COMMAND

Ishmael is an affable sort of fellow, even if overly prone to philosophical speculation. He has good reason to think deeply, for he has surrendered his better judgment to join Ahab in hunting the White Whale. He has seen the face of Fedallah, with all of the sagacity and evil of the ages stenciled into it. And he has experienced his first dangerous lowering of boats. How is one to respond to these events, unheard of on his home isle of Manhattan?

As a good intellectual, Ishmael probes this sorry state of affairs. He arrives at what he calls a "genial, desperado philosophy." Such a view begins with a realistic appraisal of circumstances. Ishmael is at sea with a captain hell-bent on pursuing Moby Dick. Disaster seems to be closing in on him, but rather than respond with panic and frustration, Ishmael opts for a different perspective. In "queer times," such as he is experiencing, perhaps it is best to take "this whole universe for a vast practical joke." If Ishmael was—in the first chapter, where he introduced himself—liable to worry and think of suicide, now his take on the universe has a gritty sensibility. He finds the wherewithal to continue, to live with a sense of things as they are. He accepts the tragic fate that may befall him—for such is the way of the world. But he will live those days that come to him with appreciation, knowing that "I survived myself; my death and burial were locked up in my chest." Gazing upon the world "tranquilly and contentedly," he also exhibits interest and engagement.

During the first hundred years in the life of *Moby-Dick*, poor Ishmael was an orphan, shunted to the side as an idiosyncratic narrator, a mere narrative device to push the philosophical action forward. Beginning in the 1940s, however, scholars began to look more closely at him and to like what they found.

Suddenly, Ishmael occupied the center of the novel's meaning. One scholar, on the hundredth anniversary of the publication of *Moby-Dick*, announced that the novel "is about Ishmael." Walter E. Bezanson, a professor at Rutgers University, explained that Ishmael is the "enfolding sensibility of the novel," the imagination and the narrator. The story, in fact, is shaped by him, thanks to his complexity of vision and openness to experience. When Ishmael ponders the whiteness of the whale, he demonstrates imagination, depth, and humor. He makes us feel his own passion for adventure, without simply falling prey to mere excitement. Ishmael's expansive sense of things allows him to accept "all that is secret, mysterious, and undecipherable in the great riddles of mankind." Ishmael, then, looms as an exemplary figure for modern times, a corrective to Ahab's action-oriented fanaticism.

A brilliant critic, Alfred Kazin, concurred in his widely distributed introduction to a 1956 edition of *Moby-Dick*. A New York intellectual, born and bred, Kazin had at a young age bounded to fame with a powerful voice in his first book, *On Native Grounds* (1942). There he had deciphered American literature and criticism from the 1890s through the 1930s as pivoting between alienation and a sense of place. In his introduction to *Moby-Dick*, Kazin continued with the theme of alienation—central to his coterie of New York intellectuals. In a poetic incantation, Kazin sounded the importance of Ishmael, making him into, well, a New York intellectual, before the fact: "It is Ishmael's contemplativeness, his *dreaming* . . . It is Ishmael's gift for speculation . . . It is Ishmael who . . . embodies for us man as a thinker . . . it is Ishmael, both actually and as the symbol of man."

For Kazin, Ishmael is the existential core of the novel, the character who personifies, through the power of language, the quest for meaning. In a chaotic world, where man was alienated from nature, where man was confronted with the ruin of civilization, Ishmael was an orphan like the rest of us, but able to transform his alienation and "homelessness" into art, able to bring forth some "meaning to existence from the inscrutable waters."

Donald E. Pease and other literary critics coming after Kazin, took a sour look at the postwar flowering of interest in Ishmael. They considered the turn to Ishmael as proof that Cold War liberal critics employed *Moby-Dick* for ideological purposes. Emphasis on Ishmael served as a form of "persuasion," pushing the agenda of consensus, along with either/or choices that led to an anticommunist paradigm. Such readings of the book see its cultural power as being enlisted for Cold War ends. Ishmael comes to represent freedom and growth as opposed to Ahab, who captures authoritarianism and destruction. Ishmael's narrative becomes a self-legitimating strategy that makes Ahab into the victimizer or the enemy rather than, for example, being considered a seeker after greater creativity or standing in opposition to the mundane presumptions of bourgeois society.

With the rise of academic criticism and the growth of departments of literature, academics were looking to establish their own reputations. They needed to find something striking. Focusing on Ishmael served them well and critics brought the character back into the consciousness of a generation of readers. Ishmael may well have been the Holden Caulfield of his own era, if not quite a "catcher in the rye," then he is at the very least the catcher of events that transpired on the sea, barely avoiding the vortex that claimed his shipmates.

CHAPTER 50

Ahab's Boat and Crew—Fedallah

FEDALLAH'S PRESENCE IS WONDERED AT

Perhaps the most unduly neglected character in *Moby-Dick* is Fedallah. Indeed, in the 1956 film version of the novel, screenwriter Ray Bradbury excised him entirely from the story, without any regret. Analysts spend inordinate amounts of time examining Ishmael and Ahab but prefer to skim the waters of Fedallah.

Fedallah and his Parsee crew are smuggled aboard the *Pequod*, and they remain below its decks until the whale-hunting begins in earnest. Fedallah's age is indeterminate, although he seems as old as the hills. His symbolic meaning is clear—he personifies the principle and reality of evil. He is a demonic worshipper of fire. Before his presence aboard ship becomes known, Ahab uses the fire ceremony with the harpoons to bind the crew together with him in effect a pact with the devil.

In Arabic, *fedallah* means "sacrifice or ransom of God." He appears to be Satan's representative, punishing Ahab for his hubris. Fedallah does bear a likeness to Mephistopheles in the Faust legend. Fedallah and his crew, we are told, are master harpooners, there to help Ahab kill the White Whale. Whenever Ahab grows distracted, whenever his sympathies for a return to home shores seem to swell, then the shadowy presence of Fedallah makes itself felt, luring him back to his nefarious and mad purpose. Fedallah exerts, unlike anyone else, conscious power over Ahab, "some sort of a half-hinted influence." When he talks with Ahab, he refers to him as "old man," hardly a term of respect for his command.

Evil may be at the heart of the universe, but it is often difficult to pin down. It is something that is sensed, something that eludes the realm of reason. It is that mysterious principle that drowns sympathy in bloody rituals and horrors. It is, in the end, as mysterious as the universe. We know that the mystery of Moby Dick remains unanswered, although we are prepped to maintain that, despite the love that surrounds us daily, the "invisible spheres were formed in fright." Like the White Whale, Fedallah, too, must continue to be "a muffled mystery to the last." He may appear in dreams—nay, in the nightmare realm—but his presence is palpable, never ceasing to litter our reality and imagination.

Figure 10.
MC Lars raps about Ahab.

CHAPTER 51

The Spirit-Spout

AHAB TAPS ON DECK AND ANOTHER WHALE IS SIGHTED

When Ahab walks the deck of the *Pequod*, he makes a sound, described in this chapter as follows: "every stroke of his dead limb sounded like a coffin-tap."

Tap, tap, tap. The sound of Ahab and his journey into the mystery of the universe, into the solitude of the soul, into the itch of revenge, has inspired many musicians. When we think of artistic journeys in music with Moby Dick, the medium of rap music does not come readily to mind.

Rap, rap, rap. Rap musician MC Lars has a cut on his CD *The Graduate* called "Ahab." It competes with other ditties such as "The Roommate From Hell," "Internet Relationships (Are Not Real Relationships)," and "Six Degrees of Kurt Cobain." Lars is nothing if not happening, hip, and attuned to a classic in literature.

Lars does not fit the stereotypical image of the rapper. He is Straight Outta Palo Alto, California, rather than Compton—a onetime student at Stanford University. He also has studied at Oxford University. He read

Moby-Dick for the first time as a college junior, in a class on Melville taught by literary scholar Jay Fliegelman. The slow pace of the novel at first failed to excite Lars. Eventually, the "layers of metaphor and allegorical references" drew him into it, and he became "a fan of *Moby-Dick*, especially because of the overarching theme of mankind's hubris in the face of Mother Nature's sublime indifference."

He calls his style of rapping "post-punk laptop rap"—rapping done by educated, wealthy white boys without any ghetto cred. But within that legion, Lars distinguishes himself by rapping about a character from nineteenth-century fiction. To further distance his rap rhapsody from those that celebrate misogyny and violence, Lars announces that he hopes that his rap song "Ahab" will "inspire kids to read more Melville and turn off their televisions."

The rap from Lars is pretty good, abounding with playful rhymes and convincing refrains.

> Call me Ahab, what, monomaniac
> Obsessed with success unlike Steve Wozniak
> On the hunt for this mammal that once took my leg
> With my warn down crew and my man Queequeg
> [CHORUS]
> (Got a low low feeling around me)
> Bad trip thanks to Moby Dick!
> (And a stone cold feeling inside)
> Peg leg, sperm whale, jaw bone, what!
> (And I just can't stop messing my mind up)
> Whale crash so fast
> (Or wasting my time)
> Oh no, oh no!
> The ship's got a hole, plug it up, plug it up!

CHAPTER 52

The *Albatross*

THE *PEQUOD* ENCOUNTERS ANOTHER SHIP ON THE HIGH SEAS

Thanks to the medium of film, many of us can say that we have, in a manner, "seen the White Whale."

A number of film versions of the novel have been made over the years, beginning in 1926 with the silent film *The Sea Beast*, starring John Barrymore. It was redone as a talkie, starring Barrymore anew, in 1930. The most famous film version was produced in 1956, directed by John Huston. A made-for-television movie starring Patrick Stewart, of *Star Trek* fame, came in 1997. *2010 Moby Dick* (see chapter 20) has Ahab (played by Barry Bosworth) in pursuit of the 500-foot White Whale (the uppermost limit for male sperm whales is estimated to be about sixty feet), who years ago had taken his leg while destroying a submarine that he was on. Now, Ahab is bent on conquering the whale. Moby, however, is one tough cookie, able to launch itself into the air to take down helicopters or to grasp submarines in its teeth. Anyway, the comely Michelle Herman, a whale specialist, alone survives to tell the tale.

In *Moby Dick* (2011), William Hurt plays Ahab, Ethan Hawke is Starbuck, and Gillian Anderson is Mrs. Ahab. The miniseries takes many liberties with the original: Ishmael, while on his way to New Bedford, rescues Pip from a beating; Ahab is hardly hidden from view as the crew readies the *Pequod* for its voyage; Ishmael is a lapdog for Ahab's mad quest; Starbuck comforts Pip as the *Pequod* goes down. While such changes and additions do not make for a great film, the scenes of Ahab and the crew engaging in demonic ceremonies are sufficiently enticing to make viewing less painful.

In the grandfather of these films, *The Sea Beast*, John Barrymore chases after Moby, one of the few parts of the novel rendered in the film with any degree of faithfulness. The chase is diminished somewhat, certainly to our modern eyes, by the weakness of the beast itself. The director had originally intended to use a life-size model of the whale, made of rubber and steel, large enough for two men to work it from inside, so that it could turn, go under, and come up again. Manufactured by Warner Brother's Studio, this whale cost the then considerable sum of $12,000. Just as one of the operators was readying himself to enter the belly of the beast to try it out, the other operator suggested that first they test how well it floated in San Pedro Bay, California. A good idea. Soon after launch, the model of the

Figure 11.
Moby-Dick enthusiasts gather for a reading of the novel and presentations on it, at the New Bedford Whaling Museum. Photograph by Arthur Matta.

whale went down. Barrymore lamented, "And so that beautiful whale of rubber and steel was lost." It was replaced by a miniature model that was set in a water tank and filmed to look larger. Suffice it to say, not much of the whale is seen in the movie.

Thirty years later, John Huston faced the problem of how to make a whale that was as spectacular and powerful as Moby Dick in the novel. From the very beginning, Huston made it clear that the whale had to look "right" and "act real." Huston's whale was impressive: Moby Dick was rendered with iron, wood, and rubber, and spanned about ninety feet. Actually three whales were constructed, each costing $30,000 to produce, no small sum in those days when most films used tiny models and different camera angles to make them seem larger. Although Huston later lamented that the whale was not outfitted with menacing teeth, overall, the beast was effective in countenance and movement. It was fearsome.

Two other film versions are in the works, both of them promising to use the wonders of computer animation and even 3-D to enhance the powerful presence of the White Whale.

CHAPTER 53

The Gam

ON THE ETIQUETTE AND MEANING OF A "GAM"

Gams between whaling ships can be marvelous occasions for mail to be received and sent home and for the men from both ships to chat about this and that. As well as an opportunity to consume alcohol. Unfortunately, Ahab has no interest in small talk or drink.

A slim volume has been written about small talk about a big book. In *Two Guys Read Moby-Dick: Musings on Melville's Whale and Other Strange Topics* (2006), Steve Chandler and Terrence (Terry) N. Hill, gam and reflect about the novel. They do not, however, dive particularly deep.

Chandler and Hill are old friends. In 1960, they were supposed to read *Moby-Dick* as high-school students. But they had other, less elevated things on their minds. In college, Chandler had relied upon a "huge dose of amphetamines" and a Cliff Notes synopsis to ace a humanities course with *Moby-Dick* as assigned reading. Now, forty years later, they decide to read with greater care. Chandler had been at a cocktail party where someone had extolled the volume. Hill decides that he, too, will join in the exercise, and they will email one another back and forth with their impressions about the novel. The plan is to read about ten chapters every two weeks, then "write our impressions as we went." They have no pretension to doing "serious literary criticism." They are, after all, just a couple of guys gamming about a novel.

Over the course of their gam, the two guys wax and wane about the novel. Sometimes, with the eyes of a naïf, they register reasonable questions: "what was Melville's point in giving us that packet of miscellany up front?" But such concerns tend to dim as they discuss the baseball exploits of Derek Jeter and Alex Rodriquez.

Critics tell us that readers are wrapped up in an "horizon of expectations," defined by the literary canon and by representations of the novel that surround them. Thus, Terry cannot shake the image of Gregory Peck as Ahab while he is reading (see chapter 109). The film has managed to "impress a scene . . . so deeply" on his mind. It is unclear, however, whether such an impression of Peck's rather stolid depiction of Ahab is for good or ill.

Hill is onto something significant. Since the 1950s, we have become a largely visual culture. Thus the continuing success of *Moby-Dick* for succeeding generations is, in part, a function of how well and widespread the novel has been reformulated in visual terms.

Sometimes the excitement of reading the book is palpable. Chandler opens one gam with, "*Moby Dick* is a thunderous book." But, "like twisted rebar coming from fragmented concrete its sentences in their stilted, lofty descriptions are not a joy to read for me." Steve would prefer that Hemingway—"the anti-Melville"—had composed the book.

The correspondence prattles on. Which brings us to the critical question— what effect did reading *Moby-Dick* have upon our two, not quite intrepid voyagers? Well, they agree to disagree on some issues, such as whether Ahab is an admirable figure. One enjoys the existentialist thrust of the novel while the other wishes that Melville resided more in the moment. Steve concludes that Melville was so ruffled with metaphysical matters that he disregarded the reader and, hence, failed to entertain. But even if the two come away from their middle-aged reading of *Moby-Dick* without being transformed by it, they are at the very least appreciative of the book's presence in American culture. As the war in Iraq intrudes upon their thoughts, Steve notes that in an editorial in the *Washington Post*, Tina Brown has wondered whether the public might be better served by viewing wartime leaders less as Winston Churchills than as Ahabs.

CHAPTER 54

The *Town-Ho's* Story

(As told at the Golden Inn)

ISHMAEL TELLS A TALE THAT CONCERNS MOBY DICK

Themes of rebellion roil through the pages of *Moby-Dick*, nowhere more centrally than in this chapter. For Melville, rebellion and religious concerns are intertwined. Ahab is a rebel against God. Or he is at the very least someone seeking to understand the ways of God and the world, to comprehend how an all-powerful God can preside over such a contingent, brutal, and chaotic world. Rebellion, of course, has its costs, as Ahab's quest for knowledge and defiance of God seems to indicate.

One tale of rebellion, however, comes to us in the oddest fashion. Ishmael relates the story of the *Town-Ho* to a group of Spanish gents in the Golden Inn in Lima, many years after his surviving the voyage of the *Pequod*. Appropriately, he tells the tale on the eve of an unidentified saint's holiday.

The lineaments of the story are simple. A most uncommon common sailor named Steelkilt, a noble steed of nature reared in the wilds of Buffalo, is nonetheless "wild-ocean born, and wild-ocean nurtured; as much of an audacious mariner as any." However, he has provoked the ire of Radney, his superior aboard the ship, a man born to the sea but preferring land; a man further contrasted to Steelkilt by his vicious ugliness and temper. Radney orders Steelkilt to do chores that are below his station and beyond reason. Faced with Steelkilt's principled defiance, Radney threatens him with a hammer. Despite being warned to desist, Radney's hammer grazes Steelkilt's cheek. With the force of righteousness, Steelkilt punches Radney, felling him with one blow and breaking his jaw so that he begins "spouting blood like a whale."

Such defiance of authority, no matter how justified, cannot escape the attention of the *Town-Ho's* captain. To make a long story short, joined by a handful of other rebels, Steelkilt warns the captain to let his trespass go unattended. But the captain refuses to relinquish his right to flog Steelkilt for his actions. At one point, Steelkilt and ten of his fellow mutineers are banished to the forecastle, deprived of light and sufficient repast.

Steelkilt's erstwhile allies either desert him quickly or betray him, and he is bound by his hands to face the whip's punishment. But somehow, Steelkilt's mysterious "hiss" (what he says is never revealed) stays the captain's hand. Eventually, he jumps ship.

Odd moments interrupt the narrative. Moby Dick suddenly appears and the men scurry after this great prize. In the midst of the fray, Radney is tossed from his boat, landing on the "slippery back" of the whale before falling into the sea and, moments later, he is "seized" by the jaws of Moby Dick, who gives him a well-earned doom.

Rebellion against authority haunted Melville. From *White-Jacket* to his final work, *Billy Budd*, the story of justified rebellion against unfair authority rings out. While Melville appreciates the justness of rebellion, he worries the issue—aboard ship, as in civil society, actions have consequences, order must be maintained. In the case of the *Town-Ho* story, Steelkilt twice manages to escape from punishment and he exercises an almost mystical control—through his hisses—over the captain. Some interpreters have suggested that the *Town-Ho* tale is a parable of slavery, however redacted. Steelkilt could not be presented by Melville as African-American, but the themes of unjustified punishment, the lash, escape, and rebellion in 1852 all had resonances that could be anchored in the port of controversy concerning slavery and rebellion.

At the same time, the *Town-Ho* story touches upon religious issues. It can be read as a case of divine justice trumping secular injustice. Here is a Calvinist God, or at least a Hebraic God, full of fury, willing to intervene. Acting through Moby Dick, God exacts punishment on the evil Radney; circumstances enable Steelkilt to escape, perhaps to live happily thereafter on some delightful South Sea island. While the overall theodicy of *Moby-Dick* may well warn us against any notion of God intervening to rectify injustice or showing any hint of sympathy, this story serves as a counter-narrative, a suggestion that God does exist and He is capable of acting nobly, when it suits His fancy.

Ishmael remarks that the "secret part of the tragedy"—which remains unspecified—was revealed by some members of the *Town-Ho* crew during a gam with Tashtego. Although he was sworn to secrecy, Tashtego's dreams are haunted by the story and one night he mumbles some of its details. His bunkmates demand a full accounting, and he accommodates them. If it is a tale that reflects the presence of God and His occasional willingness to vanquish the brutal through the agency of Moby Dick, then it never reached Ahab's ears. Perhaps he would have been unable to hear it, as deaf to this possibility as the devout Catholic priest whom Galileo, in Brecht's play, begs to look in the telescope to see how the heavens work. The churchman's reply was simple: even if I could see it, I could not believe it.

CHAPTER 55
Of the Monstrous Pictures of Whales

ISHMAEL GAUGES PICTORIAL REPRESENTATIONS
OF THE SPERM WHALE

In an influential essay, "The American Action Painters" (1952), critic Harold Rosenberg hailed the arrival and philosophical concerns of a new group of painters on the American scene. Although he mentioned no specific artists by name, the work of Willem de Kooning and Jackson Pollock immediately came to the minds of his more informed readers. In any event, Rosenberg pronounced that these painters, working in an abstract mode, were existential heroes, engaging in a strenuous relationship with the blank canvas that they confronted daily in their studios.

He invoked *Moby-Dick* to capture the nature of this precise artistic moment: "The American vanguard painter took to the white expanse of the canvas as Melville's Ishmael took to the sea." Rosenberg meant to interpret Ishmael as an existentialist; thus the action painters began with a sense of dread, "of moral and intellectual exhaustion" but also with "the exhilaration of an adventure over depths" in a search for identity and authenticity. After all, he was writing in the heyday of American existentialism.

Not all critics agreed with Rosenberg, even if they shared his enthusiasm for abstract expressionist art. For Clement Greenberg, the artist was involved less in an existential act of self-definition than in a studious attempt to confront the limits and possibilities of the picture plane, to resolve problems inherent in the nature of the medium. Yet both critics would hardly have been surprised that so many abstract expressionist painters, from the mid-1940s until 1960, confronted *Moby-Dick* in their artwork.

The roster of such painters reads like a *Who's Who* of American abstract expressionism: Jackson Pollock, Robert Motherwell, Ellsworth Kelly, William Baziotes, Sam Francis, and others. They turned to the novel for a host of reasons. Many of them came of age when the vogue for *Moby-Dick* was at its height. They found Melville, no doubt, an appealing figure, an American original. They appreciated his independence, as an outsider whose great work could not be assimilated to contemporary tastes in the nineteenth century. Beyond these surface correspondences, the metaphysical concerns at the heart of *Moby-Dick*, to dive deeper, to confront the whiteness of the whale and the darkness of evil, jibed well with the painterly and personal anxieties that motored the abstract expressionist painters.

Consider the case of perhaps the most important abstract expressionist artist, Jackson Pollock. We cannot establish that he ever read *Moby-Dick*, but he was definitely familiar with its crucial themes. At the very least he was sufficiently enthused to name his dog Ahab. His wife, painter Lee Krasner, had read the novel and may well have discussed it with him. In 1943, Pollock completed a canvas that he called *Moby Dick*. But his patron, the influential and wealthy Peggy Guggenheim, did not like the title. James Johnson Sweeney, an important art critic, was visiting Pollock's studio one day when his eye caught the work. Pollock informed him that it was titled *Moby Dick*, to which Sweeney replied, no, "That's Pasiphaë." Pollock did not know the story of Pasiphaë, wife of King Minos and mother of the Minotaur. But he changed the name of his painting to *Pasiphaë* after Sweeney told him that *Moby Dick* as a title was a "cliché." Undaunted, Pollock soon completed another painting, which he called *Blue (Moby Dick))*. Pollock offered no explanation for the odd use of parentheses, although they could serve today as emoticons of movement.

Pollock was famously reticent about interpreting his works. It can be established, however, that at this time Pollock was deeply influenced by Jungian psychotherapy with its emphasis on myth and symbolism. He was actively plowing through the rich fields of his own dreams. Thus, critics Evan Firestone, Elizabeth Schultz, and others are correct in positing that in *Pasiphaë* Pollock was relating to Ahab's search for the White Whale in Jungian terms, as a *nekyia*, an archetypal sea journey, undertaken in the dark of night, as a search into the self. Nonetheless, all that can be stated with certainty about this large oil painting is that at its center is a shape that could be read as a twisting whale, caught up in the chaos and energy of the swirls that surround it, which, in turn, may represent the sea. More important than the pieces of the painting is its overall effect, which powerfully distills tension, movement, anxiety, and expansiveness onto the confines of the canvas.

Blue (Moby Dick)) is a much smaller work, gouache and ink on composition board. It is dominated by a rich blue, upon which are various shapes in white, orange, black, and yellow. These shapes look to be caught in a current, being pushed to the right outside edge and beyond of the canvas. There is a greater sense of calmness to this work than in *Pasiphaë*. Indeed, the shapes sometime resemble the mobile constructions of Alexander Calder, and one can imagine them being blown by a gentle breeze. Yet, *Blue (Moby Dick))* may just as easily be viewed as depicting pieces of the just-destroyed *Pequod* being drawn into the vortex, forever drowned in the great expanse of the deep blue. The heavy concentration of shapes at the bottom of the canvas might be indicative of this possibility.

As Melville remarks in this chapter, "the living Leviathan has never yet fairly floated himself for his portrait." Pollock's work, too, refuses to float easily for comprehension.

CHAPTER 56

Of the Less Erroneous Pictures of Whales, and the True Pictures of Whaling Scenes

MORE DISCUSSION OF ARTISTIC REPRESENTATIONS OF WHALES

Artist Red Grooms's *Moby Dick Meets the New York Public Library* is a monumental installation piece; at 45 feet long, 15 feet wide, and 25 feet high, it has the size of a young adult male sperm whale. The artwork is so large that it has found only a couple of venues able to accommodate it since it was first built for exhibit in Grand Central Station in New York City in 1992.

The work is agog with images as absurd and enticing as in *Moby-Dick*. One can peer into the wide-open, reddened mouth of Moby. Inside one finds various sailors that seem to be less than amused by their current habitat. From one angle, the whale can be viewed as bursting forth from the museum. From another perspective, the whale seems to be protecting the library. Perched above a sculptured seascape to either side of Moby are the library's famous marble lions, Patience and Fortitude, one with a life-preserver flung about its neck. Rather than impassive, the jaws of these lions are mechanical and move up and down—perhaps trying to express the inexpressible or to register their disbelief at what is happening around them.

Inside, Grooms's library is a long table, which sways—as does a chandelier above. You can imagine yourself aboard the good ship *Pequod*, redesigned as the library reading room. A globe rotates, the library's ceiling is a humorous reference to Michelangelo's Sistine Chapel mural, while liquor bottles and books adorn the shelves. As much as Melville jostles with the variety of meaning, Grooms plays with perspective.

Although the library was built more than half a century after *Moby-Dick* was published, a figure in it appears to be Melville working on a manuscript.

Elsewhere, Captain Ahab is intently hunched over one of his charts trying to locate the White Whale. Behind him "normal" library patrons read away, oblivious to the madness that threatens to engulf them. In this manic tableau Queequeg can be found, with his bare foot perched on a library table, drinking a beer. This only begins to describe the ruckus that Grooms has depicted.

If Ishmael is concerned in this chapter to discuss the "less erroneous" depictions of whales, then he would do well to shy away from Grooms's piece. But for anyone looking for an artistic equivalent of the book, this work is perfect.

CHAPTER 57

Of Whales in Paint; in Teeth; in Wood; in Sheet-Iron; in Stone; in Mountains; in Stars

ISHMAEL CONTINUES ABOUT REPRESENTATIONS OF WHALES

Between 1985 and 1997 artist Frank Stella produced over 138 artworks in various media, each with a title corresponding to a chapter in *Moby-Dick*. Painting, sculpture, lithography, silkscreen, collage—all were modes that Stella employed with an Ahab-like concentration and determination.

The idea for the series started at the Coney Island aquarium in Brooklyn, located beside the Atlantic Ocean. Stella would visit with his young sons, and he was fascinated by the movement of Beluga whales. He had already been experimenting with a wave shape in his painting, which reminded him of these whales. He then reread *Moby-Dick* and used it as a sort of template to direct his utterly ambitious project.

A surprising project, since Stella had long been quite vocal about the power and purity of abstraction. Heretofore, his most famous works had consisted of black canvases with lines running on them—darker and more foreboding, despite formal affinities, than the works of Mondrian. Could abstract imagery convey the power and movement of *Moby-Dick*, or would the boundaries of abstraction demand expansion to inch towards realistic representation? Perhaps Stella would need to realize what he had stated in his Norton Lectures at Harvard University, shortly before he began the series. There he had imagined abstraction, "flexible and expansive. It has no need to be exclusive, even perhaps of representationalism itself."

Stella recognized these challenges. As we saw with abstract expressionists such as Pollock, while they eschewed representation, they were open to attempting in their work to evoke deep feelings or to make references to literary works. Abstraction could be a mode of entering into the unconscious as well as a heroic way of engaging with the canvas. Stella did not intend his work to correspond exactly with Melville's narrative content in each chapter. At best, it would achieve "some kind of equivalence" concerned with "image, perception, and word." His artworks would not be "too close" to the chapters. He preferred to work in something like a trance, which would help him to avoid "analysis and ideas."

What he wanted to capture was the sense of movement and space in *Moby-Dick*, terms that were of excruciating concern to him. It was, he determined, not "so far-fetched" to use the "gestures" involved in abstract art to "have a possibility of coming close to what somebody like Melville might have been seeing." Stella decided "to let myself go, to see where he [Melville] sent me, and what I found is that he left me at sea."

Of course, being at sea with Melville and *Moby-Dick* can make for an exciting voyage. Stella's overall take on the book departs from many other interpreters who have stressed its tragic sensibility. While Stella recognized the presence of tragedy and Ahab's "paranoia" in the work, he remarked that "You can be tragic without being depressing." Hence, he focused on the "action and rhythm" of the book which he found "always alert." Perhaps a tragic sensibility might have jibed better with the perceptions of the 1950s abstract expressionists and Stella's own dark canvases from that period. But now Stella wanted imagery and activity that was colorful and turbulent—after all, it would have been well-nigh impossible to do all of the chapters of *Moby-Dick* in black paint.

The work that corresponds to this chapter is Of Whales in Paint, in Teeth, &c., done by Stella in 1990; it is in mixed media on aluminum, measuring approximately 7 feet by 5½ feet by 3 feet. Orange, blue, and yellow are the predominant colors. Black paint with intersecting lines, reminiscent of Stella's work from the 1950s, is also present. Suffice it to say, there is plenty of movement and chaos in this piece, and it is hard to find a center—either for vision or for meaning. In the chapter, Ishmael tells of the various modes that have been employed, across many cultures, to depict whales. Certainly, one can view the cacophony of colors and shapes in Stella's work as suggestive of the content of the chapter. As Robert K. Wallace insightfully points out, there at the top of the work a shape appears that resembles the head of a whale, with mouth agape. Another shape, phallic in composition, is covered with lines, perhaps representative of etching on scrimshaw or of the lines that are attached to whales once they have been harpooned. A pattern at the lower left of the piece could be feathers, such as might adorn Tashtego, or they could be the teeth of a saw or even a whale. In sum, a lot is happening and it is terribly difficult to stick the harpoon of understanding into the work. One imagines this is precisely how Stella would prefer it to be.

Interpreters of the series are divided about what to make of the correspondence between Stella's individual works and the chapters to which they refer. Is there a real or simply a capricious relation? In an intelligent commentary on this question of correspondence, Elizabeth Schultz, who has authored a wide-ranging book on pictorial representations of *Moby-Dick*, agrees that Stella is only mildly concerned with capturing the "narrative integrity" of each chapter in Melville's novel. Yet he manages, "through the interplay and repetition of forms" in his work, to achieve "the illusion of narrativity" overall.

It is fair to say that Stella captures the vastness of Melville's project and through various media achieves a sense of expansiveness and turbulence without violating the strictures of abstraction. The shapes can be read for meaning, and it is obviously true that the recurrent wave shape is suggestive both of the ocean and of its immense inhabitant, Moby Dick. As to the rush of other shapes in this gushing medley of artworks, the interpreter can proceed to uncover meaning with either abandon or reticence.

To gain a sense of the ambition and scope of the project would require one to view it whole, but the works, created over a long period, are scattered around the world in various collections, and they have never been exhibited together. In that sense, the gusto of Stella's achievement, much like Moby Dick, may well "remain unpainted to the last."

Note: Along with Stella, an immense roster of painters and sculptors have been attracted to *Moby-Dick*. Richard Serra, Leonard Baskin, LeRoy Neiman, Gilbert Wilson, Ann Wilson, Mark Bradford, and Felix Gonzalez-Torres, to name a few.

CHAPTER 58

Brit

THE OCEAN AS AN HORRIFIC PLACE

Melville paints a frightening picture of the ocean in this chapter. He details the "universal cannibalism of the sea," with strange creatures devouring one another in a carnival of carnage. He admits also that the sea must remain "an everlasting terra incognita." True, at least in the metaphysical sense that its depths will forever prove too deep for our own diving. Yet Melville seems clear that the choppy waters of the sea are hardly "incognita"; they are agog with death.

Rivers and oceans, as Heraclitus remarked, are in constant movement. It is a fitting metaphor for the movement of life and thought. This was translated, centuries later, by William James into a psychological insight of the highest import; the stream of consciousness becomes the modern way for describing the nature of reality. James regularly took to the sea, to voyage to the European continent, to be away from the responsibilities of his family and to have time for thought. In this sense, he and Melville were joined in sailing the same seas and in not fearing their presence. They offered a mode of escape from the chafing that they both associated with the maternal realm.

Melville is right, certainly, when he describes the predatory nature of the creatures of the deep. Even the dolphin, seemingly the most beneficent of beasts of the ocean, according to writer and surfer Thomas Farber, is predatory, living on "squid, lantern fish, shrimp," and more. Is the cannibalism of the sea any more immense or upsetting than that which stalks terra firma? Nowadays, we bring the sea to the land, not simply in terms of making drinking water out of the ocean, but in using it in waterboarding as a torture method. Here the horrors that Melville imagined have been fully realized.

Yet, waters also remain the stuff of dreams in religious ceremonies, they anoint and purify. With an almost religious impulse Farber is prone to what is called "calenture," the need to jump into the sea. It is for Farber, a way of experiencing freedom, of connecting with the maternal, of feeling oneness with the universe. As he awaits the breaking of a wave that will take him toward shore, he is in a Zen state, at peace with himself and buoyant upon the water. Yet, the sea is a favored mode for committing suicide, witness the many leaps made from the Golden Gate Bridge into the chilling waters of the San Francisco Bay.

The ocean was the hiding place for Ahab's deepest fears and his mortal enemy. It furnished him with a good livelihood but, in the end, it served as his burial place. None other, I suspect, ever occurred to him as quite so proper.

CHAPTER 59

Squid

A GREAT WHITE MASS IS SEEN

As the *Pequod* sails the Indian Ocean towards Java, Daggoo thinks that he has sighted the White Whale. It turns out, however, that he has seen the equally rare "great live squid," which is a "vast pulpy mass, furlongs in length and breadth, of a glancing cream-color . . . an unearthly, formless, chance-like apparition of life." Squid are sustenance for the sperm whale— a case of one phantom of the deep devouring another.

Tim Severin, a man of adventurous spirits, went whaling with natives of Lemalera, a town of 2,500 on the Indonesian island of Lembata. After a successful excursion, he watched in awe as the villagers stripped the sperm whale for everything that they could use. Precise cuts were made, according to ancient custom, and then the hacking and sawing began in earnest. Whale pieces, looking like parts from a "thick foam rubber mattress," Severin relates, are taken from the whale and distributed to various members of the village. The smith who forged the harpoon head receives, for instance, "flesh from above the whale's eyes." By the close of the day, only the carcass remains, even the lungs and entrails have been savored for some use. The oil from the whale will be employed in cooking, flavoring the leaves of local plants that would otherwise be too bitter to consume.

Severin is surprised to notice that the "glistening translucent body of a large squid" swallowed by the whale has been left abandoned on the beach. "Can't you eat that, too?" he inquired. A native remarks that the inside of the whale's stomach is incredibly salty and the squid is probably too saturated with salt to be edible.

What has brought Severin to this isolated place? He is a man who regularly embarks upon adventures at sea and then writes about them. He has, he tells us with no small degree of pride, "built and sailed a leather boat across the North Atlantic to test whether Irish monks could have reached

North America a thousand years before Columbus" and he has attempted the Sinbad-like exploit to captain "a replica of a ninth-century Arab ship from Muscat on the Arabian Gulf to China."

Now he is following the course charted by Ahab in search of the White Whale, albeit without any desire for revenge or any madness bubbling to the surface. On Pamlican, in the southern sector of the Philippines, Severin asks about sightings of a white whale, and he accompanies the villagers as they hunt sperm whales. Their method is rooted in ancient traditions and a far cry from modern modes of whale-hunting, which rely upon canon-fired harpoons armed with an explosive device that detonates once it has entered deep enough into the whale's flesh. But in Pamlican, the method employed is known as "whale jumping." It is as the name indicates—small boats get as close to the whale as possible, then a brave soul, armed with a sharp hook attached to a line, leaps from the boat onto the back of the whale. If all goes well, he plants the hook into the back of the whale and swims back to the boat. If all goes poorly, the whale can dive down, taking the "whale jumper" below. Or worse.

While Severin hears many stories in this part of the globe about white whales, he does not encounter such a whale himself. He has traveled over 6,000 miles, from his initial point in Nuku Hiva in the Marquesas, in search of a white whale. Though no doubt disappointed with its elusiveness, he is convinced that white whales are extant; they have survived just as Moby Dick had in the novel. Why not?

CHAPTER 60

The Line

HOW HARPOON LINES ARE COILED AND READIED FOR ACTION ALONG WITH SOME PHILOSOPHICAL REFLECTIONS

Moby-Dick is one of the great works of existential literature. Many ignore this obvious fact because existentialism is often narrowly considered a European phenomenon, probably due to the hard-held belief that Americans are too upbeat, unphilosophical, and optimistic for any European-flavored philosophy of gloom. Kierkegaard, Dostoevsky, Unamuno, Sartre, Camus, and Beauvoir—all charter members of the existentialist tribe—talk about *the* human condition. All of us—whether born in Europe or the United States— enter a world of contingency, a world without inherent meaning.

By our actions, we impose meaning upon an indifferent world. For the existentialist, we do so under the shadow of our own mortality. Keeping that cognizance of our own demise close to hand, the existentialist assumes, opens us up to a life potentially well lived. But it is a difficult life. In many ways it is easier to live inauthentically, as we do when playing a role, assuming certitude about the nature of things, maintaining that we are saved by the assured grace of God. Men and women are free, then, but it is a terrible freedom because with it comes responsibility for our actions. We are, in essence, the sum of our actions, no more, no less.

Ahab, as much as King Lear or Raskolnikov in *Crime and Punishment*, attempts to push the limits of his freedom and power. He refuses to accept a life of comfort with wife and son on Nantucket. He rebels against the limits placed upon his mortality and mind. He will have his answer, once and for all, or die in the attempt. There is much that is heroic in Ahab's quest, and much that is tragic. Melville was appreciative of both sides in Ahab, perhaps because he shared them.

Existentialism, however, in its humanistic guise, might not rest comfortably with Ahab. He is too caught up in refusing to recognize that all individuals—precisely because they are also free—must respect the lives of others. As Simone de Beauvoir understood, an existentialist ethics begins with the individual and his or her mortality, but it reaches out to others. We are all in the same boat, full of leaks that together we attempt to repair.

In this chapter, Melville spins some wonderfully powerful existential lines: "All men live enveloped in whale-lines. All are born with halters round their necks; but it is only when caught in the swift, sudden turn of death, that mortals realise the silent, subtle, ever-present perils of life."

We live death—our own demise—however much we seek to avoid such recognition. Melville asks us, in effect, to join with him in acknowledging that life is a rough ride, whether we are on a whaleboat in pursuit of Moby Dick or sitting at home stoking an evening fire. Accept the presence of death and allow yourself to live your life. Easier said than done, as Melville well recognized.

CHAPTER 61
Stubb Kills a Whale

A WHALE IS KILLED, NO THANKS TO ISHMAEL'S INATTENTIVENESS

Sometimes, in the sweet roll of the waves, it is easy to become indolent, to enter into a "dreamy mood," to feel that while the body exists, the soul has fled. The mind becomes passive, sleepy, and unable to function. Ishmael enters into this state until roused by the piercing cry of a fellow crewman that a whale has been sighted.

It is hard to associate indolence with Melville. Between 1849 and 1852, he wrote four thick novels—*Mardi* and *Redburn* in 1849, *Moby-Dick* in 1851, and *Pierre*, the following year. Inkwell after inkwell was dried by the swift movements of Melville's pen trying to keep up with the agitations of his mind and spirit.

But indolence was on his mind once he had finished his Herculean labors of writing. These books had been poorly received, overall, both by critics and the public. In 1853, he published a story that is redolent with his own frustrations.

"Bartleby, the Scrivener: A Story of Wall Street" appeared in *Putnam's Weekly*. The story haunts. Ostensibly, it is about Bartleby, a clerk who has been hired recently to copy law documents at a middling law firm, run by an elderly and kind lawyer, who serves as the narrator for this tale. Soon after being hired, Bartleby refuses to proofread or transcribe documents that are brought to him. He offers no explanation for this odd refusal to do the work that he is being paid to do, other than, "I would prefer not to." We learn, as the tale unfolds, that Bartleby is alone in the world, spending his nights in the law office, distanced from the hubbub that is the world around him.

As a good Christian, the lawyer tries almost everything to be accepting of Bartleby's eccentricities. Alas, Christian charity can go only so far when it comes into conflict with the impression that Bartleby makes upon potential clients. In the end, Bartleby's anhedonia, catatonia, or just plain tiredness, are too much, and he is consigned to the Tombs, a prison. There, the kindly lawyer attempts to outfit Bartleby with extra portions of food, but Bartleby refuses sustenance. He literally wastes away. All that we learn further about Bartleby's sad life is that for a time he had been employed in the Dead Letter Office, perusing missives that would never be read by their intended audience.

How much like Bartleby must have been poor Melville as he composed this woeful tale. In *Moby-Dick* and in *Pierre*, he had attempted to break away from his previous work. In effect, to do something other than to copy, with slight changes, the themes and style of his earlier works. He was trying to distance himself from his reputation as "the man who lived among the cannibals."

His efforts, however infused with art and bellowing with brilliance, met with some soft applause and much grousing. He had been working in his own sort of Dead Letter Office and by 1852 it was clear that some of his books would not be read, at least not in his lifetime. Melville might well have wanted to fade away, to retreat into a state of passivity, to never place pen to paper again. Melville ends "Bartleby" with the plaint—"Ah Bartleby! Ah Humanity!" How well might he have just as easily sighed, "Ah Melville! Ah Humanity!"

CHAPTER 62

The Dart

STUBB KILLS A WHALE

In the years when the *Pequod* sailed the seas, to kill a whale was mighty hard and dangerous labor. Stubb gets his whale but it takes tremendous effort. We are told in this chapter that the harpooner rows furiously with other crewmen in pursuit of the beast. All the while, he shouts out, above the roar of the ocean, "push men, push men!" Then, even if exhausted from this toil, he must rise suddenly, "drop and secure his oar, turn round on his centre half way, seize his harpoon from the crotch, and with what little strength may remain . . . pitch it somehow into the whale." Not surprisingly, Ishmael tells us, the force of such pitching sometimes results in the harpooner taking to the air and landing in the water, with an angry whale nearby. Given such dangers, it seems natural to speak of harpooners as noble and heroic.

As noted earlier, a handful of places remain in the world where the killing of whales is done in the manner of the nineteenth century. But within a few years of the publication of *Moby-Dick*, the method of killing whales changed markedly.

In the 1860s, Svend Foyn, a Norwegian, began to perfect earlier forms of harpoons armed with explosive devices. An ad for Patent Rocket Harpoons and Guns promised to "Fasten To and Kill Instantly Whales of Every Species." The device, held above the shoulder of the "harpooner," resembled a bazooka type of weapon. It proved to be a tremendous success. The weapon, which in later versions could be fired from the home ship, launched a harpoon into the thick skin covering the whale. According to historian of whaling Richard Ellis, "[i]mmediately behind the [harpoon] head there were four toggles folded back and fastened with a cord. Upon entering the whale's body, the barbs sprang open and crushed a vial of sulfuric acid detonating an internal explosion and embedding the head of the harpoon in the flesh of the whale, an often lethal blow."

An American whaling man, Thomas Welcome Roys, developed a rocket harpoon, which went through various versions over the years. In 1856, he "ignited the powder" in the shell and it exploded aboard deck, sending him back eight feet. He recalled, I "saw lying upon the deck a finger with a ring upon it which I knew, and looking I saw my left hand was gone to the wrist." Chalk up a small victory for the whales against their relentless pursuers.

In the last century and more, these devices (as they continued to evolve) helped to wipe out various species of whales. Nowadays, among renegade crews—mostly from Japan and the former Soviet Union—onboard ship canons are highly sophisticated and accurate. Modern harpoons have timers rather than sulfuric acid, and they are deadly accurate. Using sonar devices that can follow a whale half a mile into the deep, gunners fire harpoons to latch on and kill their target. The harpoon is four feet in length and weighs 185 pounds. As one mate put it on a whale-killing excursion witnessed by naturalist Peter Matthiessen in 1969, "With us they stand no chance."

CHAPTER 63

The Crotch

ON THE POSITIONING AND USE OF HARPOONS

"Out of the trunk the branches grow; out of them, the twigs. So, in productive subjects, grow the chapters."

"So, in productive subjects" such as *Moby-Dick* emerges the necessity of a scholarly, standard edition of the text. Not only because the book's trunk is thick, its branches many, and its twigs innumerable; its history of composition and publication is shaded by leaves of complexity and complication. Imagine the challenges to compositors trying to set the type from the scrawl of Melville's pages, which he was turning out at a heated pace.

The British edition of the book, published in October 1851 and titled *The Whale*, omitted chapter 25 ("Postscript") and the Epilogue. The editor for this edition also excised many presumably offensive phrases. There are something like 700 differences (ranging from single words to sentences) between the English and the American editions. The need to publish a critical edition was pressing, especially by the early 1960s when *Moby-Dick* had established itself as the leading ship in the armada of American literature.

The early 1960s was the great age of Standard Editions. Multivolume editions, carefully annotated and designed to be definitive, were undertaken for the works of Emerson, Hawthorne, Twain, Crane, Irving, Whitman, Thoreau, and Howells. In this pantheon, Melville's works, of course, were included.

Beginning in 1965, after intensive lobbying for federal funding and with an affiliation between Northwestern University and the Newberry Library, the Standard Edition began to emerge of *Moby-Dick* and other volumes composed by Melville. The undertaking was immense. Editors and assistant editors had to be hired, office space acquired, and editorial principles established. One of the first orders of business was to get a copy of *The Whale* so that its text might be compared carefully with the text of the first American edition. For two thousand dollars a copy was obtained and work began. Tedious and laborious work, for the texts had to be carefully checked one against the other, decisions about which words were intended by Melville in the face of botches by compositors. Work began in 1965 but, like the growing branches bespoken in this chapter, the project took twenty-three years to reach fruition.

The entire project was under the editorial supervision of Harrison Hayford, professor of American literature at Northwestern. A bibliophile of immense proportions—famous for recruiting students to drive him around Chicago to used bookstores in search of treasures—he was also an able scholar of American literature. Hershel Parker, who had been a graduate student of Hayford's, was quickly hired as associate editor. He was an indefatigable worker, devoted to the task and armed with strong views. He had recently completed a dissertation on Melville and politics and would, in time, establish himself as the leading scholar of Melville. The third member of the editorial team was G. Thomas Tanselle, a professor of literature at the University of Wisconsin. He was a master of the theory and practice of editing. How, for example, does one prepare a definitive text when there is no copy-text upon which to rely? How then can editors "reconstruct" a text, one that would presumably be true to the intentions of the author, while recognizing that intentions can often be murky, multiple, and meandering?

The final product was over 1,000 pages in length, with just a wee bit more than half devoted to the text itself. That meant that the editorial commentaries comprised about 480 pages of text—historical notes and commentaries, notes on the vagaries of the text and the decisions made about how to resolve them, a long list of emendations, and much more.

Despite the bulk, why did it take these learned and able men so long, over two decades, to complete the task of breaching *Moby-Dick*? The editors were conscientious to a fault, irritably aware of the importance of their undertaking and cognizant of their responsibility to get it as right as possible. They reached out from the first to involve other scholars of the volume. This meant that they received an endless flow of information and leads that needed to be pursued. They then debated among themselves and decided how new facts affected the final text. Parker, in particular, tracked down any information relevant to the composition of the book and Melville's influences. Henry Murray, a Melvillephile of no small degree, referred to Parker as "a bloodhound for facts." The editors, along with graduate assistants, spent countless hours in the basement of Deering Library, poring over various texts, reading aloud from them, and searching and cataloging all textual discrepancies.

In the midst of the larger editorial project, Hayford and company produced the Norton Critical Edition of *Moby-Dick*. After reading it with "great satisfaction," Melville scholar T. Walter Herbert Jr., in May 1972, wrote to Hayford about some concerns. For instance: on page 493, "You change 'In thoughts of the visions of the night' to 'In visions of the night,'" Herbert found the decision troubling, for the editors had changed it "without adequately marking the first phrase for deletion. . . . You are also assuming, quite rightly, that the phrase as it stands in the earliest English and American editions seems redundant."

"But," continued Herbert, "Melville was alluding, by this awkward construction, to the opening words of Eliphaz' vision at Job 4:13: 'In thoughts from the visions of the night.'" Not to belabor the point, and its significance, "The allusion is appropriate to Melville's interests in this passage inasmuch as Eliphaz goes on to urge Job to take an attitude of humility before the Lord, asking 'Shall mortal man be more just than God? Shall a man be more pure than his maker?' In 'A Squeeze of the Hand,' of course, Ishmael appears to resign from Ahab's blasphemous quest, and to forswear the hope of direct knowledge of the divine nature. 'I have perceived that in all cases man must eventually lower, or at least shift, his conceit of attainable felicity; not placing it anywhere in the intellect or the fancy.'"

Ten days later, Hayford replied to Herbert's erudite concerns. He found the point enumerated above valid, remarking that "Another correspondent had written us about it, and certainly our faces are red! I wrote her, 'Ignorance, madam, pure ignorance.'"

Avoiding other cases of "ignorance" and being caught red-faced vexed the editors. It was more than a question of having their reputations questioned. It was also that the community of Melville scholars, of which they were a contented part, was so careful and discerning that it fed into their own obsessive compulsiveness to get every fact right, to examine every possible lead, to make the edition as definitive as possible. If the editorial problems were frustrating, the status of Northwestern University Press, which had contracted to bring out the volume, was at times shaky. Might all of the editors' work amount to naught if a publisher for the edition failed to be secured? Problems with institutional support for the long-term project also proved troubling.

In 1975, the standard edition had still not set sail. Lawrence W. Towner, president of the Newberry Library wrote to Hayford that "We are getting a lot of flack from all sides about the Melville edition: irate subscribers with standing orders; the American Association of University Presses (which feels its relationship with the National Endowment is at stake); our own staff [and] . . . people who simply want to use the edition." He inquired with some consternation, "How can we get it back on the road, and how soon?"

Work and problems continued apace. In 1987, the editors were worrying about how to deal with the Hebrew quote in the Etymology section Melville's use of Hebrew was mistaken, but the issue was to explain why.

Was it deliberate, wondered Hayford? Unlikely, he concluded, Melville "was not a scholar, of languages, or anything else, including whaling and whales. He found the foreign words in dictionaries and copied them as best he could, and his copyist and compositors probably made errors in copying his copies. At least we think that is the most plausible line of explanation."

By the mid-1980s, the standard edition seemed to be heading to port. "We are in flurry of finishing MD," wrote Hayford in fall 1986, "this is IT." Might his correspondent quickly check some problematic references? A year later, Hayford and company were still fretting about this and that aspect of the volume. Some of the concerns, he admitted, "have bothered me for years." Thus, he asked fellow *Moby-Dick* scholar Stanton Garner: "In ch. 80, 'The Nut,' is the sentence, 'I rejoice in my spine, as in the firm audacious staff of that flag which I fling half out to the world.'" Alas, wrote Hayford, "I've always been bothered by 'half out'—what does that mean? As a flag expert . . . what do you make of it? Is some flag usage or jargon involved? Why not, as with Tashtego in Ch. 135: 'the red flag . . . streamed itself straight out from him'? (And similar passages elsewhere.)" Might Stanton clear this up?

Finally, the Standard Edition, in its Moby Dickian immensity and erudition, appeared. Moody Prior, then eighty-seven years of age, wrote Hayford, "All's well that ends well. I never thought I would live long enough to see" the standard edition published. One of the editors, G. Thomas Tanselle, admitted that he never imagined that "it would take us this long. But I, for one, am not sorry, because the edition is much better as a result of our investigations and discoveries of recent years. I'll avoid the usual cetological metaphors—but the magnitude of everything about the book applies to the textual problems as well."

CHAPTER 64

Stubb's Supper

FLEECE PREACHES TO THE VORACIOUS SHARKS ALONGSIDE THE *PEQUOD*

Holger Meins called himself Starbuck, Gerhard Müller was Queequeg, Horst Mahler was Bildad, Jan-Carl Raspe was the Carpenter, and Andreas Baader was, of course, Ahab. Gudrun Ensslin, who had chosen these code names for her comrades, called herself Smutje, German for "ship's cook," a way of referring to the character of Fleece. These young Germans were members of the *Rote Armee Fraktion*, more popularly known as the Baader–Meinhof Gang, a group of urban terrorists that stalked West Germany in the late 1960s and 1970s.

The gang's ideology was cobbled together from Maoism and Marxist-Leninism, spiced with anarchism and Gramscian ideals about how states manage to control their population. In the world of the late 1960s and 1970s, as the United States bombed Vietnam mercilessly, as former Nazis still occupied places of influence in Germany, and as fascist regimes around the world maintained their power, the Baader–Meinhof Gang decided that peaceful protests simply played into the hands of existing power structures. As an ultra-left revolutionary group, they believed that acts of violence—ranging from assassinations to robbery and arson—would ignite a revolution that would topple what they considered to be the corrupt, capitalist, fascist government of the German Federal Republic.

The gang and its leaders became the subjects of a massive manhunt. By June 1972, most of its leadership had been arrested. Their trial was chaotic as the members used the occasion to condemn the procedure and the system. But this time there was no chance of them escaping a guilty verdict and prison—they were now confined in the high-security Stammheim Prison, not far from Stuttgart. In May 1976, six years after she had cast her lot with the revolutionary group, Ulrike Meinhof committed suicide in her cell. She hanged herself by tearing a prison towel into strips, piecing them together and making a noose. "Suicide is the last act of rebellion," she had once written.

The remaining members of the group listened attentively to radio broadcasts in the fall of 1977 detailing the hijacking of Lufthansa Flight 181 by four men who demanded the release of the Baader–Meinhof gang and two Palestinian political prisoners, and payment of fifteen million US dollars.

The hijacked plane hopped from one destination to another while West German authorities summoned a crack commando group to storm the plane and free the hostages, when the opportunity should present itself. After refueling in Aden, the plane next landed in Mogadishu, Somalia. There the leader of the terrorists, known as Captain Mahmud, executed the plane's pilot, Jürgen Schumann, for defying his orders. While negotiations continued to free the hostages, the commando unit arrived in Mogadishu and prepared to attack. With daring efficiency, they stormed the plane, killing three of the hijackers and severely wounding the other. The plane and its passengers, save for the murdered Captain Schumann, were freed.

In his cell, listening to a small transistor radio, Jan-Carl Raspe no doubt heard the news of the foiled hijack. He somehow communicated this information to his fellow prisoners—Baader, Ensslin, and Irmgard Möller—and they agreed that they would all commit suicide. Baader, in Cell 715, had somehow managed to procure a small pistol, which he hid in a record player. He shot himself through the neck with the bullet exiting through his forehead. Raspe also had a gun secreted in his cell, and he, too, used it to end his life. Ensslin used cable from a loudspeaker to make a noose with which she hanged herself. Irmgard Möller took a prison-issue table knife and stabbed herself, four times, in the chest. She survived.

During their years in prison, gang members had employed their Moby Dick nicknames as a code for communication, a means of confusing censors. Ensslin explained some of her choices of names for her comrades. Baader, the revolutionary fanatic, was logically Ahab—single-minded in his determination to fight against the White Whale of the imperialist powers. She further applied Melville's description of Ahab to Baader, "For all men tragically great are made so through a certain morbidness." At greater length, she discussed in a letter to Meinhof her choice of Smutje as her own code name. The cook aboard the *Pequod* is named Fleece; he is an old African-American: "You'll remember that the cook keeps the pans well scoured and preaches to the sharks." Ensslin mistakenly maintained that Fleece was an officer on the ship; she considered herself to be an officer of the Red Army Faction.

An odd choice of name for a revolutionary. After all, Fleece is presented by Melville as a shuffling old man, an early version of a Stepin Fetchit sort of character. In a comic moment, Fleece preaches with Christian love and concern to the sharks to stop the racket that they are making as they fight over pieces of whale meat. Fleece tells them that there is plenty to go around (perhaps a socialistic message!), no reason for the sharks to be uncivil in their feast. But his words fall on deaf shark ears. Thus, concludes Fleece, "de dam willains will keep a scrougin' and slappin' each oder . . . dare bellies is bottomless; and when dey do get em full, dey wont hear you den; for den dey sink in de sea, go fast to sleep on de coral, and can't hear not'ing at all, no more, for eber and eber." Fleece concludes his "benediction" by shouting, "Cussed fellow-critters! Kick up de damndest row as ever you can; fill your dam' bellies 'till dey bust—and den die."

Perhaps for Ensslin here lies the real significance of Fleece and his sermon to the sharks. Languishing in jail, she realized that her dream of revolution through direct action was a fantasy. Hope remained. If the sharks are understood to be indicative of the voracious appetites of capitalists, then they will doom themselves by fighting among one another for strips of meat until so overfed that they sink from the weight of their own appetites. From Maoism to a form of deterministic Marxism marked the journey of Gudrun Ensslin, the caged revolutionist.

CHAPTER 65

The Whale as a Dish

WHALE MEAT AS DELICACY AND TABOO

Why among civilized men and women, Melville asks, should whale meat be considered so unappetizing? Certainly, Stubb's enthusiasm for whale steaks indicates that it can be palatable. In France, we learn from Melville, whale tongue was once a great delicacy; deep-fried "billiard ball" size, spiced and seasoned whale meat was a favorite of the monks of Dunfermline. Aboard ship, whalemen have been known to dip their biscuits in whale oil, as one would smother a piece of bread with butter.

Perhaps whale meat is too rich. The whale "is the great prize ox of the sea, too fat to be delicately good . . . a solid pyramid of fat." (Recall that in chapter 31, Melville employs the term "pyramid" to connect the mysteries of the universe and the origins of monotheism.) Maybe antipathy to eating whale meat arises because humans tend to avoid eating their own kind.

Nancy Shoemaker points out that in cultures as diverse as those of the Faroe Islands, the Inuits of Alaska, and Japan, whale meat has been considered a proper food for centuries. In Japan today, many parts of the whale are used for pet food. Melville admits that he has delighted in biscuits with

Figure 12.
Whale meat—"High in protein!"

whale oil slathered over them. Many aboard ship have partaken of whale meat and announced that it reminded them of beef.

Whale meat, even when abundant, never became anything more than a curiosity or a necessity for consumption in American culture. Narrow

American eating habits do not explain this disdain. The same men that passed on whale meat salivated over Galapagos turtle soup. To be sure, the very richness of the oil encasing the whale meat made it quick to spoil, but pickling and drying could have reclaimed the meat for consumption.

During the First World War, when food stuffs were scarce, Americans were told to eat whale meat. Recipes for "stuffed whale roast," or "whale croquettes," or "minced whale with scrambled eggs," appeared in governmental reports. In the 1950s, Norwegian entrepreneurs marketed something called "Capt. Seth's frozen tenderloin Norwegian whale steak." Although directed as an "exotic" food for "elite" tastes, the campaign sunk.

To return, then, to Melville's question: why not whale meat, even before they had become an endangered species? Shoemaker finds inadequate the notion of liminality, the view that whales are mammals and special among sea creatures. After all, many in the nineteenth century, and even to this day, considered the whale a fish rather than a mammal. Whalemen throughout the nineteenth century ate whale meat, on occasion, without any sense of doing anything abhorrent; they simply considered such meals temporary and exotic.

The question of food tastes, then, may be as unanswerable as the ultimate meaning of *Moby-Dick*. Food is stuffed with symbolic meanings, but the nonconsumption of whale meat among Americans, in contrast with other cultures, is one of the questions into which our harpoon of understanding fails to stick.

CHAPTER 66

The Shark Massacre

ALONGSIDE THE *PEQUOD*, SHARKS DEVOUR A WHALE

The viciousness of sharks devouring a whale's carcass is striking and revolting. In doing his "cutting in" of the whale, Queequeg nearly loses his hand to a shark's razor teeth. He then observes, "Queequeg no care what god made him shark . . . wedder Fejee god or Nantucket god; but de god wat made shark must be one dam Ingin."

Melville is treading in dangerous waters with this statement, though it is made more acceptable to his Christian readers by having it uttered by a heathen. But the incisors of this statement cut deep into the question—is there design in the universe? The answer to this question is momentous, in two ways. If there is no design, then the presence of God comes into doubt. And if there is design, and such planning appears malevolent, then has God lost the felicity of being benign.

Rebecca Newberger Goldstein, in her novel *36 Arguments for the Existence of God* (2010), nicely sums up the arguments for design—as well as their refutation. The classical argument is that God exists because it is improbable that complex things, such as an eye, could appear without a designer. Another, connected argument is that natural selection fails to explain the irreducible complexity of various organs; hence the presence of God's guiding hand behind evolution. Even if one accepts that mutations occur, then according to the laws of probability, they should happen more for the worse than for the better. Hence, God exists because He tilts the process in favor of beneficial adaptations.

More troubling to Melville, however, than the argument from design was the other core problem with logical explanations for God. According to critic Lawrance Thompson, Melville believed that God existed and that He *had* designed the universe. Melville's ship of faith ran aground on the shoals of the problem of theodicy—how could an all-knowing and benevolent God create such a muck of a universe? He also recognized that the argument that free will accounts for evil was insufficient given the destructive force of earthquakes and other natural disasters. Even if these events happened according to natural laws, the argument for design, with God as the first cause of all things, suggested to Melville that God, ultimately, was the arbiter of such horrors. (For more, see chapter 83.)

Melville had, then, come to the same, theologically and socially incendiary viewpoint as the savage Queequeg. Along with Queequeg, Pip, and Ahab, Melville had punched through the pasteboard mask that hides ultimate reality. Their conclusion was simple, to wit, there is a God and He is responsible for the sad state of the universe. Heaven will not help us. Melville took no satisfaction in this recognition.

CHAPTER 67

Cutting In

THE CREW BEGINS CUTTING BLUBBER FROM A DEAD WHALE

It is dirty work peeling the blubber from the whale anchored next to the *Pequod*. There is a technique to the practice. First a hole is cut with a long spade, then a "semicircular line" dissects the whale further and a hook is inserted. The sailors next commence stripping the blubber, reducing the vastness of the whale into manageable pieces for rendering.

When *Moby-Dick* resurfaced as a grand tale of adventure and meaning in the 1920s, publishers moved to cut it like a whale down to consumable size. In 1926, Alfred A. Knopf brought out an edition that hacked away about half the original novel. Many chapters, mostly those dealing with Ishmael's philosophical excursions and with cetology, were excised; others were shortened. Abridger A. E. W. Blake rationalized such gutting by telling readers that when long works of literature are left untouched, considered "sacred" from editing, they languish and "grow dusty on the top shelf." Rather than allow this to happen to *Moby-Dick* (which, ironically, at that moment was quite popular in its original and proud length), Blake removed "a vast amount of digression, soliloquy and technical detail which spin out the narrative to excessive length." Blake's "Propitiatory" to the shortened version ended with the refrain, "May the shade of Herman Melville therefore forgive me the liberty I have taken."

Amazingly, the now famous opening line, "Call Me Ishmael," fell before the editor's sharp axe. It had yet to gain ascendency as the most famous opening line in American literature.

CHAPTER 68

The Blanket

ISHMAEL DISCUSSES THE SKIN OF THE WHALE

The skin of any whale, including that of Moby Dick, is hardly a blank slate. Ishmael remembers "the hieroglyphics upon one Sperm Whale" which resembled "old Indian characters chiseled on the famous hieroglyphic palisades on the banks of the Upper Mississippi." Sperm whales possess a "high, pyramidical white hump" (chapter 41) which is "a solid pyramid of fat." (chapter 65) The references to Egypt, the ancient home of hieroglyphics, are obvious. The skin of sperm whales is "engraved" with all sorts of mysterious marks, "obliquely crossed and re-crossed with numberless straight marks in thick array." In sum, the "visible surface" of the whale is a hieroglyph that needs to be deciphered.

Melville, no less than his contemporaries Emerson, Hawthorne, Thoreau, and Poe, was fascinated by hieroglyphs. In the 1820s, Jean-François Champollion had deciphered a stele from the Ptolemaic era, *circa* 196 B.C. This mastering of the script allowed others to translate hieroglyphics. The reading of hieroglyphics—and their meaning—was hotly debated in the first half of the nineteenth century. Some continued to maintain, as had Father Athanasius Kircher in the seventeenth century, that hieroglyphics were a "cabalistic science and had monstrous fancies of a refined system of Daemonism." Emerson and others maintained that hieroglyphs abounded not only in ancient Egypt but in nature, possessed of esoteric but benign meaning. Rather, for Emerson, as he made somewhat clear in his famous essay "Nature" (1836), nature was not only spiritual but also something of a hieroglyph. Thus, "Every natural fact is a symbol of some spiritual fact." Decipherment of these facts of the "book of nature," in Emerson's view, would reveal an order to things, while experiencing nature without preconceptions would help return mankind to its infancy, before such symbols became dissociated from their divine meaning.

According to John Irwin, Melville was fascinated more by indeterminacy and the indecipherability of hieroglyphic marks. The grand symbol of such indecipherability, of course, is Moby Dick. Hence, the aptness of Melville's reference to its "pyramidical hump."

The White Whale is symbolic, to be sure. But of what? Here, as Irwin notes, we have various perspectives—piled high as a pyramid. Readings of the marks on the whale, as much as the meanings associated with the doubloon that Ahab has nailed to the masthead, are varied, according to the perspectives of the individuals who look upon them. No Rosetta Stone exists, then, which can reveal the meaning inscribed upon Moby Dick.

Another interpretation, which is not necessarily at odds with the previous one, is that the marks engraved on Moby Dick and all whales are decipherable. Ahab, with his "Egyptian chest" is a modern Champollion, questing to decipher (which, in effect, would diminish or kill) the White Whale. To punch through the barrier of language, the pasteboard mask of reality, would be to comprehend, as Emerson desired, the nature of the universe, the Being of God. Melville quaked with anxiety because he sensed—from the hieroglyphics of God's creation—that the meaning of it all was meaningless at best and evil at worst, as he suggested in the previous chapter.

CHAPTER 69

The Funeral

THE WHALE'S GHOSTLY PRESENCE IS FOREVER RECOGNIZED

After cutting-in and stripping the blanket of skin from the whale, its beheaded carcass is released from alongside the *Pequod*: "that great mass of death floats on and on, till lost in infinite perspectives."

In 1866, after publication of his poems *Battle-Pieces*—which sold only 487 copies in the seven years following its appearance—Melville was appointed Collector of the Customs for the Port of New York. The job was a logical one for an old salt like Melville, and it allowed him to wander around the docks checking bills of lading and cargo holds. He was, apparently, conscientious in his work, for which he pocketed a respectable salary of four dollars per day.

The next quarter-century in Melville's life was marked by personal tragedies—the suicide of his son Malcolm, the death in San Francisco of his other son, Stanwix. He did take pleasure in reading, worked hard on his poems and the manuscript of his haunting novella *Billy Budd*, and he enjoyed the company of his granddaughter.

But these years are colored in gray. Melville's time had passed, if it had ever really arrived. He was not feted as an author of any renown, beyond that of a teller of adventurous sea tales and exotica. *Moby-Dick* was a volume that had sunk into the deep sea of neglect.

Before being pronounced dead at 12:30 a.m., September 28, 1891, Melville was already presumed to be long gone. In an article first printed in 1890 in the Buffalo *Courier*, then reprinted in the *New York Times*, it was reported—contrary to common knowledge—that Herman Melville, referred to as the once-famous author of "sea stories—stories which have never been equaled," such as *Typee*, was actually still alive. Indeed, he could be seen on the lower East Side taking a stroll most mornings. In his glory days, the article commented with some editorial license, once courted by publishers, "[Melville's] name a literary star." In contrast, today "Busy New York has no idea he is even alive."

The official funeral was held at the Melville home, with Rev. Theodore C. Williams, of All Souls' Church, officiating. Mostly family were present, from the Melville and Shaw sides. A handful of obituaries announced Melville's death, and the *New York Press* stated the obvious: Melville had, since his heyday in the 1840s, "fallen into a literary decline" so immense, that "even his own generation has long thought him dead."

Perhaps the epitaph that poet John Keats chose for his own grave might have been appropriate for Melville's resting place in Woodlawn Cemetery: "Here lies One Whose Name was writ in Water."

CHAPTER 70

The Sphynx

HOW TO BEHEAD A WHALE

Ahab stares hard at the "black and hooded" head of the whale, reflecting: "Of all divers, thou hast dived the deepest." What wonders, what knowledge, what mystery this whale must have possessed!

"The book and the whale dive down," Dan Beachy-Quick tells us in his marvelous *A Whaler's Dictionary*. He hopes that his volume of "inter-laced meditations" will "bring a reader near to the white squall of meaning that is *Moby-Dick*." To achieve this noble end, Beachy-Quick must tumble into the mysteries of meaning, into the essence of language. He is aware, of course, that he will never "exhaust *Moby-Dick* of meaning." Indeed, his brilliance is to render it ever more paradoxical, to muse about a shattered world in which we seek completeness.

A Whaler's Dictionary is a miscellany; it opens with "Accuracy" and closes with "Writing." In between are many entries, meditations on the book, the nature of language, the elusiveness of meaning, and the potential power of prose and poetry. Entries in the book can be read randomly or consecutively, according to one's inclinations. In a sense, Beachy-Quick's book is a prototype for the volume that you presently hold in your hands, or that you read on a screen. I am trying to navigate similar waters, albeit by a different means of conveyance.

Beachy-Quick dives into the text of *Moby-Dick*, coming up for air only on occasion. His book is, pardon the pun, a breathtaking performance. Listen now to the music of his prose and his meandering after meaning.

On Ahab and his motivations: "Ahab's 'defiant worship' is to recognize that unspeakable world and speak of it, to recognize that placeless world and still draw a line on a chart to sail towards it. Ahab hates the impossibility he reveres. It is his holy blasphemy."

"Ahab learns from his wounds; his injury gives him his philosophy. Happiness and wholeness may illuminate a life, but they may also mask and blind." This is exemplary of a tragic perspective. One has to survive and learn from the injuries inflicted by life. Otherwise, life is not only tragic but also without hope of even fitful redemption.

CHAPTER 71

The *Jeroboam*'s Story

THE *PEQUOD* ENCOUNTERS A SHIP UNDER THE CONTROL OF A FANATIC

Aboard the good ship *Jeroboam*, Gabriel, a prophet of uncertain mental stability, rules over the minds of its crew. He has the "measureless power of deceiving and bedevilling so many others," which makes him a sort of duplicate to Ahab. But Gabriel thinks ill of Ahab's quest for the White Whale, predicting that it will end in disaster.

As noted in chapter 48, the reviews that greeted publication of *Moby-Dick* were mixed at best. By the mid-1850s, the life of the book had seemingly all but ended; its publication history nothing short of a disaster.

Sales figures for *Moby-Dick*—in light of the praise in many of the reviews and its later status as an icon of American literature—must strike us today as paltry. The sales statement issued by Harper's at the end of November 1851 indicated that 1,535 copies had been sold, slightly more than half the initial printing. By February 1852, sales had slackened considerably, with only an additional 471 copies finding a home. Three years later, a second printing produced 250 additional copies of *Moby-Dick*, with a fourth printing in 1871 that brought forth 277 more copies. There was no fifth printing, and the book was out of print by 1887. By the time of his death in 1891, Melville had earned a miserly $1,260 from his masterwork *Moby-Dick*. These earnings accrued from 3,215 copies of the book sold, with 2,300 of those having been dispensed in the first year or so following publication.

Figure 13.
Portrait of Herman Melville.

Further disaster struck *Moby-Dick*. In December 1853, unsold and unwanted copies, nearly 400 in number, were lost to flames. A plumber, working on some pipes in the Harper and Brothers publishing office in New York City, lit a piece of paper to ignite his lamp. Noticing nearby a pan filled with a liquid that he took to be water, he tossed the burning paper into it. The pan was filled with highly flammable camphene (used to clean the rollers on the press), and before long the entire establishment had been destroyed by fire. The fire's destruction served as a sad coda to public opinion which had already forgotten Melville's book.

Gabriel would have predicted as much.

CHAPTER 72

The Monkey-Rope

A MONKEY-ROPE TIES MEN TOGETHER FOR SAFETY'S SAKE

Once again, we find Ishmael and Queequeg bound to one another, this time literally, by a monkey-rope. Worn around the waist, it allows one man to scurry along the back of the dead whale confident that his partner will pull him back to the ship should he slip into the water. Ishmael speaks of his monkey-rope connection to Queequeg as akin to being "wedded."

Herman Melville wedded Elizabeth Knapp Shaw in 1847; she was twenty-five years old at the time. She came from a distinguished family, as did Herman. The Shaws retained a good deal of their wealth and Lizzie's father, Lemuel, was a chief justice of the Massachusetts Supreme Court. He was long a close friend to the Melville family and intervened on occasion to stabilize their precarious financial position.

By most accounts, Lizzie was a cultivated and bright woman. She must have initially found Herman a welcome change from the normal run of Bostonian eligibles—few of them had gone to sea and returned home with tales about cannibals and South Sea maidens. But Lizzie was relatively advanced in years and she no doubt looked upon the vibrant Herman as a decent catch, even if his financial status and writerly occupation did not enthuse.

She was a good wife, serving as a copyist for her husband, no easy task, since his handwriting was as unruly as his imagination. Careful to give him space for his own work, never interrupting him, she brought him his meals when desired. Together they had four children, Malcolm (born 1849), Stanwix (born 1851), Elizabeth (born 1853), and Frances (born 1855). One day in 1867, after returning home at 3 A.M., Malcolm took to his room and killed himself. Stanwix lived a dissolute life, falling from one occupation to another before succumbing to heart problems at age thirty-five. And poor

Elizabeth lived a life of near constant pain because of rheumatism. Only Frances lived a full and long life.

Herman and Lizzie endured their fates together for forty-four years, but they rarely found marital bliss. A pair of letters written in 1867, one by Lizzie and the other by her half-brother Samuel S. Shaw, indicate that the time had come to slice the rope tying Herman and Lizzie together. Apparently, Lizzie had confided to her minister Henry Whitney Bellows that Herman had been abusive to her and that she needed to escape. Perhaps, it was suggested, a staged kidnapping would free her from Herman's grasp and allow her to return to the sweet bosom of her own family? Her brother nixed the idea, although he shared a concern for protecting Lizzie from what she called "the insanity of her husband." In the end, nothing came of separation plans, and they remained together for another twenty-four years.

Anecdote has it that marital violence had reared its head earlier in their relationship. Sometime between 1851 and 1856, Herman returned home, soused on brandy, and beat Elizabeth, tossing her down a stairwell. This was a tempestuous period in Herman's life, marked by the financial failure of *Moby-Dick* and the scathing reviews for *Pierre*. In 1856, Herman left for an extended period, traveling to the British Isles, the Mediterranean area, and to Asia Minor, thanks to monies from his father-in-law. Often viewed as a means of allowing Herman to recuperate his strength in the face of critical reviews and abundant work, the trip may have been more a tonic for Lizzie. Herman's absence freed her from his anger and violence and allowed her to recover and to re-tie, in some manner, the monkey-rope of their marriage.

In his fashion and despite his ambivalent sexual yearnings, Herman did love Lizzie—or at least the ideal of home as a place of comfort and stability. When separated, he wrote often, and cherished letters from his "Dearest Lizzie." As he grew older and settled into the Custom House position, he took pleasure in her company and concern for him. Lizzie may have lacked the savage grandeur of Queequeg, but she possessed her own qualities, and Herman eventually came to appreciate them.

CHAPTER 73

Stubb and Flask Kill a Right Whale; and Then Have a Talk over Him

AFTER A SPERM WHALE IS KILLED, THE MATES DISPATCH A RIGHT WHALE

Melville liked to discuss philosophy, especially with drink in hand. He fondly recalled chatting with Hawthorne about "ontological heroics." Such forays into the nature of being, into what is the essence of existence, thrilled Melville but, in time, wore Hawthorne out. When confined to ship's quarters, and given the meditative qualities associated with the sea, then philosophical discussions effortlessly arose.

Flask and Stubb engage in their own philosophical back and forth in this chapter. They wonder whether Fedallah, the Parsee stowaway, is "the devil in disguise." Stubb, with his usual light-hearted bravado, is undaunted, "Damn the devil." While the two seamen chat about deep concerns, we learn that two whales' heads hang from each side of the ship. The "counterpoise" of these immense skulls helps the ship maintain its balance in choppy seas. Our narrator suggests that one of these whale's heads might be thought of as John Locke, while the other as Immanuel Kant. Thus we have, associated with the whale on one side, the apostle of empiricism, of a close cantering with datum; while on the other side we have the great elucidator of rationalism, of systematic philosophical speculation.

We glimpse here Melville pondering the twin edges of the Enlightenment—can we be confident with Locke about what we can know, or should we join Kant in acknowledging that our knowledge of things can go only so far? Can we punch through, as Ahab desires, the mask of mystery that is the universe, that is the White Whale, or might we be better to sail with Kant and recognize that we can never bring the mystery of God to heel before our minds?

It would be lovely to imagine that the idea for composing *Moby-Dick* occurred while Melville was at sea, on his trip in the fall of 1849 to England or back to the United States that winter. He was lucky on the outgoing voyage to have had as a shipmate George J. Adler, an adjunct professor of German literature at New York University. Born in Leipzig, Germany, and two years younger than Melville, Adler had devoted years to his *Dictionary of the German and English Languages*, which in two volumes was published in

1849. The task had drained him, leaving him on the bedraggled edge of madness. On board ship, he and Melville chatted at length about German metaphysics. Perhaps from these discussions, intensified by drink and rocked by the sea, Melville whetted his own fascination about the nature of things. Certainly, Adler's life represented that of a scholar drowning in such a project. Melville described his friend as having gone "almost crazy" from overwork on the dictionary. Perhaps, again, the initial glimmer of Captain Ahab's monomaniacal search for meaning came to Melville as he pondered his friend Adler, worn down by having spent years in pursuit of the origins of words.

We do know that upon his return to the United States, in early 1850, words began to spill from Melville's mind onto the pages of his novel, sometimes with a type of glossolalia that makes *Moby-Dick* for some of its readers ascend to the heights of excitement while others tumble to the depths of boredom.

CHAPTER 74

The Sperm Whale's Head—Contrasted View

THE GREAT SPERM AND RIGHT WHALES ARE COMPARED

Melville writes in this chapter "of the grand order of folio leviathans." In the "grand order of folio leviathans" of scholarly tomes devoted to *Moby-Dick*, the writings of Hershel Parker are remarkable for their length and knowledge. This is hardly surprising since Parker has spent close to half a century sailing the seas with Melville and his work.

From the expansive windows of his study perched on a hill in Morro Bay, California, Parker can, on occasion, watch humpback and grey whales navigating the Pacific Ocean. While the study has a few pictures of Melville and other memorabilia scattered about, it is functional, intended to keep Parker productive and focused on his lifelong quest to add to our knowledge of Melville and his writings.

On the shelves are many aged volumes, often in the same editions that Melville had read in the nineteenth century. Parker has penciled in these works the marginalia that was originally in Melville's own hand. This permits Parker to go directly to the source of Melville's reading and to gauge his comments in their precise and proper setting. Interspersed with hundreds of volumes dealing with Melville and his works are the products of Parker's own prodigious labors: his two-volume biography of Melville, over 1,000 pages, along with various monographs on Melville's works, and carefully edited editions in which Parker has had a hand.

Central casting would fare well to offer Parker the role of Captain Ahab. In his 70s, Parker is tall, with whale gray hair and a moustache; he looks like he could easily handle Pacific Ocean gales. Softly spoken, he is a proud heir to an earlier generation of scholar-adventurers—Jay Leyda, Harrison Hayford, and others—who delighted in chasing after any bit of information that added to the sum of knowledge about Melville. In the days before laptops and digital cameras accompanied scholars to the archive, Parker copied out by hand thousands of pages—letters about Melville, any newspaper review of Melville's works. His appetite for Melville material is voracious even today.

He can be Ahab-like in his fierceness towards those that he considers sloppy scholars or mistaken readers of Melville. He has a long memory for slights and, alas, occasionally replays them, not only in print but also in a blog.

Parker loves his meat-and-potatoes scholarship. He shows little patience for deconstructive and other interpretive conceits. From his perspective, the responsibility of the scholar is to get at the truth, to mine the available materials to know—or to conjecture based on available evidence—if Melville originally had a comma rather than a semicolon in one spot, or whether it was possible for Melville to have run into Nathaniel P. Willis on a particular afternoon on a specific Manhattan avenue in 1851. There is no fooling around with the facts for Parker. Probably no one else in the world possesses anything near Parker's familiarity with Melville.

Born to a poor Oklahoma family, with Choctaw and Cherokee blood in his veins, Parker was an unlikely candidate to develop into a preeminent Melville scholar. He left high school in the eleventh grade to support his family. Working with the railroad in the 1950s as a telegrapher, he managed at various times to attend Contra Costa Junior College. Later, while he worked the night shift in a railroad freight house in Port Arthur, Texas, Parker took classes at Lamar State College of Technology.

In part, Parker's early schooling was erratic because, in addition to his work responsibilities, he was afflicted with tuberculosis. Often he would be given painful shots in the stomach and forced to bed to recuperate. While a student at Contra Costa in 1957, he decided one day to read Melville's *Moby-Dick*. He experienced what Melville had referred to as a "shock of recognition," albeit in an unexpected manner. The previous year, while bed-ridden with his tuberculosis, Parker had worked through all of Shake-speare's plays, committing chunks of them to memory and reveling in the writing. When he read *Moby-Dick*, he immediately recognized the Shake-spearean influence and intonations in it. He was hooked, and soon wrote his first paper on Melville. Quite by chance, an instructor at Lamar sug-gested Parker go to Northwestern University for graduate study. Thanks to a Woodrow Wilson Fellowship, Parker arrived there in the fall of 1959. He imagined working with Richard Ellmann, the great biographer, but was too shy to meet with him. Parker's life gelled nicely, however, when he came into contact with Melville scholar Harrison Hayford. He sped through his course work, publishing an influential article on Melville, "The Metaphysics of Indian Hating," before completing his dissertation, "Melville and Poli-tics," in 1963.

The pace of publication has continued unabated for nearly fifty years, for Parker shares, however in a benign manner, a bit of the monomania that Ahab had for the White Whale. You can tell by the twinkle in his eye, the excited rise in his voice when he regales you with a recently discovered fact about Melville or a scholarly conundrum that he must attempt to solve.

Figure 14.
A White Whale's head of a birthday cake, by pastry chef Donita Terry, commissioned by Larry Reynolds for his wife, Erica.

CHAPTER 75

The Right Whale's Head—Contrasted View

A DISQUISITION ON THE HEADS OF RIGHT AND SPERM WHALES

How do you fathom the age of your average whale? According to Ishmael, "In the central blinds of bone, as they stand in their natural order, there are certain curious marks, curves, hollows, and ridges, whereby some whale-men calculate the creature's age, as the age of an oak by its circular rings."

Looking at the ridge of baleen or the ear bone of whales is like examining the rings of an oak tree. However, in the case of baleen, it can erode over time, making it less dependable. In any case, these methods are inexact, at best.

Scientists have long preferred to examine amino acids in the eye lens tissue of whales. It is all rather complicated but the proteins contained in this tissue synthesize before birth, and they do not involve themselves in active metabolism. By calculating the rate of accumulation of such amino acids in the eye, scientists can, presumably, accurately state the age of the whale under study.

According to this methodology, the estimated lifespan for whales varies according to species. However, as a general rule, whales live between twenty and sixty years (the upper limit for the sperm whale is estimated to be about seventy years), with some lasting to the hundred-year range and one remarkable specimen estimated to be close to 200 years old!

Other studies have concurred that some whales may be more than a century old. Bowhead whales, which swim in the Bering Sea and Arctic Ocean, are hunted by various Eskimo tribes from Alaska. On occasion, while engaged in the process of "cutting into" their captured prey, Eskimos have found odd, old remnants of harpoons in the bodies of these fifty-ton mammals. Once analyzed, these pieces have been found to have come from a particular type of exploding harpoon that was no longer in use by the twentieth century.

Bowhead whales navigating today in the icy waters of the Arctic may well be as much as two hundred years old. If so, some Bowhead whales might have swum alongside Moby in the 1840s and 1850s!

Ishmael posits that Moby may be immortal—both physically and symbolically. Perhaps he is, but we know that some of his brethren are nearly so as well.

CHAPTER 76

The Battering-Ram

THE WHALE'S HEAD IS A POWERFUL, PERHAPS UNFEELING, WEAPON

Charles Olson was a Moby Dick, battering-ram of a man. Standing six foot eight, he weighed over two hundred and fifty pounds, and intoned with a bellowing voice. His appetites and passions were huge, and he could be obsessive in their pursuit. Olson spent much of his life near the sea. He was born in 1910 in Worcester, Massachusetts, of Swedish and Irish background. With his parents, he spent summers in the coastal town of Gloucester, northeast of Boston; later he would reside there much of the year. In his massive work *The Maximus Poems* (1960), Olson composed something resembling a poetic topology of the town. He imbibed young the sea and whaling and they remained with him: "There is this rock breaches / the earth: the Whale's Jaw / my father stood outside of."

Olson's father was a postman who gave Charles, on his nineteenth birthday in 1929, a copy of *Moby-Dick*. He dedicated the 1926 Modern Library edition with a pun, "When o'er this book, you cast your eyes / Forget your studies and Moby-lize." Olson would Moby-lize for much of his life. Reading Melville made Charles Olson "burn to know, to possess the man completely."

After many interruptions and career twists and turns, including a stint as a graduate student in American civilization at Harvard, Olson finally published in 1947 his book *Call Me Ishmael*, which was as slim as *Moby-Dick* was massive. Olson stomped his foot on the text. He adopted a certain style, which he later claimed, "can be boiled down to one statement . . . ONE PERCEPTION MUST IMMEDIATELY AND DIRECTLY LEAD TO A FURTHER PERCEPTION." Here is a typically gnomic passage which shouts out his key themes:

> Melville did his job. He calculated, and cast Ahab. BIG, first of all. ENERGY, next. PURPOSE: lordship over nature. SPEED: of the brain. DIRECTION: vengeance. COST: the people, the Crew.

ENERGY, SPEED, SPACE, MYTH: these are terms that Olson made central to his view of the world and in his poetry. While working on his *Moby-Dick* book, Olson had his own epiphany through reading. He became convinced from his understanding of Heisenberg's Uncertainty Principal, in particular, that

The inertial structure of the world is a real thing which not only exerts effects upon matter but in turn suffers such effects. [emphasis in Olson]

Olson's journey into Melville touches on some of the same concerns that possessed Hart Crane's reveries. The "MYTH" is that America was of discovery, a virgin territory agog with possibility for those willing to take it in hand. Olson, no less than Crane, seeks to ground this mythology of America and the workings of *Moby-Dick* in the world of what he calls "FACT." The American story, as the narrative of *Moby-Dick*, is then about exploration and domination of vast spaces, of imposing one's will upon Nature. "Like Ahab, American, one aim: lordship over nature." This act, however, can be alienating and destructive—predicated as it was on the settlers' actions against Native Americans. Thus, Americans "are the last 'first' people. We forget that. We act big, misuse our land, ourselves." Melville did not forget these elementary facts.

Olson rhapsodizes about "SPACE." He is in awe of America's immensity, bounded by two oceans and with a Great Plains that has sea-like qualities. America is about expansive spaces, about a nation whose people are pioneers and exploiters that cannot stay put; they must venture forth to make "MYTH" into reality. To Olson, America is "a people of Ishmaels." Melville's genius, in part, is recognizing this and realizing it in *Moby-Dick*.

Olson's emphasis on "NATURE" and "SPACE" in the mythology of America is linked with themes that were central to the work of historian Frederick Jackson Turner and that, by the 1940s, had become part of the American mythology of self. Olson was certainly familiar with the view from his graduate training under one of Turner's students, Frederick Merk, and he had been assigned to read "The Significance of the Frontier in American History" (1893) in one of his history classes at Harvard. Turner argued that the West served as a safety valve for urban discontents and poverty. It also molded those who crossed into it, in effect transforming them into something new, into the species American.

The myths that Melville mines in *Moby-Dick* are varied. First, the book may be read as about "DEMOCRACY"—the American ideal. Of course, such an ideal is compromised by the sweated, industrial nature of the whaling venture, as Olson contended. Ahab, the American willing to stare nature squarely in the face, a man of steely disposition, "is no democrat." Democracy falls to the wayside when Ahab is in pursuit of revenge or in his quest to overcome nature. The captain is inclined towards a democratic fellow feeling with the crew, and he generally treats them with respect.

But Ahab is a "great man," the individual who imposes his will, who towers above the crowd. Because Melville "was no naïve democrat," the whaleship under Ahab's command teaches us that democracy can easily be subverted by "overlords" and that "the common man, however free, leans on a leader, the leader, however dedicated, leans on a straw." Hence, Melville's story of Ahab is about the power of the leader and the dangers of leadership to democracy—for the narrative is, after all, structured as a tragedy. The crew is democracy imagined—a set of skilled workers, from all sorts of different backgrounds. But from his Shakespearean reading lessons, Melville has added tragedy to the pot of democracy. Democracy, alas, does not free men from the reality of aristocracy or power, either earned or ingrained. What Melville does in *Moby-Dick* is to "MAGNIFY" such problems, such "MYTHS" and make them relevant to our own time. Magnified in the figure of Ahab, is the power of "hate-huge." It rages, transforms, and mesmerizes.

The conclusion is apparent for Olson: "That HATE, extra-human, involves his Crew, and Moby-Dick drags them to their death as well as Ahab to his, a collapse of a hero through solipsism which brings down a world." Thinking and writing about Ahab in the era of totalitarianism allowed Olson's engagement with the volume to expand beyond mythologies of pure space and energy into object lessons for present-tense politics, at home and abroad. But he managed to do so without compromising his essentially poetic vision of *Moby-Dick*. And in that vision, quirky and creative, he has opened up space for others to wrestle imaginatively with a whale of a book.

CHAPTER 77

The Great Heidelburgh Tun

THE MARVELOUS IMMENSITY OF THE SPERM WHALE'S HEAD

The White Whale and the book *Moby-Dick* have become metaphors for bigness. The first associations between the girth of the novel and the largeness of other things began in the early 1930s. A story about boxer Jack Dempsey's potential opponent, Primo Carnera, referred to him as "fistiana's Moby Dick." With good reason. Carnera, an Italian heavyweight, stood close to six and a half feet, with great punching power but limited ring skills. A bookstore in Los Angeles named the Moby-Dick Book Shop boasted about its collection of 50,000 titles, all of them discounted twenty percent. Another newspaper piece, from the period, noted that a file about Pan American airways "bulges fat as Moby Dick."

In the 1960s, the metaphorical power of Moby Dick as bigness still reigned. Relief pitcher Ed Roebuck called his Los Angeles Dodgers teammate

Figure 15.
Moby Dick bar the Castro District of San Francisco. Photograph by Marta Peluso.

Frank Howard, who was 6 foot 7 inches tall and weighed about 250 pounds, "Moby Dick, the great white whale." Popular comedienne Phyllis Diller, not only poked fun at her husband, "Fang," but also skewered her overweight mother-in-law, whom she referred to as "Moby Dick." Everyone got the reference.

When Amazon introduced its Kindle book-reader, many of its advertisements featured *Moby-Dick*. What could have been more appropriate than to link up with an American classic? Now a thick book could be downloaded and contained in a digital reader—and for only eighty cents. According to a report in the *Los Angeles Times*, the Kindle version of *Moby-Dick*, on an iPhone, required 9,461 screens for viewing! An advertisement for *Moby-Dick* on Kindle suggested that the whole megillah of the novel could be downloaded at 3G speeds in less than sixty seconds. How long it would take to read the volume in this form was wisely left unsaid.

Finally, in the gay Castro district of San Francisco is a bar called Moby Dick. There one imagines that some patrons, after imbibing a few stiff drinks, might begin to brag about the size of their own Moby Dick. Not surprisingly, tall tales abound.

CHAPTER 78

Cistern and Buckets

TASHTEGO FALLS INTO THE TUN BUT IS RESCUED BY QUEEQUEG

Great works of literature when brought to the screen often fall into a vast "queer" world.

In 1926, the first film version of *Moby-Dick*, called *The Sea Beast*, appeared in theaters throughout America, helping to boost sales and interest in the novel. The movie starred John Barrymore, then forty-three years old and America's leading heart-throb. He had yearned to do the film because he loved the novel. And he was tired of playing too "many scented, bepuffed, bewigged and ringletted characters—princes and kings." He longed, at last, to "revel in the rough and almost demented character" of Captain Ahab.

The Sea Beast was immensely popular. Eight weeks after its opening, 300,000 people had seen it. Newspaper reviews were glowing. This despite the fact that the film bore little resemblance to the novel that Melville had composed.

Figure 16.
John Barrymore as Ahab, with famous profile, from the 1926 movie *The Sea Beast*.

The film transformed the novel into a love story, a tale of revenge (although not solely against the whale). It even paraded a happy ending! Ishmael is absent from the story, ditto any theme of male bonding between him and Queequeg (who appears simply as one of a handful of harpooners). All of the momentous symbolism of the novel is stripped from this silent version.

The screenplay, by Bess Meredyth, presents us with a deep love between young and vibrant Ahab Ceeley, a sailor who adores the sea, life, and his love, Esther. She is the daughter of a minister, and she returns Ahab's affection. They promise, during a moonlit night of passionate but chaste embracing, that they will forever be devoted to one another. Lurking in the shadows, however, is Ahab's half-brother Derek, who lusts after Esther, played by Dolores Costello.

While at sea, Moby Dick is sighted. Taking after him in a small boat are Ahab with harpoon in the front and Derek rowing in the rear. Ahab's harpoon hits its mark, but the whale turns back upon the boat, cutting the line. At this moment, Derek scurries to the front of the boat and pushes Ahab overboard. The whale bites off his leg. He is rescued and survives the ordeal. Once aboard the main ship, Derek begins a subtle strategy of undermining Ahab's confidence and winning Esther for himself, once he has returned to port.

To make a long story short, Ahab hobbles to meet his beloved at a dance, which nicely juxtaposes the joy of movement with Ahab's pained steps. Esther retains all of her love for Ahab, but he imagines pity in her response. Derek stokes Ahab's fears, until Ahab decides that it is best to allow his brother to love Esther since he regards himself as a wrecked man. But a glimmer of doubt enters into his mind—might he be mistaken in his sense of Esther. He goes to her house, only to behold in silhouette her and his brother appearing to be intimate. He leaves the scene an embittered figure. Of course, he is mistaken.

Years pass and Ahab is now captain of the *Pequod*, determined to wreak revenge upon the whale that robbed him of his leg and his love. He decides to obliterate Esther from his life in a particularly effective scene. Using the surface of a red-hot harpoon, Ahab burns away her tattooed name from his arm. With a grinning and cunning Fedallah, consistently presented as his evil twin—a racist depiction of the Oriental, common to this period— Ahab plots the currents of the oceans and the history of whales to find his quarry. But things get complicated, as he learns finally that it was his brother that pushed him in front of the whale's path. He then tells the crew that they are going to return to port, much to the dismay of evil Fedallah.

In the interim, Derek has fallen overboard from a ship returning him, Esther, and her father to New Bedford. Miraculously(!) he is found floating by the *Pequod*. When he is picked up, he lies, telling Ahab that Esther has drowned. Ahab and Derek fight. By planting his ivory leg in a hole in the ship, Ahab manages to overcome his brother, sending him overboard to his proper death in the sea.

Next Ahab takes off after Moby Dick. He manages to toss his harpoon into the whale, but his small boat is capsized. Ahab grabs the line, and with lance in hand, he triumphantly holds onto Moby, killing him. With the whale and his brother both dead, Ahab is redeemed. He returns to New Bedford to find Esther (who at various points in the film is shown to be pining for her honey) at home. Their eyes meet and their love triumphs over evil designs and white whales.

This somewhat mocking summary ignores the successes of the film. It opens nicely, focusing on a copy of *Moby-Dick, or the Whale*, with Melville's name displayed as author. The book opens not to the passage on Ishmael, but to lines about the brave and heroic lives of whalers. The greatest scenes of excitement come when the small boats speed along in pursuit of the whale. Another well-done scene occurs when the *Pequod* is caught in a typhoon, with only Ahab's determination keeping her afloat. Barrymore does more than simply offer his famous profile for viewers to admire. He shows himself well as an agile and lively young man, and he is effective as the dark and demonic Ahab. Woven into the film are a number of scenes that effectively depict the business of whaling; the crew is shown industriously stripping the blubber and later rending it into valuable oil. The sparks between Barrymore and Costello are real, for he had fallen in love with her literally at first sight, and pushed to have her play the lead role.

The only hint that the story of *Moby-Dick* may be something more than an ultimately sappy adventure story occurs at the height of the action. The *Pequod* is shivering against the sea during a typhoon. A crazed Ahab wants the crew to continue its mad hunt for the White Whale. A seaman, unidentified but probably modeled on Starbuck, urges Ahab to desist: "The White Whale is the devil's self. God warns you away!" Upon hearing this, Ahab strikes the sailor down with a single blow, then exclaims: "God is the lord of the Sky, but I am the Captain of the Ship. Avast."

The Sea Beast was an accessible and sentimental adventure story. However odd in its tracing the storyline, it helped to make *Moby-Dick* an icon of the American public, no matter how serious and scholarly readers might simultaneously find themes of tragedy and symbolism in the text. The "horizon of expectations" of the American public, as indicated by the film, could accept a dose of tragedy, as when Ahab loses his leg and, initially, the love of his life. But as William Dean Howells famously remarked to Edith Wharton, "what the American public always wants is tragedy with a happy ending." The American public got it, without protest, in the final scene of the movie, where Ahab and Esther embrace in front of the house with a white picket fence.

CHAPTER 79

The Prairie

ISHMAEL ON THE PHRENOLOGICAL ASPECTS OF A WHALE'S HEAD

Ishmael wonders what it would be like to run his fingers, as if he were a phrenologist, along the bumps and wrinkles on a sperm whale's head.

The best way for children to encounter the delights of *Moby-Dick* is by running their hands along a pop-up book version of the novel.

Sam Ita calls himself a "paper engineer," which hardly begins to capture his artistry and imagination. He combines cartoon panels and pop-ups to illustrate the story of Ahab, Moby Dick, Ishmael, Queequeg, and the *Pequod*.

As you open the volume, the *Pequod* pops up, in all its three-masted glory. The next pages are magnificent. We find Father Mapple atop his ship's prow of a pulpit, pointing to the heavens, in full fury holding his Bible, which has the symbol of a fish on its cover! In the pop-up pews we see Ishmael, Bible in hand, Queequeg, harpoon nearby, sleeps through the sermon.

Figure 17.
Sam Ita's marvelous *Moby-Dick* pop-up book.

Ahab has, of course, his own pop-up. He holds a mallet in one hand and a bottle of rum in the other—Ita is depicting the scene where Ahab seduces the crew with his heated rhetoric and the doubloon to search the seas for the vaunted White Whale.

The penultimate scene presents the *Pequod* after it has been rammed by the whale. The sea is in the process of claiming it forever. In an imaginative aside, a tab can move Moby in a circular manner as the vortex he has created drives sailors down to their watery graves.

Speaking of reading bumps. In 1949, a Braille edition of *Moby-Dick* was published.

CHAPTER 80

The Nut

THE MYSTERIES OF THE WHALE, LIKE THE SPHINX, REMAIN

The whale, we are told, "wears a false brow to the common world." The world, it might also be said, is often presented in a false guise of happiness and contentment. Rejection of such a sanguine view of the world propelled some readers of *Moby-Dick* to find a tragic sensibility of heroic proportions in its pages.

Lewis Mumford started to write about Herman Melville and *Moby-Dick* in his early thirties, close to Melville's age when he had composed his own great work. Both were born in Manhattan, and they shared shady family histories. Melville's life had been forever tainted by his father's financial failure and death. Mumford's own family history may have helped him to identify with Melville. Until he was well into his forties, Mumford avoided direct confrontation with what he had long suspected, that he was the illegitimate child of a Jewish businessman named Lewis Charles Mack. His mother, of German Protestant stock, had been a housekeeper at the home of an uncle of Mack's. His father and mother had a brief affair, resulting in Lewis Mumford's birth. Mumford also, at the moment of undertaking his biography of Melville, was similarly hobbled with the need to support a growing family by his writing. Thus, both Herman Melville and Lewis Mumford wrote with a sense of liberation but also with financial crisis near to hand.

Mumford was a complex character. Like many intellectuals of his era, he was alienated from the present, but he identified strongly with the American past. He emerged from service in the Navy during the First World War with a firm view that evil lurked behind the façade of civilization and that irrationality bubbled up from below the veneer of rationality. He was supportive of progressive politics but without an absolute sense of certitude. Civilization was not marching forward; in fact, it was entering "a new Dark Age." Little did he realize at the time that the First World War was only a warm-up for a larger conflagration, one that would claim the life of his son Geddes, who fought on the Italian front.

Mumford was not the first to write a biography of Herman Melville. Raymond Weaver's biography had that status, but no one presumed that it was definitive in any fashion (see chapter 92). It was also a bit thin on analysis of the stylistic and philosophical questions that had engaged Melville. An Englishman named John Freeman had published a brief biography of Melville in 1926, and Harvard psychologist Henry A. Murray was beginning his long-term work on a biography that would never be published (see chapter 113). Mumford later said that his time in the Navy had helped prep him; he had rowed a whaleboat and been subject to military discipline, which he imagined made him something of an old salt.

Mumford identified with Melville as a fellow traveler along the tragic path of life. As with almost everyone who had, or would, tackle Melville and *Moby-Dick*, the book he produced was as much about himself and his concerns as anything else. They spurred him forward, pushing him to do some of his finest work.

He wanted, as had Emerson and Melville in the previous century, to examine moral and personal issues that were at the heart of the American and human experience. Mumford's pace would have thrilled Melville himself. Yet in May 1928, he wrote to Raymond Weaver that "Melville is a very whale to handle . . . My task waxes as my energies wane." By late summer of 1928, however, he had a completed draft. When his book appeared in the spring of 1929, it was a financial godsend for Mumford and his family.

According to historian Casey Nelson Blake, Mumford's work on Melville was critical for his intellectual development. It helped Mumford sharpen his critique of "the moral flabbiness of American liberalism." It committed him to the development of a "democratic community" based upon "an ethical middle ground" that recognized the tragic nature of existence and "personal boundlessness." In sum, he had moved to a philosophy of spirited liberalism, peppered with Ahab's purposefulness and zest.

Mumford characterized Melville as a refreshing realist, meaning that he embraced a tragic sense of life. In Mumford's understanding of the term, Melville had in *Moby-Dick* realized that "the highest human flight is sustained over an unconquered and perhaps an unconquerable abyss." The struggle to create a work of greatness, to peek with unflinching courage into the abyss, these were the attributes of heroism. Such heroism shunned contentment and material rewards. Out of the process of wrestling with the devil of life, the individual—should he survive—retained something "precious," something "impregnable."

Mumford argued that *Moby-Dick* offers readers "a parable of the mystery of evil and the accidental malice of the universe." The whale is representative of "the brute energies of existence, blind, fatal, overpowering." Ahab, in contrast, is heroic, exemplary of the "spirit of man, small and feeble, but purposive, that pits its puniness against this might, against the blank senselessness of power." Fine and dandy, but unhelpful in explaining the multiple layers of the symbols. After all, if the White Whale is indifferent, then is it evil? Does evil require a sense of purpose, a malice at its heart, to be evil? And, for all of Ahab's determination, at what point might he be viewed as monomaniacal to the point of rashness in leading his crew to doom?

Moby-Dick was a tome valuable for Mumford's times. It closed the books on the Victorian fantasy of tragedy with a happy ending (did he see *The Sea Beast?*), plunging the reader into the existential realm of true, unrequited suffering. This world—the real world of flesh and blood men and women—is agog with "destruction, that meaningless force." Destruction comes with a hurricane, a volcano, an earthquake, or, one might add, totalitarianism and racist repression. Call God the power that summons these forms of horror, if you will. But also accept God as absent, uninterested in the heady and high purposes of humanity. In such an inhospitable world what is to be done? Mumford wanted Americans to jettison simplistic confidence about their exalted place within the scheme of things and accept that they were part of a wild, chaotic universe. In such a contingent and chaotic world, a man's value is in his defiance of the gods and in his attempts to be virtuous.

Perhaps Ahab's heroism was narrowly symbolic for Mumford himself. Might Ahab be heroic for his willingness to glance into the blinding whiteness of the whale? If so, is he then, unlike most in polite and complacent society, willing to think more deeply, to commit himself to living most "intensely"? Rather than a simple tale of monomania and revenge, Ahab's quest is about creativity, scientific and artistic, which is the essence of a "formative . . . expressive" existence. The spirit of art, the heroism of the quest, when undertaken with others, represented, for Mumford, the "utmost spirit" that in its best moments, allows man to "meet Leviathan on even terms."

"Even terms" mean no certain victories, no edifices that will withstand the shaking of the foundations that constitutes the tragic cycles of existence. Reading *Moby-Dick* ("the best tragic epic of modern times") in this manner, concludes Mumford, can help us to face life with determination. For the novel makes us aware of the power of scientific explanation (the cetology sections) without reducing all of life to certitude. There is something lurking at the edges of knowledge. Hence science must be joined by the "illumined eye of imagination and dream." The book, with its tragic sensibility, its complex symbolism, and its wisdom presages "part of a new integration of thought, a widening of the fringe of consciousness, a deepening of insight, through which the modern vision of life will finally be embodied."

CHAPTER 81

The *Pequod* Meets the *Virgin*

THE *VIRGIN* OFFERS SOMETHING TO THE *PEQUOD*

In his wildest fantasies, Melville would have been unable to conjure up that his character Starbuck would achieve worldwide renown as the name for an immensely successful chain of coffee shops.

It is an odd name for the store. Starbuck is steady and moral, but he is unable to summon up a sufficiently strong brew of will to defy Ahab's mad plan. All we know about Starbuck is that he risks danger in pursuit of his profession, that he has a wife and family back on Nantucket, that his last name is common on the island, that he is a fine first mate, and that he does not—at least within the confines of the novel—drink a single cup of coffee.

The only connection between Starbuck and coffee occurs in this chapter. The mates of the *Pequod* wonder what the captain of the *Virgin* is waving in his hands. "[It's] a lamp-feeder," opines Starbuck. No, replies Stubb, "it's a coffee-pot, Mr. Starbuck; he's coming off to make us our coffee." Flask finally resolves the question in Starbuck's favor. He carries no coffee pot, but forever will Starbuck and coffee be intimately associated in the public mind.

Certainly more than this mere drip is responsible for Starbuck's name coming to grace coffee shops around the world. Accounts differ, but the first Starbucks opened in 1971 in the Pike Place Market in Seattle. It was the brainchild of Jerry Baldwin, an English teacher, Zev Siegl, a history teacher, and a writer named Gordon Bowker. Apparently, Bowker wanted to name the shop Pequods, after the ship. An odd choice, in its own right, since the Pequot was an Eastern Indian tribe nearly wiped out in battles between 1634 and 1638; many of those not killed were sold into slavery in the Bahamas Islands (see chapter 16). Terry Heckler, a creative partner, thought it a poor choice, less for historical than for linguistic reasons: "No one's going to drink a cup of Pee-quod." Probably right.

Bowker and Heckler went back to the drawing board. Might they name it after a mining camp that had been on Mount Rainier in the early twentieth century, called Starbo? The result, an amalgamation, became Starbucks. Howard Schultz, who came aboard the Starbucks company ship in 1982 and oversaw its expansion to over 16,000 shops in 49 countries, maintains that the original name is drawn from the novel, perhaps because he thinks it bequeaths the brew a more literary pedigree.

Why not, then, have called the first café The Gam, a place where persons or ships, passing alongside one another, share a cup of coffee? Or would the order, a "double gam," sound strange? There are many seafood restaurants known as Moby Dick's, as well as the gay bar in San Francisco that goes by that name. Would getting a double espresso at Moby Dick's have sounded better than one at Starbucks?

CHAPTER 82

The Honor and Glory of Whaling

A RAMBLING DISCOURSE ON WHALING THROUGH THE AGES

Books came quickly, if not always easily, from Herman Melville. One December evening, after spending a day working on *Moby-Dick*, Melville described the writer's life in a letter to his friend Evert Duyckinck. Living during the winter season in Arrowhead (so named because of the prevalence of Indian arrowheads still to be found in the area) gave Melville "a sort of sea feeling" as he looked out from his window upon the snow- covered landscape. Continuing with nautical metaphors, he described his room as like "a ship's cabin." At night, when awakened by "wind shrieking," he almost felt compelled to "go on the roof & rig in the chimney."

Melville combined something of the farm life with the writer's existence. First thing in the morning, he went to the barn to feed his horse and cow. Then after breakfast, he made for his "work-room," which afforded him a spectacular view of the "gigantic shape of Greylock" mountain—massive in winter like a White Whale.

Let Melville describe the rest, for his prose sparkles and crackles like his study fire:

> [I] then spread my M.S.S. on the table—take one business squint at it, & fall to with a will. At 2 ½ P.M. I hear a preconcerted knock at my door, which (by request) continues till I rise & go to the door, which serves to wean me effectively from my writing, however interested I may be. My friends the horse & cow now demand their dinner.

Another jovial description of Melville at work comes from his wife. Speaking of the time in 1847 that they lived on Fourth Avenue, New York City, in 1847, while Melville composed *Mardi*, Lizzie noted that after breakfast at eight, Herman took a walk north to Washington Square. While he was out, she hurried to his upstairs room to tidy it up a bit so that he might "sit down to his desk immediately on his return. Then I bid him good bye, with many charges to be an industrious boy, and not upset the inkstand."

Plenty of times, no doubt, the ink from his quill splattered, the inkstand tipped. Melville wrote at a furious pace, the words tumbling like Niagara Falls water. When they evaded him, he was frustrated and fallen. But in the years of his greatest output, the spout of his creativity—although hampered by expectations and demands from his public and by the need to provide an income—gushed with abandon.

Was a "careful disorderliness" the "true method" (see chapter 84) employed by Melville in composition? Disorderly, certainly. Careful, well, less so if we note how Bulkington suddenly disappears or how Ishmael, our intrepid mariner and narrator, is not only privy to conversations out of ear range but also to the inner mind of Captain Ahab.

Whatever his method in the "work-room" of his thoughts, it succeeded.

CHAPTER 83

Jonah Historically Regarded

ONLY A PERSON OF FAITH COULD ACCEPT THIS WHALE OF A STORY

Lawrance Thompson argued vehemently that *Moby-Dick* was about evil and that the source of evil was to be found in God. Melville had not written an atheistic tract (that would have been the easy way out), but one that put the onus for the suffering of man squarely at God's own altar (see chapter 66).

In a striking and controversial interpretation, Thompson attempted to demonstrate how Melville remained beholden to his Calvinistic origins. But he transformed them, and he absolved Adam and Eve for original sin. Thompson charted the development of Melville's religious disillusionment and search for answers as it developed in each of his novels prior to *Moby-Dick*. Because of his family position and the religiosity of American society in the mid-nineteenth century, Melville cloaked his theological views with irony, satire, and indirection. Symbolism and allegory made his meanings often seem contradictory or unclear. In Thompson's view, Melville had picked a "quarrel with God." It was to be a battle of the titans.

In *Moby-Dick* and other writings, Melville demands answers from God to the following questions: Why do we exist in a death-saturated world? Why at an impressionable age was he (Melville) robbed of his father? Why should an infant die of hunger in the hell-hole of the Liverpool slums? Melville wanted answers to these questions, and he wanted a direct dialogue about them with God.

Ahab sets himself up as a countergod. In the famous doubloon ceremony aboard ship, he engages in his own form of catechism, binding the men to him by avowal and then by the sacrament of wine. This is, of course, blasphemy. It may be responsible for bringing down upon Ahab and his crew God's wrath, via Moby Dick.

Another reading suggests that Ahab enlists himself and his men in a holy quest—to know God fully. Melville, through Ahab, is storming the citadel of heaven in *Moby-Dick*. The conversation that Melville sought with God will be realized in his "wicked book" through Ahab's desire to get at the reality of God, once and for all.

What, then, is the nature of God and his creation? Ahab may be viewed as a nineteenth-century Job, an upright man hobbled by God's malice. Whereas Job remains complacent in the face of God's apparently unreasonable tortures, Ahab rebels against such afflictions. He decides to sink his harpoon into the symbolic presence of his enemy, to find out what is what. This is not done in an obvious fashion, according to Thompson, because Melville was often confused about his overall theology and because he feared the repercussions of making his views explicit. By the use of "sustained irony in the focus of narration," with the regular employment of "Biblical allusions," then, Melville theologizes in more subtle fashion.

But the conclusion is clear to Thompson: *Moby-Dick* is an antireligious book. It presents God, incarnate in the White Whale, as at best indifferent, more often malicious, hateful, a tyrant in His absolute power over His domain. In contrast, Ahab is heroic in his search for answers, in his belief in the sovereignty of man. He knows that death is his due, but if that, or madness, is the cost of asserting his equality with such a God, then so be it. He is, to the end, defiant. His death is a form of "anti-Christian victory."

It is important to recognize that readers experience Mapple's sermon through Ishmael (see chapter 9). This young man is no conventional Presbyterian, but he is curious and open to possibilities, religious and otherwise. What does he do immediately after the sermon? He returns to his room to find Queequeg involved in a pagan ritual. Ishmael is as intrigued with this blasphemy as he is with Christian belief. In fact, the implication is that Queequeg's religious sentiments, when tied to his strong sense of fellowship and generosity, make him a better Christian than most self-professed Christians. As Ishmael remarks, "I must turn idolater." The world contains many possibilities, and Queequeg's is deserving of recommendation. In a satirical comment, bursting with meaning, Ishmael famously states, "We cannibals must help these Christians."

Ishmael's openness, his biblical waywardness, may be the source of his salvation; he is the only one saved. Thompson responds that the Epilogue, while amenable to such readings, is misleading. It opens with a quote from the book of Job: "And I only am escaped alone to tell thee." Fine, but what is it that Ishmael has to tell the reader? One answer that Thompson provides is that both Ishmael and the reader of this novel exist in the same space in relation to God. They are alive but they are "god-bullied." Moreover, the coffin image at the conclusion of the novel harks back to an earlier reference when Ishmael meditates on his own suicidal thoughts.

Pip the cabin boy had also drifted in the sea; he came to recognize the indifference of God, and it drove him mad. A type of madness also comes to Ishmael, contained in his recognition of "the paradox of God's simultaneous malice and indifference." In the matter-of-fact telling of the story's ending, Thompson sees Ishmael as mimicking God's own indifference. Perhaps the conclusion of the novel is less about redemption than about how all of us are, like Ishmael, adrift, orphans looking to be rescued from the meaninglessness of existence.

CHAPTER 84

Pitchpoling

ON THE SUBTLETIES OF HARPOONING TECHNIQUE

Imagine a moment in time, say a day in early May 1851. Herman Melville is at his desk, flailing away at *Moby-Dick*, while Gustave Flaubert is entrenched in his Rouen home, ever so carefully composing *Madame Bovary*. Of course, neither knows the other exists.

Melville was born in 1819, Flaubert in 1821. Both came from well-established families and both rebelled, in their fashion, against the proprieties of their social backgrounds. Melville took to the sea to earn a living and in search of adventure, to encounter the exotic other. Flaubert, although famously embedded in a comfortable bourgeois lifestyle, also sought escape. He traveled to Egypt, where he delighted in the flavors of the land and in the favors of prostitutes.

Both sought to channel their restless souls onto the page, albeit in different manners. Flaubert famously remarked that a writer must "Be regular and orderly in your life like a bourgeois, so that you may be violent and original in your work." He was able to embrace this ideal with success; Melville less so since the violent and rough seas of his temper spilled out into his personal life, all too often.

Flaubert is famous—or infamous—as the stylist extraordinaire. He hunted for *le mot juste*, willingly spending an entire day to pin it to paper. His appetite for revision was enormous and his perfectionism vaunted. Peruse the letters he wrote to his lover, writer Louise Colet, and you will find a compendium about the craft and concerns of an obsessive writer. Flaubert maintained that style could transform, enliven, sort of drop magical dust upon, the most mundane subject matter.

This is what he wanted to achieve in *Madame Bovary*, a novel about a provincial young woman who is dissatisfied with her life and who enters into an illicit affair, with dire consequences. It is a work of vivid realism, which challenged the romantic conventions of the novel when it first appeared in 1857. Its reception was rocky, to put it mildly. Flaubert found himself brought to court by the government on charges of immorality, after sections of his novel had appeared in a newspaper. Flaubert beat the rap, and by the 1870s, as literary styles shifted in his direction, his place in the pantheon of modern authors became firmly established.

Melville had his moments of stylistic brilliance but his method of composition was hurried. He eschewed careful revision and he did not, so far as can be established, spend many hours worrying about the appropriateness of a particular phrase or word. But we should not presume that Flaubert would dismiss Melville's occasionally bombastic style out of hand. After all, Flaubert once remarked, "Exuberance is better than taste." Melville had the former in ample supply.

Despite their differences, both writers helped to establish the modern novel. Flaubert dove deep into the nature of the beast; style became the water upon which the novel sailed. Melville, especially in *Moby-Dick*, dives deeply into the very nature of existence.

Figure 18.
Publicity campaign for Johnson City, Kansas, public library. Yes, some thought fresh fish could be bought at their local library.

CHAPTER 85

The Fountain

THE WONDERS AND DANGERS OF THE WHALE'S SPOUT

Whalers know one truth: it is dangerous to be hit by the spray from a whale's spout. It can blind you, if it gets in your eye.

As a young man, Paul Metcalf felt the blinding mist of Melville and his writings. Born in 1917, around the time that Melville's reputation was resurfacing, Metcalf was on his mother Eleanor's side the great-grandson of Herman Melville. Metcalf was already a published author when he realized that he had, for his entire life, "been blocking out" the works of his great-grandfather. He then determined to "sit down and engorge Melville"—"in chronological order."

The shadow of Melville was always present as Metcalf grew up. His mother's side of the family had considered Melville a poor husband and a wild drinking man (he was called "the beast"). But they upheld his reputation as a writer. Eleanor, a difficult woman, was described by her son as the "den mother" of Melville scholars. Few dared to cross her for fear of having significant research sources closed to them—some of which she stored in a breadbox in the attic.

Metcalf's novel *Genoa: A Telling of Wonders* (1965) is his accounting with the Melville family legacy. He describes it as "a documentary novel. Although a fictional (or semifictional) story provides the central structure of the book, a great deal else is incorporated; particularly material from the life and work of my great-grandfather Herman Melville, and material from the accomplishments of Christopher Columbus." Metcalf sails with Hart Crane and Charles Olson in alluding to such connections (see chapter 76).

Genoa is the story of two brothers, one a "moral monster," emotionally and physically crippled in a Japanese prisoner-of-war camp. Carl becomes a predator, before the state executes him for horrible crimes. Michael, his younger brother, is a scholar, whose interests encompass both Melville and Columbus. Perhaps like one of the characters in the novel, Paul Metcalf came to believe that "maybe Melville, as history, had impressed himself into the fiber and cells of which Carl was made, had become part of his makeup."

Michael, the narrator of the novel, is a nonpracticing physician, hobbled by a clubfoot. He compares his problem with Ahab's severed leg, which he considers far less offensive than his own disability: "A sudden fury lashes me, a desire to mutilate myself, to amputate the great, round, ugly glove of a clubfoot—to make it not me." Allusions, sharp and muted, continue throughout the novel to Melville's texts and family history. In a way, Metcalf is doing what his narrator seeks: "There is an experience that I must try to understand, and it has to do with awareness, with a point in time and perhaps also in space where the awareness may be fixed, a time-space location, such as, say, a whale-ship."

The novel is a montage, interweaving quotes from Melville's work, the story of two brothers, Melville family history, material on Columbus, and much more. Sometimes links are made with cunning abandonment: "it is not so much that Columbus may have been a Jew, or Melville at war with Christ, as it is that both men ran upward to the sources . . . men who, like the first king of Atlantis, imagined and predicted, and from whom, therefore, action flowed. . . ." Both Columbus and Melville were "men of vision."

The cabin in which Michael composes resembles a ship, with its masts and beams: "The house, the attic, are once more become a ship." The metaphor of a vortex recurs often, as well as thoughts of suicide and mutilation. Metcalf takes us through the rough waters of personal and family history, and we emerge raw from the experience. Tragedy is the hallmark of the recounting, which ends with the swirl of poison gas claiming the life of one of the characters in the novel.

CHAPTER 86

The Tail

DISSECTING THE IMMENSE TAIL BUT ITS MYSTERY REMAINS

As noted earlier, *Moby-Dick* has been censored and chopped up over the years. Sometimes, its dissection has been, as far as can be found, inadvertent. In the English edition, published as *The Whale*, one chapter and the Epilogue were omitted. Published by Richard Bentley, *The Whale* lacked the lines, "hell is an idea first born on an undigested apple-dumpling." Another famous line that fell to the cutting room floor was the one uttered by Queequeg, "de god wat made shark must be one dam Ingin." Nor was it acceptable to refer to Ahab as having "a crucifixion in his face." More proper for the English sensibility was to have Ahab bearing "an apparently eternal anguish." Sexual references were dropped: old whales could not be found "warning each young Leviathan from his amorous errors."

In the 1956 film version of *Moby-Dick*, John Huston wanted to convey Ahab's blasphemy. He filmed, however, in a period when Hollywood films, especially anticipated blockbusters, were expected to depict the glory of God and religion rather than to plant seeds of blasphemy. Moreover, in an era when film censorship, from within the studios and from outside, remained a force, the very idea of a movie dedicated to capturing Melville's "quarrel with God," was a pipe-dream at best. As Ray Bradbury, the screenwriter, noted while making revisions of the confrontation in the cabin between Ahab and Starbuck, "blasphemy will be censored, best to cut it out" (see chapter 109).

Joseph Breen headed the Motion Picture Producers and Distributors of America, from 1933 until 1954. His role, quite simply, was to censor film content that audience would consider, salacious, antireligious, or anti-American. He read the script for the film and found that the "basic story . . . seems to meet the requirements of the Production Code." Hardly a rousing endorsement of an American classic!

Breen then outlined his concerns with the version of the script before him. While some uses of the words "damn" and "hell" were "legitimate," at least when they were direct quotes from the novel, any other uses of the words were unacceptable according to the code. In addition, the phrase "In the name of God" should be struck from the script because it was "not used entirely reverently." Ditto for the use of the terms "Oh, God" and the expressions "Good Lord," "Thunder and Hell," and "ye damned whale." Breen also stated "of course, that our final judgment will be based on the finished picture." One of the producers, within a day of receiving the letter, wrote back promising to "proceed to adjust the dialogue in question."

A detailed form, "Analysis of Film Content," noted that liquor was consumed in some scenes, that other races were portrayed, and that crimes were depicted. The film passed the scrutiny of the censors and the studio; the Legion of Decency rated it A-1 for content, while the Protestant Motion Picture Council, Harrison's Report, and the "Green Sheet" from the Film Estimate Board of National Organizations found the film acceptable for adults and young people. Nonetheless, it was still thought necessary that in reel eight, the scene where Queequeg fights a Portuguese sailor who would harm Ishmael, "the display and use of a knife in the fight on the deck be reduced."

Perhaps Ray Bradbury had anticipated such censorship problems with his script. In 1953, he had published a brave book, *Fahrenheit 451*, about the dangers of censorship that was aimed straight at the heart of McCarthyism and the Red Scare in America. It is a frightening parable about the burning of books (which incinerate at 451 degrees Fahrenheit) and the yearning that some have for the knowledge within them. Firemen are trained to set fire to books that are deemed dangerous to serene minds. A mechanical hound, with the determination of Ahab, is capable of hunting down readers, those who defy the edicts of the totalitarian state. While Bradbury mentions by name some of the books that are consigned to flames, he does not single out *Moby-Dick*. Perhaps that would have been hitting too close to home.

CHAPTER 87

The Grand Armada

KILLING WHALES, INCLUDING A MOTHER

According to the dazzling literary critic Harold Bloom, *Blood Meridian* (1985) by Cormac McCarthy is the only American novel to approach the grand sublimity of *Moby-Dick*. For his part, McCarthy has acknowledged his indebtedness to *Moby-Dick*. The two novels share much. Both are written in an intricate, at times baroque style. Each novel grapples with the challenge of theodicy. Both novels are inked with symbolism and with characters who are frightening and unforgettable. Both are bathed in blood.

Blood Meridian tracks the round-the-clock murder rampage committed by the Glanton gang. Such a horde did exist in the period around 1850, and their initial charge—at the behest of the Mexican government—was to kill Comanches around the border between Mexico and Texas. They were paid by the number of scalps that they turned in. The gang is a varied lot, joined only by their taste for blood and ability to endure a hostile environment. In time, they depart from their focus on massacring Indians and begin to murder Mexicans. This brings upon them the wrath of the Mexican government—the hunters become the hunted.

One member of the gang, in particular, etches himself in the minds of the novel's readers. The Judge (named Holden) is a massive presence, described as being close to seven feet in height, weighing 300 pounds, an albino with a bald pate. He never sleeps and he takes pleasure in killing and raping. This "great pale deity," after dispatching a life, plays his fiddle or does a nimble dance. He is more than a dynamo of destruction; he is also the life of the party and a man of heightened sensibilities, learned to the extreme. He appears to know almost everything. He spouts a rather simple overall philosophy of life—namely, that life is about death. There is, he opines, "meanness in the least creatures," and the only thing that seems to endure is war. The Judge has certainly found his calling as a killer of epic proportions.

Early in the novel the Judge is called the Devil. And he may well be, given his glee in bringing death and destruction wherever he travels. He is also described as ubiquitous and immortal. He may be symbolic, then, like the White Whale of the meaning of the universe. If Ahab was trying to punch through the pasteboard mask that he determined was Moby Dick into the nature of things, then McCarthy's Judge Holden is the descendent of the White Whale, come onto land. And behind the mask stands revealed the true nature of the universe—it is blood and bodies, all the way down.

Intonations of *Moby-Dick* in *Blood Meridian* are also apparent in the character of the Kid. He comes to the gang at the age of sixteen; he is an adept killer but he lacks a lust for blood that is typical of the others. Like Ishmael, he will survive the manic mayhem of the 1850s. The novel ends, as does *Moby-Dick*, with an accounting. The Kid is now forty-five years of age. He walks into a bar, orders a whiskey, and suddenly sees, at a table nearby, the Judge. They are the only surviving members of the gang. The Judge tells the Kid, "Drink up. This night thy soul may be required of thee." The Judge worships at the shrine of "the sanctity of blood." He has, like Ishmael, been part of the crew, but almost always a bit apart, unwilling or unable to give his full assent to the madness of the quest. Later that evening, the books will close on the Kid. The Judge rapes and murders him. The Judge, as is his wont, celebrates by dancing naked, "huge and pale and hairless, like an enormous infant. . . . He is dancing, dancing. He says that he will never die."

The whale vanquishes Ahab and the Judge devours the Kid. Are we bereft, then, of a world that is reasonable and pacific? Melville's Epilogue, as we shall see, has intonations of the possibility of redemption—Ishmael survives to tell his tale. An epilogue also graces *Blood Meridian*, but it is strange in the extreme. In a handful of italicized lines in a single paragraph, McCarthy conjures the vision of a man "progressing over the plain." He is using an instrument to dig holes in the ground, "striking the fire out of the rock which God has put there." One assumes that his task is to make holes for fence posts. If so, then he is fencing in the wild plains, a harbinger of the forces of civilization.

Surely McCarthy, no less than Melville, cannot mean this conclusion to play without irony. If the Judge and the rule of war apply in ubiquitous, never-ending fashion, then can there ever be surcease? McCarthy's later novels point in this direction. Anton Chigurh is a modern Judge, a dispenser of death in the novel *No Country for Old Men* (2005). The time may be recent, but the southwestern landscape remains stained by blood. When McCarthy peers into the future, as in *The Road* (2006), we find a postapocalyptic world that has ripped apart at the seams, where only survival, at a minimal level of existence, rules.

We are, like the vanquished whale that hangs over the side of the *Pequod* in this chapter, at the mercy of the sharks that revel in blood. Did Melville, like McCarthy, imagine that we are those sharks, maddened by blood, willing to eat our own entrails?

Between 1900 and 1989, wars claimed 86 million people. That is a killing rate of about 2,600 each day or 100 people every hour of the day. The albino Judge's dark shadow remains over the landscape.

CHAPTER 88
Schools and Schoolmasters

VARIOUS VIEWS ON THE HABITS OF WHALES

From the late 1940s through the 1960s, *Moby-Dick* was everywhere in American popular and middlebrow culture. W. Somerset Maugham, an influential British novelist, edited a series, "The Ten Greatest Novels in the World"; Melville's *Moby-Dick* appeared alongside Austen's *Pride and Prejudice*, Dostoevsky's *The Brothers Karamzov*, and Dickens's *David Copperfield*.

Moby-Dick was secure as an American classic, a reading habit to be cultivated early and often, entrenched by 1950 in the junior and high-school curriculum. Thirteen-year-old Vincent Taliercio stated that he enjoyed the story because "it shows adventure and excitement. It shows how a great white whale lived and died his fantastic life." Junior high schools around the country participated in a Great Books program, with students in the

Figure 19.
Classics Illustrated Comic version of *Moby-Dick*, attracting young readers since 1942.

seventh grade reading *Moby-Dick*, or at least part of it. Harvard required its students to read *Moby-Dick* as part of their general education program.

Teachers and parents in the mid-1950s were aghast at the presumably deleterious effects of comic-book depictions of violence upon youngsters. Thus, librarians in Santa Barbara made paperback copies of *Moby-Dick* available for young readers to divert their interest in comic "trash" toward better literature. This was the era when fear of comic books reigned. Sometimes for good reasons, as many of them were gory, misogynist, and plain gross. Social reformers, such as psychologist Frederic Wertham, appeared before congress to warn against the deleterious effects of comic books upon youthful minds.

One suspects, however, that most youngsters first encountered *Moby-Dick* in its Classics Illustrated Comic book version. The first edition of the comic appeared in September 1942, priced at a nickel a copy, just in time for soldiers to read, alongside an armed-forces edition of the novel. A new edition appeared in 1956, when most of the baby-boom generation had turned reading age. Now priced at fifteen cents, the comic's cover shows Ahab standing in a small boat, harpoon at the ready. Alongside him swims the whale, teeth sharp and eye with a hint of evil. The young reader begins with Ishmael, depicted, full-page, shown from behind, as he carries his napsack while looking for a place to spend the night. The dialogue box closes with the prescient line, "For there is death in this business of whaling." No scene depicts Queequeg's arm around Ishmael, but the two, after a puff from the pipe, we are told, become "blood brothers." Even if the homosocial aspects of the scene were deleted, the mere camaraderie between a figure who is dark-skinned and the light-skinned Ishmael was socially refreshing and controversial.

One particularly effective moment happens when Starbuck tells Ahab that the leaking casks of oil aboard the *Pequod* must be repaired. As the ever-prudent and money-conscious Starbuck leaves the cabin, he says, "But let Ahab beware of Ahab. Beware of thyself, old man." In the next box, Ahab thinks to himself, "What's that he said? Ahab beware of Ahab. There's something there."

Something there, indeed. And librarians were openly building upon the novelty of youngsters reading *Moby-Dick* in comic form. Following the final box with Ishmael being rescued, the comic—no doubt in a wise nod to educators and parents—stated: "NOW THAT YOU HAVE READ THE CLASSICS *Illustrated* EDITION, DON'T MISS THE ADDED ENJOYMENT OF READING THE ORIGINAL, OBTAINABLE AT YOUR SCHOOL OR PUBLIC LIBRARY."

CHAPTER 89

Fast-Fish and Loose-Fish

SOMETIMES A DISPUTE OCCURS OVER WHO HAS CAUGHT A FISH

The Genesis device is biggest fish in the universe—at least in *Star Trek* films. It is capable of transforming matter! Whoever possesses it has over-whelming power. We know from this chapter in *Moby-Dick* that many battles—legal and otherwise—obtain between warring parties, each claiming the right to a whale. Possession, in the end, is a matter of law and power. But possession to what end?

No one wants the device more than Khan Noonien Singh. Khan, played with brio by actor Ricardo Montalban, is a genetically engineered superbe-ing sort of guy from the late twentieth century. He has earlier crossed paths with Captain Kirk of the Starship *Enterprise*. Much to his dismay, Khan has been exiled by Kirk to a barren planet. He has survived there, along with a handsome medley of males and females from a ship that crash-landed, building a colony of sorts. In his heart Khan desires only one thing—revenge against Kirk. On this lonely planet, Khan rules and reads. The book most prominent in his bookcase is, of course, *Moby-Dick*.

Khan is a re-engineered space-age Ahab. When his second in command tells him to break off the engagement with Kirk because they have already gained their freedom, Khan quotes verbatim from memory Ahab's words, with some amendments: "*He tasks me. He tasks me*, and I shall have him. I'll chase him 'round the moons of Nibia and 'round the Antares Maelstrom and 'round perdition's flame . . ."

Khan and Kirk will cross swords or starships—that's for certain. Khan gains possession of the Genesis Device. It is able to create life but when directed towards life, it is a ray of death. With his crew dying around him and his own starship disabled, badly wounded Khan activates the Genesis Device, well aware that its power will destroy not only him but the Starship *Enterprise*, with Kirk aboard. There seems nothing that can be done; revenge will be Khan's and he succors that thought. Indeed, once again, he quotes Ahab, from chapter 135, "to the last I grapple with thee; from hell's heart I stab at thee."

Mr. Spock, Kirk's longtime second in command, takes matters into his own hands. He beams himself aboard Khan's vessel, the *Reliant*. Unlike humans, he can better withstand the radiation emanating from the Gene-sis Device. He is miraculously able to do something before it explodes.

When it does, it begins the creation of a new universe, right before the amazed eyes of Kirk and his crew.

Alas, poor Spock, we knew him well. He manages to beam himself back to the *Enterprise*, but he is a goner, riddled with radiation. He summons up enough energy for a farewell chat with Kirk. "Don't grieve for me," Spock tells Kirk. After all, what he has done is purely logical, sacrificing himself for the sake of many. His final words, hardly a surprise to the myriad fans of the Star Trek series are: "Live long and prosper."

Through transformations of the story of Ahab and the White Whale, as in *The Wrath of Khan*, the memory of *Moby-Dick* promises to "Live long and prosper."

CHAPTER 90

Heads or Tails

"De balena vero sufficit, si rex habeat caput, et regina caudam."
Bracton, l.3, c.3.

A DISQUISITION REGARDING OWNERSHIP OVER WHALES

A good question is asked in this chapter, "By what right is sovereignty invested?" Such a question could apply as well to the status of *Moby-Dick* upon the throne of the classic works in American literature.

The coronation of *Moby-Dick* occurred in the 1930s. In 1929, a then assistant professor at Harvard, F. O. Matthiessen (see chapter 26), announced: "It is time for the history of American literature to be rewritten." Inklings of this imperative abound. In that same year a journal, *American Literature*, was founded to reinforce the academic importance of American works of literature.

Although critics differed over how successful Melville had been in achieving his aims in *Moby-Dick* (and they also differed about what constituted those aims), by the 1930s a general consensus had emerged. In the words of Henry Seidel Canby, editor of the influential *Saturday Evening Post*, *Moby-Dick* is "the most magnificent [novel] I think in modern English."

Matthiessen's *American Renaissance*, published in 1941, cemented this view. For him, and generations of literary critics to follow, the novel's greatness revolved around its heady use of symbolism, its immense ambition (much of it realized), its embrace of paradox and a tragic perspective, and its narrative and stylistic complexities.

Fair enough. But should such sovereignty rest simply upon qualities favored by highbrow professors sitting in their wood-paneled Ivy League offices?

In 1851, the same year that *Moby-Dick* appeared and that it was ignored by most Americans, another book entered the world at a propitious moment. Harriet Beecher Stowe's *Uncle Tom's Cabin* was, after all, clearly designed to tug at the heartstrings of antislavery, or potential antislavery, types, by presenting the abuses of slavery against the family, morals, and happiness. The success of the novel was aided by other factors. *Uncle Tom's Cabin* was an immediate bestseller in the North and Midwest, selling 100,000 copies in the Midwest alone within eight weeks of publication. Richard Henry Dana reported being in a train car traveling between Boston and New Haven when he noticed that four passengers in the compartment were reading the book.

Uncle Tom's Cabin arrived brimming with proper literary form and content. In contrast to Melville's novel, Stowe's was rather uncomplicated. Characters were either good or evil. She was able through her depictions of them to elicit the expected response from readers (tears and anger, empathy and disgust). Most of her readers were already inclined towards antislavery sentiments, and Stowe's novel gave them what they wanted. The novel trafficked in the conventions of what is now referred to as the "literature of domesticity," and it paid special attention to women characters and their circumstances. Often in such works, moral young women were led astray by immoral older, more powerful men.

Critic Jane Tompkins finds Stowe's work firmly embedded within traditions of the sermon and social-reform literature of the American mid-century. The death of little Eva in the novel is expiating, commonplace in women's literature where sacrifice for another is a sign of saintliness and salvation. In a period when women were viewed as moral exemplars, Stowe was clinging to that mantle. And unlike Melville, she studiously dusted away any hint of metaphysical speculation.

This description is not intended as a putdown of the author and her work. Quite the opposite. *Uncle Tom's Cabin* has power, what Tompkins describes as "sentimental power," meaning the ability to move the reader, to even push that reader towards political action. Hardly surprising, then, that Abraham Lincoln once said, "So you're the little woman who wrote the book that caused this great war." Not that far-fetched and a testament to the book's power. Suffice it to say, none of Melville's works came near in the nineteenth century to equaling sales for Stowe's *Uncle Tom's Cabin*; it reportedly sold over a million copies, with those copies being passed hand to hand for countless others to read. The train upon which Dana had traveled would have been able, no doubt, to seat all the readers of *Moby-Dick* comfortably.

CHAPTER 91

The *Pequod* Meets the *Rose-Bud*

"In vain it was to rake for Ambergriese in the paunch of this Leviathan, insufferable fetor denying that inquiry."

Sir T. Browne, V. E.

ON THE AROMA OF AMBERGRIS AND AN ODD ENCOUNTER AT SEA

As already noted, the size and digressions of *Moby-Dick* have spawned a bunch of heavily expurgated editions (see chapter 67). Orion Books offers an edition of *Moby-Dick* reduced to 336 pages. It allows youthful or lazy readers an easier ride through the novel, with all of the action retained and all of the metaphysics deleted.

Perhaps the oddest edition to grace the shelves of Mobyiana is Damion Searls's *; or The Whale* (2009).

Say what? Here's the catch. Searls has printed everything that the Orion edition omitted, from missing commas to abandoned chapters. One of Searls's chapters might contain a sentence or two, or less. Here, for instance, is his chapter 117, "The Whale Watch," in its entirety:

> ,
>
> ,
>
> , face to face,
> " "
> —
>
> in the gloom
> " "
> — —

Is this a hoax, a postmodern joke on Searls's part? He contends, in contrast, that it is in the discarded passages, marked by "bizarre vocabulary" and exciting effects, where readers will find the ambergris of brilliance buried in the novel.

Actually, Searls wants "to generate a real conversation about: What is literary value? What is worth reading for, so if you're going to abridge for what's important, what do you keep? I was honestly setting out to see which demi-book would preserve more of what makes Melville Melville." He is offering a wry comment, too, on the process and politics involved in the editing of a great work of literature (see chapter 63).

But what can be said about a book with the title *; or The Whale*?

CHAPTER 92

Ambergris

ON THE HISTORY AND APPEAL OF AMBERGRIS

As a fragrance is extracted from the "decay" of the whale, so did Raymond Weaver manage to reclaim the magnificence of Melville and *Moby-Dick*, after both had languished for over half a century.

It all began one June evening in 1919. Raymond Weaver, then a lecturer in the Columbia University English department, was attending a departmental dinner. Sitting beside him was Carl Van Doren, a literary editor for *The Nation* and at work on a history of American literature. Van Doren leaned over to his colleague and remarked that August 1919 would be the centennial of the birth of Herman Melville. "He was a wonderful old boy," said Van Doren. According to one of his students, Van Doren had been urging his students to read *Moby-Dick* as early as 1915. Since he was busy with various projects, and could ill afford to spend time with Melville, he recommended that Weaver write about Melville.

Why not begin with an article for *The Nation* and, if further inclined, then produce a long-needed biography of Melville? Weaver had already tasted a bit of Melville—a mention of him in a course with Brander Matthews at Columbia, as well as a brief dip once in *Typee*. In a spirit of giving it the old college try, Weaver agreed to take up Van Doren's offer. He considered it an advantage that he was "unhampered with information."

Weaver strode to the Columbia University library and started reading Melville's South Sea adventure tales. He was soon climbing the monument of *Moby-Dick*. He read with "gaping wonderment and incredulity," feeling like he had entered into "a great opium dream." Weaver was surprised and frustrated, however, when he found no existing biographical treatments of Melville listed in the massive *Poole's Index to Periodical Literature*. While this ignored Stedman's introduction of 1892 to *Typee*, it was largely a fair characterization. Weaver quickly surmised that since he would be unable to crib from previous accounts, he would have to go to the sources on his own.

He located relatives of Melville's, finding his grand-daughter Eleanor Metcalf willing to assist him in all matters biographical—even hinting about deep family scandals caused by Melville's melancholy and temper. Soon Weaver was grabbing up first editions of *Moby-Dick* for less than a dollar apiece, filling his ornate, dandyish room with Melvilliana and notes. Within a couple of months, at Van Doren's behest, he had published a short piece on Melville in *The Nation*. The scuttled boat of Melville's reputation was about to be raised.

In some ways, Weaver was a surprising choice to take up cudgels for Melville. He was born in Baltimore in 1889 and attended Columbia as an undergraduate, receiving his B.A. degree in 1912. Over the next three years, he lived in Hiroshima, Japan, teaching English. Upon returning to the United States, during a time of professorial purges at Columbia with the outbreak of the First World War, Weaver got a job teaching introductory literature classes. He did not have an especially firm background in American literature, nor had he published anything of note. Like a fish to water, he would swim comfortably and busily in Melville's sea. In a remarkably short period he produced an enticing and popular biography of the until then forgotten figure and book.

Writing late in his life, as his alter ego "Pierrot Philosophique," Weaver attempted to capture the essence of his personal take on life. Comfortable neither as pagan nor Christian, Weaver opted to live as a "spectator," someone who delights furtively. He was an "observant eye," finding in the "phantasmagoria" of the cosmos and civilization an "epic absurdity." Rather than reveal much of himself, and to keep his distance from others, he became a man of masks, unwilling to "declare upon the good or evil consequences of any act," finding his own balance in the roles of "the tireless idler, the sad comedian, the tragically sincere poseur." A self-admitted failure in life, Weaver felt that he had carried it off with a certain élan, perhaps with a soupçon of *grace*!

We should not swallow his self-representation whole. Weaver was, after all, a teacher of young men, and a strikingly able one by all accounts. Bennett Cerf, later to become a leading publisher, had the luck to find himself suddenly in one of Weaver's classes. Weaver had replaced Professor Henry Wadsworth Longfellow Dana, dismissed by Nicholas Murray Butler, the president of Columbia, for perceived antiwar agitation. Weaver faced a class that had been primed, as Cerf recalled, for a rather unchallenging semester. Weaver immediately dispelled all such notions, as he within "three weeks . . . had the football team reading Dante, Cervantes, and discussing Boswell, discussing them in class with deep interest."

To be such an inspired teacher required more than an ironic and masked presence. Everyone recalled Weaver's extraordinary voice: "very deep, sonorous, mellifluous," while another described it as "stentorian." And yet a third found it thunderous." He was "utterly serious," a "formidable gentleman" who was a "spellbinder" as a lecturer, impressing the students with both his erudition and his commitment to a life of the mind. Unlike his predecessor in the class, he did not raise political hackles; he no doubt challenged all sort of Victorian proprieties—while upholding the civilities of his time. Weaver welcomed a select group of budding scholars, such as Cerf and the radical Joseph Freeman, to his rooms at the university for talks that lasted well into the early morning hours. Along with Richard Simon, later to found the publishing house of Simon and Schuster, Cerf would marvel at Weaver's collection of oddments from his residence in Japan and relish his chattiness. Weaver was an "inspiration" to Cerf, although at the time, he admitted, he sensed that something was "irregular" about Weaver's life. As Cerf became more sophisticated and closer to Weaver, he realized that Weaver was a homosexual.

Weaver turned out to be a fine biographer of Melville. He could exult with Melville in the pleasures of diverse cultures without committing himself to them fully. As Melville had castigated the presumptions and policies of missionaries in *Omoo*, so did Weaver. In a faintly autobiographical novel of his time in Japan, Weaver showed how a missionary spirit crimped fellowship and understanding. He had, in his own life, touched the bottom rungs of hell through depression and thoughts of suicide. A self-professed dandy and semicloseted gay man, Weaver identified with Melville's rage against bourgeois culture and its confines. Although he was unable to confront homoeroticism openly in his book on Melville, he rushed to join Melville in a world of male musing and adventure.

Weaver presented Melville as a lonely voice crying out against the materialism, conformity, unhealthy sanity, and artistic timidity of his age. Confronted with an America that wanted its artists to echo its own prejudices, Melville sought escape; indeed, "His whole history is the record of an attempt to escape from an inexorable and intolerable world of reality." In the South Seas and aboard ships, Melville sought experiences not to be had in the counting-houses and parlor rooms of his culture. As an outsider, as an artist at odds with his era, and as a man who relished his role of the "devil's advocate," Melville, according to Weaver, was to be applauded for his vision of "corrosive pessimism" and "convictions repugnant to the herd." Having "sinned blackly against the orthodoxy of his time," Melville paid the price in unsold books and hints of personal insanity. This theme echoed in Melville and *Moby-Dick* criticism throughout the decade: the cost paid by Melville to produce a great novel and the destruction of its author by an unenthusiastic public.

According to Weaver, *Moby-Dick* was Melville's "undoubted master-piece," no matter how ill treated it had been by Americans. In eight raptur-ous pages early in his biography, Weaver laid out the claims of *Moby-Dick* to greatness. Weaver called the book a "fabulous allegory" that demon-strated that the world, rather than a place of love, was conceived in hate. This was Melville's challenge to the heady optimism of the Transcenden-talists of his era, and Weaver was happy to employ it against Chamber of Commerce boosters and oligarchs of optimism in the 1920s. To face the world honestly is to see it as a place of suffering and tragedy. Ahab's hero-ism resided in recognizing this sad state of affairs and then summoning up "all the rage and hate of mankind" and fixing it upon Moby Dick, that "ancient and vindictive monster." In Weaver's account, all attention is riv-eted on Ahab. The ultimate meaning of Ahab's quest—and hence of the whale—is relatively simple. Melville wanted to preach that "There is a wis-dom that is woe, and there is a woe that is madness." In Ahab, wisdom and madness are mingled, part of "the history of the soul's adventure." This is the meaning of Ahab.

It was, of course, a meaning that resonated deeply with Weaver. This accounts for his excitement researching and writing about Melville and his masterwork. Weaver had an intense relationship with Melville, exulting in finding a precursor and a familiar spirit. Weaver's life as an outsider—in both his homosexuality and his aesthetics—set him apart from his own culture. The masks that he wore, the presentations of self that he flaunted, both hid and exposed his deepest wellsprings. His life had moments of joy, but they were, as he admitted near the end, riddled with ironic detach-ment. Depression and madness became the tokens of his existence. As early as the 1920s, Weaver lessened this burden a bit not only by writing about Melville, but by embracing Melville's troubles as his own. As many American artists in the 1920s proclaimed, America was inhospitable ground for artistic development—a "lost generation" took to Europe to find community and freedom. Weaver stayed near to home, content to teach and to relax in the wisdom and woe that Melville communicated.

CHAPTER 93

The Castaway

PIP FLOATS IN THE OCEAN AND DISCOVERS MUCH—PERHAPS TOO MUCH

Nobel Prize-winning novelist Toni Morrison has inquired deeply about the African-American presence in American literature. She seeks to lift the veil that often hides it, concluding that "the presence of African-Americans has shaped the choices, the language, the structure—the meaning of so much American literature." We saw how this functioned, for example, in the ring shout (chapter 40), where African-American rhythms and racial tensions board the *Pequod*. As Morrison realizes, African-American characters are central to *Moby-Dick*, perhaps none more interesting than Pip, the cabin boy. Pip is all about what Morrison terms "the unspeakable things unspoken."

Pip refuses to bend to stereotype. Compared with Dough-Boy, the white cabin boy, who is "dull and torpid in his intellects," Pip is "at bottom very bright," although of a jolly countenance that we are told is "peculiar to his tribe." Pip embraces life and freedom with zest.

In need of an "after-oarsman," Stubb orders Pip to fill the slot. As Melville phrases it, full of resonance to slavery controversy, "Pip was put into his place."

It is not a place that Pip cottons to. In pursuit of the whale, Pip is nervous and with good reason, as quickly becomes clear. He jumps from the boat, in fear of its being upended by the whale; he immediately gets caught up in the line connected to the wounded whale. The rope "had taken several turns around his chest and neck," a certain allusion to bondage, one of Morrison's "unspeakable things unspoken." Thankfully, Pip is not in the slave South, so Stubb issues the command, with great reluctance, to cut the line, saving Pip by releasing the whale.

Stubb then lectures Pip about staying in the boat and not undermining the purpose of the whaling enterprise, which is to fatten one's purse. Should Pip leap anew from the boat he will be left behind while the others pursue the whale. As fate would have it, Pip "jumped again" from the boat, to find himself "in the hands of the Gods." He bobs up and down. But unlike Kierkegaard's man of faith floating alone in the vast ocean, Pip is without such faith. Alas, "poor Pip turned his crisp, curling, black head to the sun, another lonely castaway, though the loftiest and the brightest."

Pip remains afloat until another small boat rescues him. In that interim, things have changed. The natural buoyancy of the sea has saved Pip's body, but his mind has become unhinged. He has been "carried down alive to wondrous depths," encountered strange creatures and things heretofore unimagined. Let Melville narrate what has happened: "Pip saw the multitudinous, God-omnipresent, coral insects, that out of the firmament of waters heaved the colossal orbs. He saw God's foot upon the treadle of the loom, and spoke it; and therefore his shipmates called him mad. So man's insanity is heaven's sense; and wandering from all mortal reason, man comes at last to that celestial thought, which, to reason, is absurd and frantic; and weal or woe, feels then uncompromised, indifferent as his God."

Oh, Pip. Oh, humanity.

The abandonment and insight that Pip has experienced render him mad in the eyes of his shipmates. It also makes him into a spokesman for the black presence in American literature and life—consigned to the periphery, hidden within, refused a presence and when gaining it, condemned as mad, bound in ropes of various sorts.

Toni Morrison has read her Melville carefully. Like so many, she has followed in his monumental wake. In perhaps her finest novel, *The Song of Solomon* (1977), all sorts of allusions to *Moby-Dick* can be uncovered. The main character, Macon Dead Jr. (are his initials mere coincidence?), is like Pip adrift for much of the novel. Only when he accepts his past does Macon dig into his roots to discover the sense of belonging that has evaded him. He has abandoned his cousin and lover, Hagar. The name is Biblical; Hagar was a servant to Abraham's wife. She gives birth to his son, Ishmael. But Hagar, along with Ishmael, is forced to wander. Rejected by Macon Dead, Hagar is madness maddened, as she stalks her former lover, attempting to kill him. Her intense desire for vengeance, however, is tempered by the still-burning embers of love. Her efforts are bound to fail until, finally, her hatred turns inward and she dies instead.

Almost all of the characters in *Song of Solomon*, then, are emotionally crippled because they are cut off from family and tradition, banished to the periphery, abandoned to the vast oceans of displacement. It is a *Moby-Dick* of a novel.

CHAPTER 94

A Squeeze of the Hand

THE JOY OF SQUEEZING WHALE SPERM

The homosocial aspects of this chapter are overwhelming as Ishmael and others squeeze away at sperm collected in a large vat. The experience is ecstatic in nature: "A sweet and unctuous duty!" As he squeezes away, thoughts of the dangerous voyage fall away. "I felt divinely free from all ill-will, or petulance, or malice, of any sort, whatsoever." If this were not enough, Melville squeezes home the implications: "Come; let us squeeze hands all round; nay, let us all squeeze ourselves into each other; let us squeeze ourselves universally into the very milk and sperm of kindness." Sometimes, lost in the process, Ishmael and the other sailors find themselves squeezing one another's hands.

In a famous essay, "Come Back to the Raft Ag'in, Huck Honey!" (1948), critic Leslie Fiedler discussed "innocent" homosexuality—always "chaste"—as a dominant theme in American literature. Male bonding typically occurred between a young white male (orphaned, searching for his identity) and an older man (usually an outsider, African- or Native-American). Most famously, Huck Finn and the escaped slave Jim fled from polite society to take to the country. At one point in the novel, Huck's affection for Jim is tested sorely when he ponders his social responsibility. Should he return Jim to slavery, as required by law? Or should he allow friendship to rule? "I knowed very well I had done wrong," Huck admits. But he also "knowed" he had done right by saving his friend from slavery's chains, despite the "raft of trouble" that he soon found himself in because of his action. Huck had confronted a moral dilemma; he chose friendship over law, compassion against custom. What made his choice momentous was that Huck and his social milieu teemed with racist ideas and was untroubled by the institution of slavery. Ruminating on the burden of his choice, Huck concludes: "All right, then, I'll *go* to hell."

Years later, Fiedler returned to this theme in his monumental volume *Love and Death in the American Novel* (1960). Now, among other works, Fiedler examined the homosocial relationship between Ishmael and Queequeg. He again found chaste, innocent love between orphaned young white Ishmael, escaping from the bonds of normal society, and an alien, the Pacific Islander Queequeg. It is a symbolic marriage between males, hence immature, "juvenile and regressive," typical of how American fiction avoids dealing seriously with adult love between a man and a woman.

Despite his negative characterization of such relationships, Fiedler was something of a pioneer, at least, in noting the centrality of homoeroticism in the American novel. His take on the erotic bonds between Ishmael and Queequeg was more explicit than Matthiessen's and Arvin's in stressing homoerotic themes in *Moby-Dick*. Of course, as a rousing heterosexual, Fiedler could get away with it more easily, too.

CHAPTER 95

The Cassock

THE WHALE'S PRIVATE PART

A "cassock," readers need to know, is the penis of the whale. As described in this chapter—as well as in reality—it is behemoth in size. No doubt Melville took extreme delight in chatting about such an organ.

Readers may wonder at this point about the connection between homosexuality and fascination about Melville and *Moby-Dick*. This nexus applies in some form to Weaver, Crane, Matthiessen, and Arvin, to name but the most famous of Melville's gay interpreters. On an obvious level, these closeted gay writers and critics viewed Melville as a sympathetic figure who battled against Victorian sexuality in both his life and fiction. Most alluring to them in *Moby-Dick* was obviously the amorous relationship between Ishmael and Queequeg. If male love were not allowed to speak its name in the period when Arvin held his position at Smith College, then at least it could be encountered—even if only in the form of innocence that Fiedler found—in the greatest of American novels.

Of this much we can be certain. All writers read themselves onto texts, and texts are submissive to varied readings. Given its ambiguous symbols and characters, *Moby-Dick* was a perfect vehicle for homoerotic appeal. The all-male world of the ship must also have been imagined by homosexual readers as a sort of paradise. Many of these men faced a society that denied them an identity, forcing them into a closet of hidden sexuality. They sought escape. Small wonder, then, that Melville's novel begins with Ishmael fleeing from the melancholy confines of his own spiritual imprisonment.

The next question that demands consideration is the obvious one—was Herman Melville gay? To a degree, all revolves around definitions. In the mid-nineteenth century, as historian George Chauncey and others have shown, it was not uncommon for males to engage in sexual activity with boys and other men, especially aboard ship. Is it fair to presume, then, that Melville partook in such relations? Who knows, but his descriptions of life among the "savages" during his ocean sojourns have a distinctly homoerotic content, as do relations between Ishmael and Queequeg. We also know that Melville had lots of issues with his mother, wrote about sexual uncertainty, and was attracted to young men, such as Arthur Stedman, who befriended him late in his life.

Of course, throughout much of his life, Melville was married, fathering a handful of children, and devoted, in his manner, to Lizzie. Yet one senses that he would rather have spent his days with one of his yeoman male companions, embarked on a life of adventure or lolling around on a Pacific island, engaging in his "squeeze of the hand" form of play.

CHAPTER 96

The Try-Works

THE CREW LABORS TO EXTRACT WEALTH FROM A WHALE

Boardman Robinson's illustrations for a 1943 edition of *Moby-Dick* pay careful attention to the men laboring aboard the *Pequod*. This is hardly surprising, given that Canadian-born Robinson was a committed radical who had worked as an illustrator for radical publications such as *The Liberator* and *The Masses*. In addition to illustrating *Moby-Dick*, Robinson's artwork graced editions of Dostoevsky's *The Brothers Karamazov*, Edgar Lee Master's *Spoon River Anthology*, *King Lear*, and *Leaves of Grass*.

Robinson's thirty-one drawings and paintings for *Moby-Dick* are striking. Produced for the Limited Editions Club in a two-volume offering, the press soon made them available in a one-volume edition. As Elizabeth Schultz remarks, Robinson wanted most to convey the inner states of the characters in the novel, about their fears and hopes, their anguish and heroism. The illustrations serve up *Moby-Dick* as a depiction of the human condition. At the time of his writing, the notion of "the human condition" was central to both representational works such as Robinson's and the emerging school of painters grouped around abstract expressionism. Key concerns were the interplay between the primitive and the civilized, the unconscious and the conscious, and the role of myth.

Robinson barely confronts Moby Dick. One illustration does show the immense size of the beast against a boat. Within the frame of the painting all that is visible is the whale's tail. Another depiction of the whale shows it as a swirl, dark in color, with the caption, taken from the text of the novel: "It was the whiteness of the whale that above all things appalled me." This contrast between the dark whale and the quote about its whiteness jibes nicely with critic Clifton Fadiman's observation in the volume's introduction that the Whale and Ahab are two sides of the same coin,

Figure 20.
"The Candles," by Boardman Robinson.

that in fact the whale exists to a large degree in Ahab's overheated consciousness.

Most of the illustrations depict sailors, both the major characters and the minor ones. In keeping with the socialist realism of the period and Robinson's own convictions, the men are invariably shown as strong and gritty. If Melville possessed "confidence in mankind," then the same spirit pervades Robinson's drawings and paintings. Queequeg is simply a dark, muscular fellow, without tattoos on his flesh. Even Fedallah is a powerful figure, shown in one illustration as flinty-eyed, watchful, angular, and inscrutable. As Schultz remarks, there is a focus on the eyes of the crew members, as if they are looking into their fates, thinking about the fires of home, or focusing on the tasks at hand.

Ahab appears a few times, usually with profile right, glancing off to the side. In one depiction, he is enraged, looking like Moses at the moment when he destroyed the holy tablets; he may be crying out in anguish to God. Other times, Ahab is calm, with full white beard, powerful body; his mind and eyes always fixed on the White Whale. Ahab is not without his humanity. In one particularly strong illustration, Robinson presents Ahab comforting Pip, with his arms around the maddened cabin boy, who has been rescued from the deep. Even in this moment of bonding, Ahab's mind is elsewhere, as he looks away, thinking of his final encounter with the whale, perhaps. None of the illustrations deals with Ahab and his crew's final accounting with Moby Dick.

Boardman produced some mighty drawings, eliciting hyperbolic praise from Lewis Mumford: "His pictures would remain as precious evidence of Melville's genius even if the words that prompted them had been destroyed."

CHAPTER 97

The Lamp

ISHMAEL IS ELOQUENT ABOUT SPERM OIL LAMPS

How can *Moby-Dick* be transformed or illuminated as if by the wonderful whale oil in the lamps that burn aboard the *Pequod*? Can it be made into something different, something palatable for postmodern tastes? We saw one example in chapter 91. Here are two others.

First, the 6,438 sentences of *Moby-Dick* will be rewritten into Emoji, the "picturesque emoticons" found on "most headsets in Japan." The project began with plans to obtain three different translations for each sentence in the novel. A popular vote will then decide which rendering deserves inclusion. Work on the project will take place online so that hundreds of individuals may participate. According to an article in the London *Daily Telegraph*, if you contribute ten bucks to the project, then your favorite Emoji will appear at the end of the book; if you donate two hundred smackers, then you will receive a "limited edition colour hard back version" of the emoticon *Moby-Dick*.

The book, compiled and edited by Fred Beneson, was completed and can be bought online at *http://www.emojidick.com.*

ENGLISH: Call me Ishmael.

EMOJI:

Second, for those of a certain sensibility, there is excitement in the games that French novelist Georges Perec and his Oulipo group perfected, such as writing a 300-page novel without ever employing the letter "e" in it. Well, Mike Keith has rendered *Moby-Dick* as an anagram, according to the rules of the "N + 7" procedure. Word replacements are as follows:

Each replacement word must (no exceptions!) have the same number of letters as the original. If possible, it should have the same initial letter as the original. If possible, it should have the same final letter, though this is less important than the initial one. If possible, it should have the same number of syllables. *A given word in the original is changed in the same way every time it appears.*"

Having fun yet?
Here is some more explanation:

Most nouns, verbs, adjectives, and adverbs having more than four letters have been replaced, the only exception to the more-than-four letters rule being *Moby* and *Dick* in the title. Note that replacement words were *not* steered towards synonyms (while they may occasionally be, this is just luck). This strategy helps to give the anagram the surrealistic flavor of an N + 7 text, while the other replacement rules tend to make it *less* bizarre than a typical N + 7 story. Most proper names were left alone, except for the title of the book and its main characters, who become Ishrael (really, "Israel", but he has a speech impediment), Caption Arab, Starbuks, Queenegg, Butts, and Tushhomo.

Get it?

What follows are a couple of sentences, one from the original text, the one below is the anagrammatic text. For those desiring the full anagrammatic text, the website address is given in the endnotes.

Chapter 1

Loomings

Call me Ishmael. Some years ago—never mind how long precisely—having little or no money in my purse, and nothing particular to interest me on shore, I thought I would sail . . .

Chapter 1

Lemmings

Call me Ishrael. Some years ago—never mind how long perchance—having minute or no monte in my pique, and nailing. . . profligate to fragment me on sense, I typeset I would sail . . .

CHAPTER 98

Stowing Down and Clearing Up

"THE DIN IS DEAFENING" WHEN WORK IS DONE ABOARD THE SHIP

In the 1920s, after Raymond Weaver's biography (see chapter 92) of Melville had appeared, interest in *Moby-Dick* surged in American culture.

Critics pounded home the importance of *Moby-Dick* for American readers. Carl Van Doren published three pieces, two of which focused exclusively on *Moby-Dick*. In *The Century* magazine in 1925, Van Doren introduced readers to the novel, under the headline "Lucifer from Nantucket." Melville was a Yankee Lucifer or Faust, a man with "an obscure distemper [that] gnawed at him" and translated itself into his great work of art. In a fuller and more penetrating analysis of *Moby-Dick* than the one undertaken by Weaver, Van Doren found plenty of Melville in Ahab. Both searched for truth and meaning, the reality of existence.

Within two years of the publication of Weaver's biography, *Moby-Dick* was commonly referred to as a classic. In a letter to the editor of the *New York Times* in 1923, Samuel W. Banning announced off-handedly that the book, which is "acclaimed the greatest novel of modern times," is so popular that "libraries can't meet the demand for" it and other seafaring novels. A story about the huge crowds at Coney Island on Memorial Day, 1923, espying a spout of water gushing a few hundred yards out to sea, mentioned *Moby-Dick* with sure apprehension that readers would catch the reference. Everyman's Library advertised its new edition of *Moby-Dick* under the heading: "The Books That Never Die."

References to *Moby-Dick* abounded. In a story designed to boost sympathy for the poor, it was reported that one boy decided to forgo his desired Christmas present of a copy of *Moby-Dick* to donate instead the money for charity. When not partying to Moby-inflected themes, some of the wealthy named their yachts after the now-fabled whale. An ad for home furnishings indicated that their furniture and accoutrements could evoke "the days of Moby Dick." The mayor of New York City, James J. Walker, after struggling to catch a rather large fish, told reporters, "We went out after swordfish, but we must have hooked Moby Dick." In the early 1930s, a gray gelding named Moby Dick, owned by John J. Farrell, achieved success on the show-jumping circuit. Included in a story about the American Kennel Club competition was a picture of a Great Dane named (what else?) Moby Dick.

Popular culture references in the 1920s and early 1930s were almost always to the whale rather than members of the crew or the larger-than-life figure of Captain Ahab. Moreover, the whale was rarely equated with the mysteries of existence, the paradoxical nature of its color, or with the discussion of its captain that fascinated highbrows like Weaver and Van Doren. The focus on Ahab would only emerge in American culture in the late 1930s, in league with the rise of concerns about totalitarian leadership, the ability of such leaders to sway a crowd, and the psychology of fanaticism. When references to Ahab appeared in 1920s literary criticism, they often dealt with him as a tragic figure, a symbol of "defeat and ultimate extinction."

Between 1922 and 1930, eleven new editions of *Moby-Dick* tumbled from American presses. Most of them had some sort of introduction and illustrations. Raymond Weaver contributed an introduction to a popular 1925 edition published by Albert and Charles Boni. A year later, a revised version of this introduction graced a new edition from the Modern Library. We already encountered the lavish Lakeside Press edition of 1930, with 280 engravings by Rockwell Kent (see chapter 28).

Dutton's Everyman's Library edition arrived in 1921, priced at one dollar. An ad for it announced that *Moby-Dick* was no longer "unobtainable" for readers. A more expensive edition was heralded as "the perfect gift for children," available at the Santa Claus Toyland in a New York City department store in 1922. Artist Mead Schaeffer's color plates made it a perfect Christmas gift, since he had "entered thoroughly into the epical magnitude of the chase of the White Whale." By 1926, thanks to the Modern Library edition, readers need spend only ninety-five cents to have an edition of the classic work, to take on "vacation," with "large clear type" in an "attractive limp binding" capable of being placed in one's pocket.

Rowland Hilder, in an abridged edition published by Knopf in 1926, dazzled with his illustrations. A full-color plate next to the title page greeted readers with a dose of excitement. With the *Pequod's* sails in full bloom in the background, Hilder depicted Queequeg (as dark skinned as Tashtego), harpoon at the ready, on a small boat. Among the twenty-nine other drawings, some showed Ishmael as a stout and strong young man and Queequeg almost in minstrelsy garb and features. Striking were the number of drawings that depicted blacks—Pip, the cook, Tashtego. Perhaps, Hilder was drawn to the contrasting skin tone on the white paper for his drawings. Or maybe such depictions added to the exoticism of the whaling venture.

A second abridged edition came two years later in 1928 from Scribner's. Sylvia Chatfield Bates, affiliated with the journalism department at New York University, cut with a monumental pair of scissors, reducing the mighty work to 116 small pages with decent-sized typeface. Eight illustrations, one in full color, by I. W. Taber, accompanied the truncated text. Stripped from the original was everything that made it monumental—the symbolism, the winds of blasphemy, the cetological discourse, the ambiguities of the whale, and the philosophical discussions. Instead, Bates distilled the action. We are left with Ishmael's (no hint of his suicidal inclinations) and Queequeg's friendship and with Ahab seeking revenge against a monstrous sea-beast that had gouged his leg off. We have parts of the vivid descriptions of the crew, especially the exotic harpooners. But mostly the abridgment focuses on the excitement of the chase, on the enthusiasm and danger associated with the hunt.

The introduction to this slim volume, by John H. Finley, promised to bring readers into contact with America's own version of Homer's *Odyssey*. Ahab was Ulysses reborn in American garb. In the appendix, Finley referred to Ahab as "strange" but familiar. For Finley, the book captured humanity's "wild anger against that which has hurt us," as well as its "will to dare the blind brute force of the universe." For all of us, then, "we do not wonder at the fiery chase." Indeed, we want to join it.

America, by this time, had joined with Ahab and Ishmael on a voyage in search of the White Whale.

Figure 21.
A "madness maddened," Woodcut by Rockwell Kent.

CHAPTER 99

The Doubloon

VARIOUS PERSPECTIVES ARE OFFERED ABOUT THE DOUBLOON'S MEANING

To voyage with Melville in *Moby-Dick* is to be tossed into a world of tragic happenings, a deeply flawed universe. The world appears as an inhospitable place, without any surcease in the offing.

Melville is aware, as all good novelists are, that one's vision of the world is particular to the individual—we all encounter and interpret the world from our own perspective. Thus, in this chapter, Melville describes the variety of points of view of how various men aboard the *Pequod* regard the prized doubloon.

The coin is described, much like the skin of the whale or the tattoos on Queequeg's body, as being almost hieroglyphic, marked by "strange figures and inscriptions" which open themselves up "in some monomaniac way whatever significance might lurk in them."

For Ahab, the coin reveals "grand and lofty things" with its images of "mountain-tops and towers." The volcano and tower are perceived as Ahab, "the courageous, the undaunted, and victorious" in search of the White Whale of meaning.

For Starbuck, the coin is inscribed by the "devil's claws." While there is a "vale of Death, God girds us round; and over all our gloom, the sun of Righteousness still shines a beacon and a hope."

For Stubb, almanac in hand, the coin is a zodiac of meaning; it is imbued with his typical comedic take on the nature of things.

For Flask, the doubloon is marked by its cash-value. It is "worth sixteen dollars . . . and at two cents the cigar, that's nine hundred and sixty cigars . . . I like cigars, and here's nine hundred and sixty of them."

Others give their own readings to the piece of gold hammered to the mast, the Manxman, Queequeg, even Fedallah (with his "tail coiled out of sight").

But Pip offers the strangest lines, the most beguiling interpretation of all, three times:

I look, you look, he looks; we look, ye look, they look.

Pip mutters some more. He must be insane for his words seem bereft of meaning.

Or are they?

Pip's conjugation is puzzling, to be sure, but it nicely sums up the varying perspectives of those gazing at the coin. It jibes with the descriptions of Moby Dick that have glittered variously throughout the novel.

Meaning, no less than the whale, is nearly impossible to harpoon. Does this mean, as Melville seems to suggest, that science, God, and reason fail us as well as language?

K. L. Evans brilliantly summons the philosopher Ludwig Wittgenstein to put a helpful point upon this old discussion of whether our glass is half full or half empty with language. She quotes Wittgenstein thusly (although the line is probably from Otto Neurath):

Philosophy is a leaky boat which must be repaired while at sea.

Concludes Evans, we are aboard that leaky boat of language and meaning. It often fails us, as we have to bail out to stay afloat. But it keeps us going, nonetheless, taking us places, allowing us to continue—intrepid sometimes, flummoxed other times, yet still afloat.

Ah, if only Ahab had curbed his madness with Wittgenstein's reason on this matter. Of course, then, the story would have been less exciting in many ways.

CHAPTER 100

Leg and Arm

The Pequod, *of Nantucket, Meets the* Samuel Enderby, *of London*

THE CAPTAINS OF THE *PEQUOD* AND *SAMUEL ENDERBY* HAVE A GAM

Tragedy elicits various responses. Consider Boomer, the English captain of the ship *Samuel Enderby*. He has tangled with Moby Dick and lost his arm in the fracas. Boomer had grabbed hold of his harpoon then sticking into

Moby's side. The whale flailed about and went underwater with the sharp edge of another lance ripping through Boomer's arm, just below the shoulder. He was lucky since he would have been drowned, had not his arm become forever separated from his shoulder. Boomer's "shocking bad wound" was "as ugly gaping wound as a surgeon ever saw," longer than two feet. His arm has been replaced by an ivory appendage, with a hook at the bottom.

Boomer has suffered a great loss, but he accepts it as part of the business of whaling and the vagaries of the universe. He has "lowered" for Moby Dick once and that was sufficiently costly. While there would be pleasure in killing Moby Dick and tapping into his copious sperm bank, Boomer concludes that the white whale is "best let alone." He prefers to move on, to live and let live. Why would he want to risk his other arm in such a mad adventure?

In contrast, Ahab is consumed with his desire for revenge; he is incapable of considering forgiveness as a response to his own tragedy. Yet, forgiveness seems to be a perfectly valid response to what happened to both Ahab and Boomer.

Forgiveness does not require that justice be jettisoned; indeed, it is predicated upon it. Is there any justice in a mad chase after a presumably senseless beast of the ocean? Perhaps Boomer has learned an important lesson from his bout with Moby—bad things happen in life, sometimes as a result of bad intentions, more often by dint of pure contingency or blind fanaticism. When faced with acts of contingency, the best attitude is to recognize what has happened and to forgive the blind chaos of the universe or the God behind it. Otherwise, bitter vengeance eats away at the victim's humanity.

Even if vengeance could be brought to bear upon the White Whale, it remains unclear how satisfying it might be. As Milton notes in *Paradise Lost*, "Revenge, at first though sweet / Bitter ere long back on it self recoils."

In South Africa, Rwanda, and elsewhere, truth commissions attempt to establish the facts behind the horrors that had happened, to examine who did what when. Often, individuals who committed atrocities account for their actions. Once these essentials have been undertaken, then the victim can claim that justice has been done (at least in terms of getting to the bottom of things) and decide to forgive.

In order for forgiveness to take hold, understanding and truth need to come first. This is where Ahab is destined to run aground. Ahab's problem is that his desire for vengeance is linked with his need to gain a hold on the nature of the universe. Here he is bound to be frustrated. Thus, forgiveness is absent from his moral compass; all he can seek are answers and revenge, which are balled up together in his maddened quest against the White Whale. Bitterness and defeat are the only ports of call where he can cast his anchor.

CHAPTER 101

The Decanter

ISHMAEL RECALLS THE BRITISH SHIP *SAMUEL ENDERBY*

Opinion concerning *Moby-Dick* was somewhat different in Great Britain and Canada than in the United States in the late nineteenth century. British writer W. Clark Russell, a well-known composer of adventurous sea stories, found *Moby-Dick* "a medley of noble impassioned thoughts born of the deep," a work of poetry that well evoked its Shakespearean inspiration. H. S. Salt, in a piece appearing in the *Scottish Art Review* in 1892, gave a full accounting, perhaps the first in forty years, of the crucial themes of the novel. He recognized the White Whale as an object at once "metaphysical and ideal," as well as a concrete reality, and he marveled at the "mysterious personage" of Captain Ahab.

In an important reconsideration published in 1899, Archibald Mac-Mechan, a professor of literature at Dalhousie University in Canada, proclaimed *Moby-Dick* "the best sea story ever"; it was the quintessential American novel, marked by its expansive and picturesque style, generously ladled with humor. Melville was, in essence, "a Walt Whitman of prose," able to communicate to the "landsman the very salt of the sea breeze."

John Masefield, at one time the British poet laureate, thrilled to the sea and to *Moby-Dick*. His famous poem "Sea Fever" captures the allure of the sea for him:

> I MUST go down to the seas again, to the lonely sea and the sky,
> And all I ask is a tall ship and a star to steer her by,
> And the wheel's kick and the wind's song and the white sail's shaking,
> And a grey mist on the sea's face, and a grey dawn breaking.

This theme, with specific reference to *Moby-Dick*, recurs in Masefield's "A Wanderer's Song,"

> Oh I am tired of brick and stone, the heart of me is sick,
> For windy green, unquiet sea, the realm of Moby Dick;
> And I'll be going, going, from the roaring of the wheels,
> For a wind's in the heart of me, a fire's in my heels.

For Masefield, Melville's success in *Moby-Dick* was both simple and profound: he had captured the "very secret of the Sea."

Why, we must ask, was there a relatively earlier retrieval of *Moby-Dick* in Britain and Canada than in the United States? Perhaps in Britain, with its rich and problematic colonial experience long under way and still expanding, readers found less need for the exotic. Some of them had experienced life in the colonial empire, had encountered other cultures. Unlike American readers they had little need to focus on the more accessible tales of the Pacific natives from Melville's pen. Perhaps, too, given their long history as a naval power and tradition of sea tales, they were more naturally drawn to Melville's classic account of a whaling expedition. Finally, the British literary tradition, then on the cusp of modernism, found in Melville's masterwork the symbolism and depth that soon came to dominate high literature.

CHAPTER 102

A Bower in the Arsacides

EXAMINING THE INTERIOR OF THE WHALE, LIKE NO ONE SINCE JONAH

The outbreak of the First World War deeply disturbed British writer D. H. Lawrence: "The war is just hell for me." Europe was where "the autumn of all life has set in," he wrote to American poet Harriet Monroe in 1915, right after his novel *The Rainbow* had been suppressed. Soon he found himself harassed for his militant antiwar statements and accused by some of being a German agent. For a number of years he had contemplated escape from the old continent to America. He finally migrated in 1922, staying for a couple of years before ill health drove him back home.

Lawrence had already taken the pulse of America from afar, writing *Studies in Classic American Literature*. He revised the essays, while living in New Mexico, for American publication in 1923. His views on American literature attracted much attention in the popular press. Among the "American literary pearls" that he discovered was *Moby-Dick*. Lawrence's attention to it helped solidify its reputation as an American classic.

Lawrence enthusiastically discussed *Moby-Dick*, mostly in an odd manner. Much of what he had to say was at best skeletal, a set of orphic pronouncements along with various long passages quoted from the novel.

Sometimes his views, as one analyst put it, seemed "hysterical." But it was a creative encounter, one great author taking the measure of another, with them sharing a fondness for "all matters of barbaric vertu."

Lawrence encased what he had to say about *Moby-Dick* within his larger take on America, its social mores, foundational assumptions, and current concerns. According to Lawrence, Americans naïvely embraced newness as the end-all of fashion. Alas, America's foundation stone was sunk not in freedom but in enslavement, the murder of the Indians, and religious fanaticism.

Despite all of his venom (much of it drawing blood), Lawrence delighted in some aspects of America. America is at its best when it is truest to its wilderness, open to the tragic unfolding of nature, and when it keeps its moralizing to a minimum.

Melville, Lawrence tells us, "was neither mad nor crazy. But he was over the border . . . like those terrible yellow-bearded Vikings who broke out of the waves in beaked ships. He was a modern Viking." Hmmm.

Lawrence further informs us that Melville "instinctively hated human life," that he was "mystical" at his core, and that he found the white man "the ugliest beast on earth." Melville was trapped. However much he despised civilization, he could not become a savage himself. Thus, "he was born for Purgatory. Some souls are purgatorial by destiny." Even when landlocked at home, he was lost at sea.

From such a vantage point, Melville composed *Moby-Dick*—"a great book," according to Lawrence. But why is it great and what is the meaning of the symbol of the White Whale? "I doubt if even Melville knew exactly," but Lawrence will, no doubt, explain it for us, in due time.

Lawrence marvels at the adventure aspects of the story, more in the nitty-gritty of whaling details than in the symbolism of the whale or the soul-quest of Ahab. Melville wants to take us on a journey that is "metaphysically deep" into the ultimate meaning of things. But Melville is at his deepest when he sticks to the surface as phenomena, to his descriptions of life aboard ship and the creatures that are encountered.

"This *Pequod*, ship of the American soul" is agog with meaning, with its crew, "a collection of maniacs fanatically hunting down a lonely, harmless white whale," admits Lawrence. The leader of the expedition, Captain Ahab, "maniac captain of the soul" of America, is rather like President Woodrow Wilson, with his stiff moral idealism. The crew represents "Many races, many peoples, many nations, under the Stars and Stripes. Beaten with many stripes."

To what end? *Moby-Dick* is, in Lawrence's estimation, "the greatest book of the sea ever written. It moves awe in the soul" but it is also (one senses an "alas," in his view) "a book of esoteric symbolism of profound significance, and of considerable tiresomeness." At the core of such symbolism is doom! "Doom of our white day. We are doomed, doomed. And the doom is in America. The doom of our white day."

Lawrence considered Melville a prophet for understanding, as Lawrence puts it, that "his race is doomed. His white soul, doomed. His great white epoch, doomed. Himself, doomed. The idealist, doomed. The spirit, doomed." Why, then, hunt a White Whale? In Lawrence's estimation, Moby "is the deepest blood-being of the white race; he is our deepest blood-nature."

Thus, Ahab turns against himself, in effect, committing a sort of suicide because the white American "blood-consciousness [has been] sapped by a parasitic mental or ideal consciousness." The sinking of the *Pequod*, then, represents the death of the white American soul.

That's a whole lot of doom. Is there anything that floats atop the waves of this ocean of doom? Not in Melville, since he is the unstinting chronicler of this doom. Perhaps. Lawrence viewed Walt Whitman as the American apostle of rebirth. He was "the first white aboriginal." But that is another story.

CHAPTER 103

Measurement of the Whale's Skeleton

TAKING THE MEASURE OF A WHALE AND MORE, OF COURSE

It is difficult to take the measure of outsider or primitive art. It defies our categories, refuses to engage the tradition, and often seems informed more by ardor than by depth. While it is rarely, as Ishmael says of the whale's fins, "weighty and majestic," it can open us up to an "unbounded sea" of possibility.

Consider the case of Matt Kish from Dublin, Ohio, near Columbus. He has no academic background in fine art, but he has been attracted for years to graphic commix illustrations.

Kish is a big fan of *Moby-Dick*. He had learned about Zak Smith's project of doing a drawing a day for each page of Thomas Pynchon's *Gravity's Rainbow*. Kish decided to emulate Smith by doing likewise with *Moby-Dick*. He

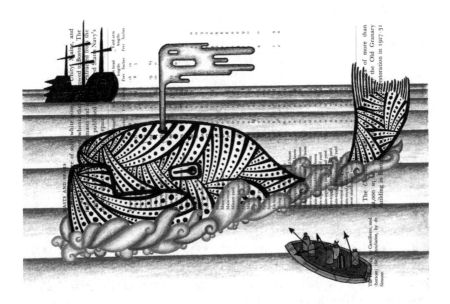

Figure 22.
Matt Kish's imaginative drawing-a-day of scenes in *Moby-Dick*. This one is titled: "'I will have no man in my boat,' said Starbuck, 'who is not afraid of a whale.'"

would use the Signet edition (1992), which boasts 552 pages. He began the project on August 5, 2009. After close to two years labor, he completed it.

Kish has avoided looking at other illustrators of *Moby-Dick*, although he is aware of Frank Stella's monumental artistic engagement with the work (see chapter 57). He draws his pictures on discarded leaves from books of all sorts—Kish is drawn to ephemera, and he attempts to recompose it into something related to the text of *Moby-Dick*.

The artwork is varied and inventive. Go to his blog: *http://www.everypageofmobydick.blogspot.com*, or check out his recently published compilation of the artwork.

You will not be disappointed. Like me, you might even take the opportunity to purchase one of the works that he has decided not to include in the series.

CHAPTER 104

The Fossil Whale

ADDITIONAL LEARNED DISCOURSE ABOUT THE BONES AND SKELETON OF WHALES

Who cannot respect "writers that rise and swell with their topic"? Modern writers wonder how Melville managed to "rise and swell." Michael Chabon, author of the Pulitzer Prize-winning novel *The Amazing Adventures of Kavalier and Clay* (2000), in answer to the party question, "What book would you want to have with you if stranded on a desert island?", chooses *Moby-Dick*. He does not explain why, and we must assume it was something more than a text that would help him to navigate away from the island. Rather, one suspects, it would afford him a reading opportunity that was endless in its possibilities, that presented depths not be exhausted over a long period of loneliness.

There is a *Moby-Dick* presence in Jack Kerouac's novel *On the Road* (1957), which is, after all, very much a moral tale, about coming to terms with reality. Sal Paradise is the Ishmael character, open to the thrill of the road but attracted to stability. Dean Moriarty has a few aspects of Ahab to him, for example, his headlong dive into experience without much regard for others. At one point in the narrative, Kerouac speaks of Dean as "that mad Ahab at the wheel" of a car, "driving at tremendous speed."

Amitav Ghosh, an Indian novelist fond of pondering sea routes for trade and intercultural connections, finds Melville "the greatest writer that America has ever produced," his work "inexhaustible in its inspiration," and thus a profound influence upon his own fiction. He revels in Melville's "open-minded" curiosity and his "level of engagement with the world that is completely absent from 19th century English writing." The *Pequod* is a United Nations of different nationalities and voices, and Ishmael is "a figure who is articulating a very challenging view of our relationship with nature, in terms of attention to nature; and the whole idea of the destructiveness—both the interest of whales and the horror of killing whales, and at the same time the joys of men working together in killing whales."

Roberto Bolaño, the brilliant author of many works of tragic fiction with a largeness of palette, has claimed *Moby-Dick*, along with *The Adventures of Huckleberry Finn*, as the source for all subsequent American fiction. He used *Moby-Dick*, a voyage into "the land of evil," as a model for his own momentous and monumental forays into that same landscape in *The Savage Detectives* and *2666*.

E. L. Doctorow recalled reading *Moby-Dick* first as a nine year old, then again as a Kenyon College undergraduate, next as a young editor at the New American Library, and finally to prepare a lecture. From it he gained a sense of writerly freedom. Thus, "whatever rule breaking I have done in my work I probably owe to Melville." Melville is also a source of "ideas for poems," given the richness of his texts. If one is looking for the beginnings of modern American literature, then in Doctorow's view, *Moby-Dick* is the fount: "that book swallowed European civilization whole. And we only, are escaped alone on our own shore, to tell our tales."

On and on goes the celebration. Augusten Burroughs, a memoirist of deep feeling, says of *Moby-Dick*, "When I read the first page I had to ask, 'Wait. Is this as cool as I think it is?' It is."

William Faulkner, not a man to mince words, considered *Moby-Dick* one of four books that influenced his own writing (especially his symbolically rich *The Bear*), and he read it aloud to his seven-year-old daughter.

Jay Parini, a very talented poet, biographer (Faulkner, John Steinbeck, and Robert Frost), critic, and novelist has long been drawn to Melville and *Moby-Dick*. Perhaps he has briefly sated that interest with his masterful novel *The Passages of H. M.* (2010), which attempts to fill in the blanks in Melville's life and mind through fiction, with special focus on Melville's wife.

Just published is an enticing novel by Chad Harbach, *The Art of Fielding*, which is on one level about baseball. Harbach tips his hat in Melville's direction in obvious ways. On the campus where much of the novel takes place is a statue of Melville and one of the key characters has written a book, *The Sperm Squeezers*. And the central character is named, Henry Skrimshander, and he plays for a baseball team nicknamed "The Harpooners." But, as one of the blurbs for the book reads, the novel is "mere baseball fiction the way *Moby-Dick* is just a fish story." Both books are about the nature of tragedy, how in the blink of an eye lives of promise can be transformed.

Most famously there is Peter Benchley's *Jaws* (1974), where three men hunt the Great White Shark that has been terrorizing swimmers near the town of Amity, Long Island. The shark hunter, Quint, is rife with affinities to Ahab.

Joyce Carol Oates says, "If you're going to spend the next year of your life writing, you would probably rather write *Moby-Dick* than a little household mystery with cat detectives. I consider tragedy the highest form of art."

By all means, reader, "spend the next year of your life" reading *Moby-Dick*, or better yet, trying to write like Melville.

CHAPTER 105

Does the Whale's Magnitude Diminish?—Will He Perish?

THE NARRATOR MUSES ABOUT THE STATUS OF WHALES AT PRESENT

In the nineteenth century, ships under the flags of all nations combed the oceans of the world "even through Behring's straits, and into the remotest secret drawers and lockers of the world." A "thousand harpoons and lances" were aimed at. Mused Melville, "the moot point is, whether Leviathan can long endure so wide a chase, and so remorseless a havoc; whether he must not at last be exterminated from the waters, and the last whale, like the last man, smoke his last pipe, and then himself evaporate in the final puff."

Yet, let us not conclude, too quickly, that Melville was a conservationist. Ishmael, after all, believes that whales will survive and he exhibits no remorse about his role in killing whales or the impact on the environment of such activity. But, as Andrew Delbanco states, "It's irresistible to make the analogy between the relentless hunt for whale oil in Melville's day and for petroleum in ours."

Although within twenty years of Melville's tale whale-hunting was to take a severe downturn because of new sources of energy to light houses around the world, the whaling industry continues on into this century. And it exacts a toll. Hardly any Bowhead, Blue, and Right Whales swim the seas today.

That some species of whales have survived is thanks to the efforts of conservationists. After the Second World War, the International Whaling Commission was formed to regulate whale-hunting. Although its edicts have been enforced erratically, the campaigns of groups such as Greenpeace brought pressure against nations like Japan and the Soviet Union, to curtail or cease their whale-hunting. They have made a difference, but a difference in degree is not the same as a complete cessation.

No one has acknowledged and acted upon this recognition more than Paul Watson. As he put it, "I have touched and been touched by the whales. I have been with them when they frolicked freely in the seas, knowing that their mighty hearts were filled with the joy of life."

Watson considers killing a single whale an abomination, a crime of the highest order. Since authorities are lax in enforcing prohibitions against whaling, he maintains that it is his moral duty to intervene forcefully to stop the slaughter.

In 1975, already a committed environmentalist with years of experience at sea, Watson attempted to halt illegal killing of whales. About sixty miles off the coast of California, he and his fellow antiwhaling activists, found the Soviet ship *Dalniy Vostok*. The Soviet vessel was 750 feet long, like the *Pequod*. It was a veritable factory, built for extracting all that was valuable from whales. Its whaling boats stretched 150 feet in length and were equipped with harpoons armed with payloads that exploded upon impact with the whale's body. The science of whale killing had progressed since Ahab's day.

Watson undertook what he called a "kamikaze" action. In Zodiac speed-boats—horseshoe-shaped and constructed of rubber, capable of quick maneuvering and capable of zooming forty miles an hour in choppy waters—Watson and his comrades sought to place themselves between Soviet harpooners and whales. They came armed only with the courage of their convictions and with motion picture cameras to capture the confrontation to gain publicity for their cause.

This attempt to stymie the Soviet hunters failed that day. One 250-pound harpoon whizzed over the protesters and found its mark. Listen to Watson's description of that mortal moment and its meaning: The whale "rose slowly out of the water, a quarter of his bulk towering above us. His eye fell upon Fred and me, two tiny men in a little rubber raft, and he looked at us. It was a gaze, a gentle, knowing, forgiving face. Slowly, slowly, as if he did not want to disturb the water unduly, as if taking care that his great tail did not scrape us from our little perch, he settled into the quietly lapping waves. I had one more glimpse of that gazing eye, and then he was gone from our world."

"What had I seen? Was it understanding? We wept, there in that boat on that ocean, we wept—for the whales and ourselves."

Watson's course was fixed and he has since dedicated himself, and his considerable powers of persuasion and energy for action, to the saving of whales. With his now stark white mop of hair, larger-than-life personality, and absolute conviction, he resembles Ahab. One imagines that Ahab—having seen the destruction rained upon the population of whales since his days at sea—might have been pleased to sail with Watson on his mission.

Or, if Ahab's thirst for revenge against Moby and his progenitors remained unquenched, then he would have found in Watson a worthy opponent.

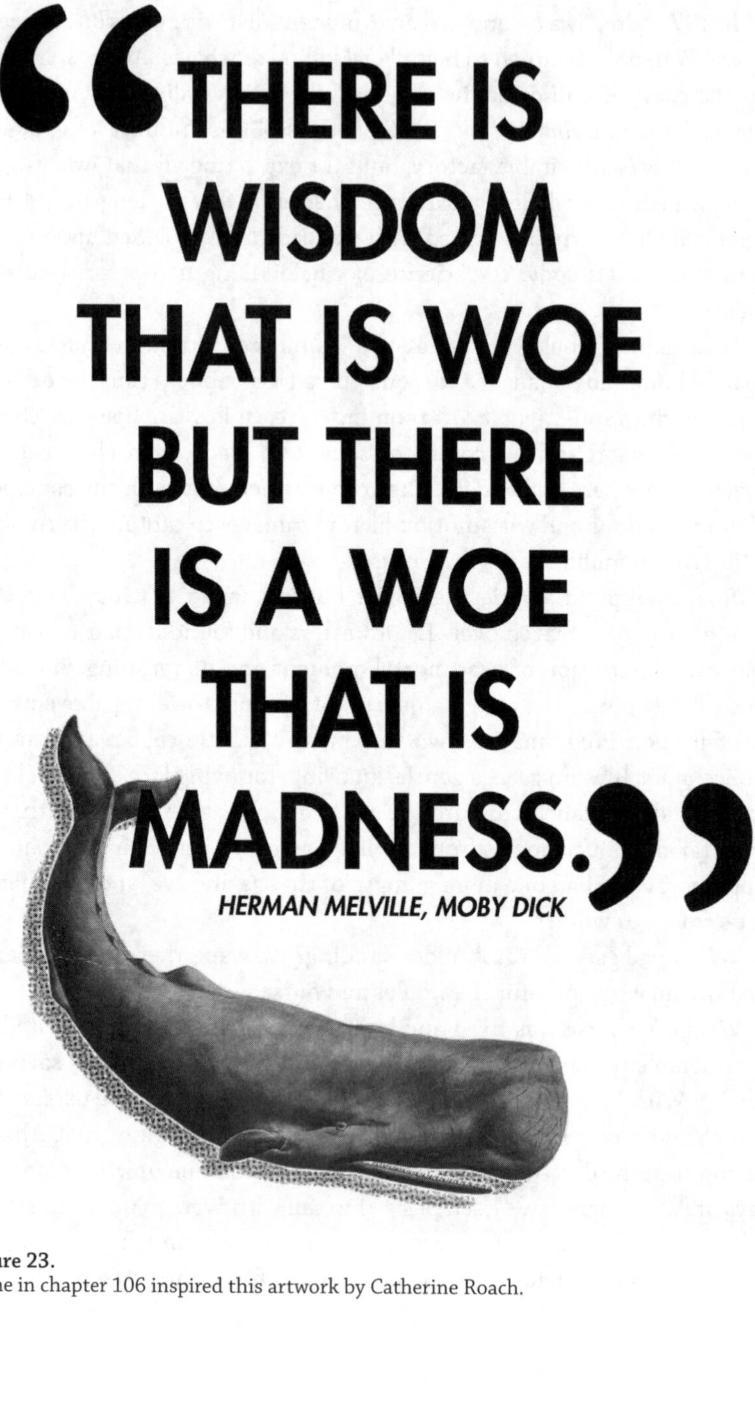

"THERE IS WISDOM THAT IS WOE BUT THERE IS A WOE THAT IS MADNESS."

HERMAN MELVILLE, MOBY DICK

Figure 23.
A line in chapter 106 inspired this artwork by Catherine Roach.

CHAPTER 106

Ahab's Leg

AHAB SPLINTERS HIS IVORY LEG

From the onset of his long, distinguished career in Hollywood, director John Huston had dreamed of making a film version of *Moby-Dick* (see chapter 109). He wanted its message blasphemous and its facts truthful to the text. Along with most readers of *Moby-Dick*, however, he wondered which leg of Ahab's had been shorn by the whale. Although Melville supplies much by way of description for Captain Ahab—we know of his looking like " a man cut at the stake" and the scar that "scorched his face and neck"—he never offers the reader any information on which limb was missing.

In 1953, while preparing for his film, Huston wrote Melville scholar Tyrus Hillway for an answer to this question. Hillway concluded that Ahab probably lost his right leg for the following reason: while giving chase to Moby Dick, Ahab would have been on a small boat, bracing himself on what was known as a "clumsy cleat." Here the harpooner would brace his left knee for support when throwing his lance at a whale. The device was devised for right-handers, so assuming that Ahab was right-handed, he would have lost his right leg.

In the film, Gregory Peck, playing Ahab, hobbles around on his ivory *left* leg. So much for cinematic veracity.

CHAPTER 107

The Carpenter

THE CARPENTER ON THE *PEQUOD* IS A BUSY MAN

Like carpenters, actors play various roles. Consider the case of Patrick Stewart. Before appearing as Ahab in a 1998 television film of *Moby-Dick*, Stewart had recently portrayed Othello, and he had earlier gained fame for his role of Captain Jean-Luc Picard in the hit television series *Star Trek: The Next Generation*.

Stewart was an inspired choice for Ahab. In his late fifties, with a powerful physique, his emotional, powerful voice could bring the dead to life. A brief foray in boxing had lent his face an altogether fascinatingly beaten shape.

In preparing for his role, like a good carpenter, Stewart honed his tools and learned how to construct Ahab. He read *Moby-Dick* and was both frightened and fascinated by the tale, especially Ahab's thirst for vengeance. "There was much about the role that appeared mysterious," Stewart related, the "obsession seems to be so absurd and the cost to him too high. I had to find ways into that man's mind, and I do remember that it was with great relief that it became clear to me why Ahab is such a tragic figure."

Ahab's self-awareness, in Stewart's view, makes him tragic. He knows precisely what he is doing at each moment. For Stewart, "He has a choice." And he has chosen, and he is "in agony because he knows how inhuman his choice is."

The tragic dimension rings, in Stewart's stalwart performance, as well as a bit of the blasphemy that compels Ahab. But, as Stewart recounts, the key to the story is that it is a fetching narrative about the hunt for the White Whale. The "fundamental duty is to communicate a narrative and to have our audience longing to know what happens next." What the audience demands and deserves is "a crackling good yarn. All the psychological complexity, the theology and philosophy in the story, all that's a bonus. The tale, after all, is about a man trying to kill a whale."

Stewart—and all involved in the film—understood the demands of television, in this regard. The show garnered, thanks to plenty of advertising and interest in the novel, an average of 5.9 million viewers for its two-night presentation, "the highest audience ever for any program other than news or sports" for basic cable television, up to that time.

Figure 24.
Patrick Stewart as Ahab, attempting to spear Moby Dick, in the 1998 television movie, directed by Franc Roddam.

CHAPTER 108

Ahab and the Carpenter

The Deck—First Night Watch

THE CARPENTER AND STUBB AGREE THAT AHAB IS "QUEER"

The pressing question for readers of *Moby-Dick* is: who is this fellow Ahab? What makes him tick? The carpenter and Stubb have concluded that Ahab is "queer." He's "queer, queer, very queer." Of course, they are not privy to all the details of Ahab's history, nor are they attuned to his fanatical quest for meaning or to find an anchor in the heady seas of existence. But because of his mad search for revenge upon the White Whale that has sheared off his leg, they feel more than justified in characterizing their captain as "queer."

The term "queer" in the days of the *Pequod* did not have the same connotations as it has today. We saw in chapter 46 that one recent writer about the novel has imagined Ahab soaked with desire for young Ishmael. While we generally associate Melville with Ishmael—both are orphans that narrate tales and more—he might also have hammered into the character of Ahab some of his own homosexual tendencies. Certainly the peg leg is a sharp phallic symbol. Another author weighs in on the possibility that both Ahab and Ishmael may be black or mulatto (see chapter 41).

Ahab is certainly queer in the nineteenth-century meaning of the word. Begin with his appearance. He sports a scar upon his face that extends down his body, like an etching from above. He is described early in the novel by one of the owners of the *Pequod* as "a grand, ungodly man," or "a swearing good man," paradoxes that fit Ahab better than the slouchy hat that he commonly wears.

Finally, this most "queer" of men may be modeled upon the tragic figure of Lieutenant Charles Wilkes (chapter 124), as well as other figures that loomed large in Melville's era (see chapter 130).

In the end, however, Ahab remains Ahab, singular and "queer" to the core.

CHAPTER 109
Ahab and Starbuck in the Cabin

**VALUABLE WHALE OIL LEAKS FROM CASKS, AND STARBUCK IS
SHOCKED AT AHAB'S LACK OF CONCERN WITH LOST PROFITS**

The fraught and tense relationship between Ahab and Starbuck is central to the novel. Ahab represents madness and power; Starbuck demonstrates reasonableness and obedience. Ahab is volcanic and deep-diving; Starbuck is temperate and surface.

In the making of the 1956 film version of *Moby-Dick*, director John Huston can be seen assuming the guise of Ahab while writer Ray Bradbury played the role of Starbuck.

John Huston was a fascinating character. Born to an actor father, Walter Huston, and a sports-writer mother, he was a sickly child, often confined to bed. As a teenager, he threw off the covers of his sickness and became a roustabout. A man of sometimes overflowing physical courage, he had been a professional boxer. Despite his impressive record of victories in the ring, his cragged face recorded many punches that had landed on him. He had even served in the Mexican cavalry for a spell. Tall and imposing, with a voice that seemed to emerge from a gravel pit, he was cantankerous and mercurial, and often took pleasure in torturing those who were not his equal in matters of the intellect or physical power. He demanded loyalty and craved affection. He was devoted to making his film and having it torched with blasphemy, veracity, and cinematic splendor. He would have made a marvelous Ahab in the film.

Bradbury was an inspired choice to compose the screenplay. By the early 1950s, he was emerging as a science-fiction writer and novelist. Living in Venice, California, with a wife and two young daughters, Bradbury was a devout film fan, and he wanted desperately to write a screenplay for John Huston. He wrote vivid, accessible prose, and he was drawn to symbolism. Bradbury was a neophyte at the business of filmmaking, and he both adored and abhorred the larger-than-life figure of Huston. Bradbury brought to the film youthful confidence and naïveté. He was, after all, signing on to transform America's greatest novel for the screen, for millions to view.

Working with Huston on the script was both exhilarating and exasperating for Bradbury. By the time he had finished, Bradbury claimed he had 1,500 pages of script, thanks to twenty rewrites. The process began on a hopeful note, as Bradbury threw himself into writing with gusto. The first scene that he confronted was Father Mapple's sermon which, in many ways, would anticipate the "blasphemy" that Huston found at the core of the novel.

After an ocean voyage and brief stopover in Paris, Bradbury and family settled in a hotel in Ireland for the long haul. The weather was horrid and the work challenging beyond Bradbury's dreams—how do you translate a great, sprawling novel into a film script? According to Bradbury, Huston was small help, advising him to find his own voice. Indeed, Bradbury later claimed that "John didn't know any more about *Moby-Dick* than I did. It was the blind leading the blind." But these blind men learned to see. Both read the relevant literature on Melville, including recent books by Newton Arvin and Lawrance Thompson. When Bradbury inquired whether Huston wanted "the Melville Society's version of *Moby-Dick*, or the Jungian version, or the Freudian version," Huston reportedly announced, "I want Ray Bradbury's version."

To his credit, Bradbury worked feverishly on the project. As the pages fell from his typewriter, he rushed them to Huston's Irish countryside retreat. Then he would be either devastated or elated by a raising or lowering of the director's prodigious eyebrows. Huston was, as someone had told Bradbury, a "son of a bitch," albeit a charming and irascible one. He enjoyed needling the forthright Bradbury about his personal fears (speeding in a car, not liking to fly or ride a horse). One night, toward the end of the project, when Huston had been particularly vicious in his joking at Bradbury's expense, Bradbury hauled off and punched Huston, an act which probably endeared him more than anything to the director.

One morning, after months of labor on the script and many meetings with Huston, Bradbury awakened early and was at work around 7 A.M. Suddenly he felt transformed: "I am Herman Melville," he declared. With enthusiasm and a sense that he was now channeling Melville into the script, he wrote a scene that had been confounding him. Ahab, he now realized, "wants the men's souls" as well as revenge against the whale.

Huston had wanted Bradbury's soul. He managed to get a good film script that he reworked until it fit his own vision of a man bent on diving deeper, confronting a God who had questions to answer.

Figure 25 and 26.
Queequeg cannot remove his tattoos but fans of *Moby-Dick* can design and don shirts, at will. Designs by Kristin Walko and Mat Hudson.

CHAPTER 110

Queequeg in His Coffin

QUEEQUEG ANTICIPATES HIS DEATH BUT THEN REBOUNDS

Queequeg, that "tattooed savage," takes ill with a fever and anticipates his own demise. He withers away to the point that there seems "but little left of him but his frame and tattooing." He orders the ship's carpenter to fashion a coffin for him, built from "some heathenish, coffin-colored old lumber aboard" the *Pequod*. Once the construction is completed, with harpoon shaft, Yojo idol, biscuits, and a flask of water in place, Queequeg readies himself for his final port of call. However, he rallies and soon regains his healthy vigor.

"With a wild whimsiness," Queequeg decides that the built coffin can be readily transformed into a sea-chest. He spends his spare hours "carving the lid with all manner of grotesque figures and drawings." These images resemble some "parts of the twisted tattooing on his body," which have the look of "hieroglyphics" somehow communicating to those in the know, the "complete theory of the heavens and the earth, and a mystical treatise on the art of attaining truth."

Queequeg's body contains in a single "volume" all of the mysteries that are associated with the White Whale. But in the form of riddles that are tantalizing and resistant to solution. If only Ahab had spent his time deciphering Queequeg's body, things might have turned out better for all involved.

Samuel Otter helps us understand Melville's fascination with Queequeg as the "tattooed savage." According to Otter, Melville wrote *Moby-Dick* when scientists and explorers were busily engaged in what he calls the production of "intense racial knowledge." Ethnology demanded attention as a science that could demonstrate human differences. Central to its presumptions was the superiority of the white race in contrast to those of a savage cast. Race, in the view of these ethnologists, was fixed and hierarchical.

In many ways, Melville challenged this emerging science. He relies not on cranial measurements, bumps upon the head, or dissections, but upon experience and observation. He reads the mark of Queequeg well by recognizing that beneath the tattoos is a man of regal bearing and humane heart. He is the equal of any white man aboard the *Pequod*.

Moreover, the marks that crisscross his body, perhaps like those upon the White Whale, are full of meaning. As we learn in this chapter, the marks on Queequeg's body are nothing less than "a complete theory of the heavens and the earth, and a mystical treatise on the art of attaining truth." Alas, the prophet that had inscribed them is "departed." They will forever remain a mystery. This is in stark contrast to the pretensions to knowledge on the part of nineteenth-century ethnologists. Fittingly, the readings of the whale and the doubloon are perspectival, deep dives into the self rather than into any fixed or accessible reality.

The tattoos gracing Queequeg and his chest, then, tantalize us with their presumed meaning, their depths, and their insights into the nature of things. But they stay afloat while the dreams of mortals to attain such certitude, to read these signs, lead only into the deep brine of the sea. This is something that Ahab, that fanatical reader of signs and seeker of truth, will learn, the hard way.

CHAPTER 111

The Pacific

AHAB'S FANATICAL "HIDDEN SOUL BENEATH" REVEALED

Ahab gazes upon the vastness of the Pacific Ocean but he imagines it existing only as a holding tank for the White Whale.

Another fictional character shares a similar monomania about a watery creature. Captain Hook is obsessed with the Ticking Crocodile, as well as with Peter Pan. The ever youthful and exuberant Pan is his nemesis, having chopped off Hook's arm in a swordfight. The missing limb was eaten by the crocodile, which found it most tasty. So delicious in fact, that it craves the rest of Hook's body. Lucky for Hook that he can hear the hungry croc approach, since it has a ticking alarm clock in its belly. But like much of life and luck, the clock will eventually wind down.

The connection between J. M. Barrie, the author of the Peter Pan tale, and *Moby-Dick* is hardly gratuitous. We know that Barrie had read and delighted in *Moby-Dick* (and *Typee*), well before he wrote his story.

Sometimes, as David Park Williams demonstrates, Barrie borrows from *Moby-Dick*. The most obvious connection is that Ahab is defined by his missing leg while Hook lacks a hand. Of Hook, Barrie states, "the grimmest part of him [Hook] was his iron claw." Of Ahab, writes Melville, "the whole grim aspect of Ahab . . . not a little of this overbearing grimness was owing to the barbaric white leg upon which he partly stood."

The Crocodile, although lacking the size and symbolic resonance of the White Whale (Barrie's audience is, after all, youngsters), does have immense power. In an early version of *Peter Pan*, the "crocodile raises its open mouth . . . the bow of the boat goes into Crocodile's mouth, which breaks it in pieces."

Both Ahab and Hook have their objects of abject hatred—the White Whale and Crocodile, respectively. They read all of the evil of the universe, all of the woes that have befallen them, onto their objects of disdain. Each man can be seen as a personification of evil, of an unwillingness to bow to convention and to care for other human beings. Both men, also, seek to control their crews, worried that they might not share in their thirst for revenge. One of those rebelling against Hook is a seaman named Starkey, named not so distantly from Starbuck, who contemplates mutiny against Ahab.

An apparent distinction, however, is that the Ticking Crocodile pursues Captain Hook while the White Whale is indifferent to Ahab. In Ahab's mind, however, the White Whale pursues him, for it is forever on his tail, shadowing his every thought, eating into every fiber of his being, conscious and unconscious. It is the ticking clock that defines the hours of his day— and ours.

CHAPTER 112

The Blacksmith

THE CARPENTER AND HIS HISTORY, A MAN SEA-SALTED WITH DEATH

The carpenter's place of birth is unstated but many aboard the *Pequod* are Nantucket Quakers. Death is a familiar presence to them, and it has "plucked down" many close to the carpenter, and he feels its cold breath upon his own neck. The eyes of men such as the carpenter are, as Melville intones beautifully, "death-longing."

Poet Robert Lowell did not hail from Nantucket, but his roots in New England sank deep, descending from the Winslow and Lowell families. His father was an officer in the U.S. Navy. The son rejected military service, opting to go to prison as a conscientious objector during the Second World War. He was a mercurial figure, awash with manic depression and alcoholism. But the waves of his region and its history beat upon the shore of his mind, as is apparent in one poem in his Pulitzer Prize-winning book, *Lord Weary's Castle*, published in 1946.

The poem, "The Quaker Graveyard in Nantucket," is dedicated to Lowell's cousin Warren Winslow, who died at sea during the Second World War. It is a dirge about death, rippled with references to *Moby-Dick*.

The poem opens with references to Winslow's death in the Atlantic while the sea is "breaking violently." Then, we are transported to the "long night" cries from the Nantucket graveyard which may be heard "Bobbing by Ahab's whaleboats in the East."

The sea has claimed many of New England's finest, most recently Lowell's cousin. But he goes back to "Quaker sailors lost / In the mad scramble of their lives. They died / When time was open-eyed." Those open eyes were peeled, at each bounce of the waves, for sperm whales, the lifeblood of these mariners of old.

Death and the sea are intimate partners.

> For water, for the deep where the high tide
> Mutters to its hurt self, mutters and ebbs
> Waves wallow in their wash, go out and out,
> Leave only the death-rattle of the crabs

Into that sea went the Nantucketers in quest of the whales. Out went Starbuck, his family's name etched deeply into the stones that mark the graveyard of Nantucket and the sea. Out went Ahab, a Nantucket man, too, but one whose exile from humanity could be read on his "void and forehead." Out went the carpenter and the other Nantucket sailors aboard the *Pequod* to the sea—"where time's contrition blues."

CHAPTER 113

The Forge

THE BLACKSMITH FORGES A NEW HARPOON BLADE FOR AHAB

Moby-Dick "changed me," recalled Henry A. Murray, one of the most influential psychologists in twentieth-century America. But how exactly, and whether it was for the better, remains unclear.

Murray was first bitten by the Moby-bug at age twenty-seven, in August 1924. The book was given to him by a friend as Murray boarded a ship heading to England. After devouring it with "a shock of recognition," Murray pronounced himself, "swept by Melville's gale and shaken by his appalling sea dragon." It evoked for him "Beethoven's *Eroica* in words."

Born into the New York elite, much as Herman Melville had been earlier in the nineteenth century, Murray's family on his mother's side were Revolutionary War heroes and scions of great wealth. His father was descended from Scottish royalty. But Murray found the plush interiors of his upbringing painful—he was forever in quiet and ambivalent rebellion against narrow propriety and in a quest for the love that he felt his mother had denied him. Brilliant and moody, Murray demanded adulation and attention beneath a veneer of sweet camaraderie. He was a complex man with a secret history.

Also aboard ship bound for England was Christiana Morgan, with her husband and son. Soon she and Murray began a torrid relationship that lasted for decades, within plain sight of their respective families, while remaining hushed to most outsiders. Although Murray destroyed many of his notes on this intense "dyad," Christiana copied some of them out. Apparently, Murray took especial pleasure in sadism, using chain and whip repeatedly to cow Christiana into subservience prior to sexual intercourse.

Upon returning to the United States, Murray ardently pursued his newborn interest in hardcore sex, as well as in *Moby-Dick*. His years of thinking about Melville and the novel were summarized in his essay "In Nomine Diaboli" (in the devil's name) published in 1951. The piece steams with near-to-the-surface hints of the tempestuous secret life that Murray had then pursued for over two decades.

Murray identified strongly with Ahab—a sort of demigod, stained with evil aspects, but heroic in many ways. He opposed the Calvinist God (exemplified by the White Whale) who denied freedom—sexual and otherwise.

Ahab personified the id, of panting sexual desire trying to break the shackles of repressive society. Why the poor whale should have heaped upon its massive expanse the sins of the fathers, the cloak of the superego, remains unclear. The imperative behind Murray's essay is apparent: he and Melville (through Ahab) are fellow voyagers against the superego of Moby Dick and the "rational realistic Ego" of Starbuck.

Murray speaks softly about the symbolic emasculation of Ahab, which is at the core of his desire for revenge against Moby. At the same time, Ahab's final "suicidal lunge" and his becoming bound to the beast, indicate the power of parental, in this case maternal, power. Murray even whispers some comments about the unhappy nature of marriage in Melville's time, about how it was a "prison house" for incompatible couples. Thankfully, observed Murray, with today's divorce (and no doubt forbearance for trysts such as he had long engaged in with Christiana), greater freedom abounded.

Murray boasted that, as Melville's biographer, he brought scientific tools to the task: "the conceptual lance, harpoons, cutting irons and what-nots." The legacy of his many years of work on Melville remains unpublished, a jumble of a 1,000-page manuscript housed in a Harvard University archive.

No sooner had Murray returned to Harvard with family and mistress in tow, than he began to build his empire, based on the presumption that through various tests, observation, and interviewing techniques, the personality of an individual could be revealed. He gained fame for development of the Thematic Apperception Test (1935), designed to help type personalities by their responses to a series of images. During the Second World War, Murray had lent his skills to the government for purposes of screening applicants for various positions in the military, and he also drew up a well-regarded portrait of Adolf Hitler's personality, with predications about how the dictator might act in the coming years of conflict. In the Cold War years, Murray's connections with the CIA and other government agencies ripened. With governmental support, he sought to determine how various personalities respond under pressure and under the influence of the hallucinogenic drug LSD.

In one of his experiments, Murray and his assistants first gave Harvard undergraduates a battery of evaluation tests and then placed them in a brightly lit room, before verbally assaulting them. Between 1959 and 1962, a particularly brilliant and troubled young man went through this barrage, and also was administered LSD. His name was Ted Kaczynski, and he would become known in 1996 as the Unabomber, the fanatical antitechnology terrorist responsible for sending package bombs to various individuals, killing three people and wounding twenty-three others. Did Murray's dangerous research methods help to shatter Kazcynski's delicate psychological balance?

It is easy, tantalizingly simple, to find affinities between Ahab and Kazcynski—fanatics, madly wedded to their own grief and devoted to revenge. Holed up in his tiny Montana cabin, living largely apart from society, Kazcynski rails against a society that is based upon technology and science. Such values are not at the service of humanity; they exist to inculcate among people "feelings of inferiority." In his own "manifesto," Kazcynski called for a revolution, rather than reform, against the White Whale of modern society. Only by sinking his exploding harpoons into its thick skin would significant change become possible.

Kazcynski, Murray, and Ahab, each in his own manner shared a sense of a terrible indignity being foisted upon him. By wrapping themselves in personal righteousness and power, they sought to exact revenge in the name of a higher good.

CHAPTER 114

The Gilder

THE *PEQUOD* CONTINUES ALONG, IN SEARCH OF MOBY DICK

The sea and meditation, Ishmael told us in the first chapter, are forever wedded. As Starbuck gazes out upon the vast calm of the Pacific Ocean, he realizes it as "Loveliness unfathomable, as ever lover saw in his young bride's eye!"

We know so much about Ahab and Ishmael, Queequeg and Starbuck. But what do we know, for instance, of the "young bride's eye" of Ahab's wife who awaits his return?

"Captain Ahab was neither my first husband nor my last," Una offers at the outset of the story of her life. Sena Jeter Naslund has created a feminist fantasy, of bulk equal to *Moby-Dick*, titled, *Ahab's Wife*. In many ways, she had a life richer than his although both were dogged by tragedy.

Born in Kentucky, Una is sent away at the age of twelve (the same age at which Melville's father died) to stay with her aunt's family who reside on a small island, where they manage a lighthouse, not far from Nantucket. There she enjoys the wonders of nature, the love of family, and various adventures. She meets two young men, Giles and Kit, both of whom take a fancy to her.

The story meanders, but the upshot is as follows. Una goes a-whaling, aboard the good ship *Sussex*. She is, of course, disguised as a boy, serving as a companion to the captain's son. Before long, she is climbing ropes up to the masthead, where she immediately employs her superior vision to spot a whale. Alas, disaster comes quickly. Giles either falls or leaps to his death. The ship is later rammed by an enraged whale! The captain, his son, Una, Kit, and some others take to a small boat, heading for Tahiti. Supplies are soon exhausted. There is no choice but to turn to cannibalism. Una survives, thanks to ample amounts of pure gumption. Kit, who had already shown signs of derangement, falls deeper into lunacy. But they are rescued, soon to be placed aboard the ship commanded by Captain Ahab. At Una's request, Ahab marries her and Kit, although it is a doomed match that ends in reality, if not in legality, when he takes to the wilderness.

Una is not one for pining away. She lives a rich and exciting life and displays a sassy, unconventional mind. Before the novel closes, she has supported herself as a seamstress, made friends with astronomer Maria Mitchell and her family, become a soul-mate with Margaret Fuller, had a deep conversation with Nathaniel Hawthorne, viewed Halley's comet, and learned the delights of using a dildo!

As you might well imagine, Una and Ahab renew their acquaintance and it blossoms into romance. The captain uses his power to annul Una's marriage to Kit and then to marry her. They have some happy times together, but the sea calls Ahab. After one miscarriage, Una gives birth to a son, named Justice. Ahab returns from one voyage bereft of a leg and consumed with a desire for revenge. He leaves hearth and home, never to be seen again. Una, the widow, settles into life with her son.

The story does not end here—how could it? She eventually meets a young man who, it turns out, is none other than Ishmael! Boy, does he have a tale to tell. Ishmael and Una live happily ever after. Oh, by the way, Naslund reveals that Ishmael's real name is David Pollack. How disappointing.

CHAPTER 115

The *Pequod* Meets the *Bachelor*

AHAB HAS NO TIME FOR A HAPPY SHIP

Hints of Melville's short story "Benito Cereno," published in 1855, can be found scattered throughout *Moby-Dick*. In this chapter, for instance, we learn that some "Long Island Negroes" were working as if "they were pulling down the cursed Bastille." Other anticipations of black rebellion can be found in the story of the *Town-Ho*. In both cases, appearance and reality are at war with one another.

In the story, Captain Amasa Delano, upright Yankee captain of the trading ship *Bachelor's Delight* (note the title of this chapter, "the *Pequod* Meets the *Bachelor*"), comes upon a Spanish ship that has been through hell. Its passengers (some Spanish sailors and African slaves) are devastated it appears by bad weather, disease, starvation, and thirst. Delano comes aboard to replenish the ship and to help bring it to port.

As he lounges aboard the Spanish vessel, he is frustrated on a number of counts. Its captain, Don Benito Cereno, is at times diffident, scared out of his wits, exhausted, and simply odd. Is Cereno suffering "innocent lunacy" or some sort of "wicked imposture"? Delano also notes various small, strange happenings on the disabled ship that affront his sense of decorum. Over and over again, in the midst of the story, Delano tries to figure out the "sphinx-like" mysteries that confront him. These sightings wend themselves around Delano's consciousness, but time and again he dismisses them as mere speculations. After all, what you see is what is. Grabbing hold of this commonplace is "tranquilizing" to Captain Delano. But he keeps returning to the "very queer" nature of things aboard Cereno's ship, with some of its Negroes aloft loudly sharpening hatchets and the strange winks and nods that some of the Spanish sailors seem to be directing towards him.

Delano's forebodings are soothed partly by his "benevolent paternalism" about the intrinsic qualities of blacks. He is convinced that they are by nature docile, happy, and stupid. He delights in glancing at a Negress with child, remarking that "There's naked nature, now; pure tenderness and love." He later assays that Negroes are "natural valets and hair-dressers." Delano concludes, with good cheer, that he "took to negroes, not philanthropically, but genially, just as other men took to Newfoundland dogs."

Appearances hide realities. In fact, Babo, the ever-present servant to Don Cereno, controls the ship. Early in the voyage, the slaves had revolted, executing some of the passengers and commandeering the ship with the intention of bringing it to safe harbor for them in Senegal. Bad weather and other mishaps have intervened. Now, all that they can do is to wait for the moment when they can capture Delano and his ship.

Finally, in a rush of violence and recognition, things come to a head. As he prepares to leave the Spanish ship for his own, Delano's hand is seized by Cereno, who does not want to let go—it is a case of a sort of "monkey-rope" tying them and their fates together. Separated at last, Cereno jumps over the bulwarks, and some of his sailors leap from the ship—which brings forth the realization that the ship has been under the control of the slaves and that they intend to hijack the *Bachelor's Delight*, if possible.

Delano has the "mask torn" from his face, "the scales dropped from his eyes" and with a "flash of revelation," he springs to action. The slave revolt is crushed, the ship and its survivors are taken to the nearest port. Babo is tried and burned to death, his head placed upon a spike for all to examine. Cereno dies three months later.

Blind for much of this novel, ignorant of signs of doom, "incapable of sounding such wickedness," Delano lacks a tragic sensibility. Instead, he is marked by a spirit of "generosity and piety." Ahab, in contrast, is a man whose every fiber contains a sharp sense of evil, a constant imperative to read all signs as indices of malign intent, at least as regards the White Whale.

Do not rest too comfortably in the presumption that Melville is celebrating the character of Delano over Ahab. It is by nothing more than a whisker of chance that Delano and his ship escape calamity. It must be remarked, too, that Delano's self-satisfied ruminations about the inner being and character of Negroes prove to be simplistic and wrong-headed. Thus, Melville may, as was his democratic and open wont, be composing a radical testament to the Negro's desire for liberty and their machinations to bring it about.

CHAPTER 116

The Dying Whale

AHAB KILLS A WHALE AND CONTEMPLATES ITS DEATH

For all of Ahab's monomaniacal attention to the task of slaying Moby Dick, he does occasionally do what is expected of him as captain of a whaling boat. Thus, when he and the crew of the *Pequod* sight whales, they go after them. Sometimes with success.

Ahab finds himself soothed to be aloft the gentle waves of the Pacific after he has vanquished a whale. Quickly he then finds himself "only soothed to deeper gloom." Gazing at a dying sperm whale, beyond the "wondrousness unknown" before him, he begins to feel an affinity with it. He notices how the whale "slowly" and "steadfastly" turns itself, with great effort, in its "last dying motions" towards the sun. "He too worships fire," remarks Ahab. The whale is destined to be part of the eternity of the sea, with a "hushed burial" in calm waters. The sight fills Ahab with "a prouder, if a darker faith. All thy unnamable imminglings float beneath me here; I am buoyed by breaths of once living things, exhaled as air, but water now." Below, in the deep recesses of the sea, "ye billows are my foster-brothers."

It is easy to imagine ourselves, in transcendental moments such as Ahab experiences after the kill, at one with our prey. Without such a sense of identification, the impress of the chase after the White Whale would be weakened. There are dangers in such reverie, in the notion that we are at one with the beasts of the sea.

In the waning days of February, 2010 at Sea World in Orlando, Florida, the distance between humans and whales became sadly apparent. Dawn Brancheau, an experienced trainer of whales was standing by the edge of the tank that held Tilikum, a male orca that weighed over 12,000 pounds. Orcas are commonly referred to as "killer whales," but they are not known to kill humans. On that day, however, Tilikum leaped from the water and grabbed Brancheau by her ponytail, taking her into the tank. According to reports, Tilikum thrashed the trainer around and then took her under the water to her death. The whale, one witness stated, had appeared "agitated" earlier in the day.

Richard Ellis, greatly learned in matters of the sea and its creatures, when asked what happened, gave the best answer: "I think he just went a little nuts."

Maybe, then, humans and whales are joined. Both Ahab and Tilikum went "nuts" with tragic outcomes.

CHAPTER 117
The Whale-Watch

AHAB AND FEDALLAH DISCUSS MORTALITY AND IMMORTALITY

What Ahab—"with a laugh of derision"—says of himself is truer of *Moby-Dick*: "Immortal on land and on sea!"

We have seen how this novel has achieved greatness but is it, like so many works once deemed great, to be consigned someday to the dustbin of literature?

Were *Moby-Dick*, simply a literary classic taught in colleges and used in abridged versions in high schools, then its future might be dimmed. But the book thrives outside the confines of academe.

Survival depends upon adaptation. In an age of graphic depictions, *Moby-Dick* affords many possibilities. Consider the following. In 2002, Marvel (a major comic-book company) published a hardback, comic version of *Moby-Dick*, adapted by Roy Thomas and Pascal Alixe. Its glossy pages are alive with action and interest. When Ahab comes to the quarterdeck to address the crew, his glare is frightening; his facial features sometimes resemble those of Gregory Peck, while at other times Ahab evokes a wolfman, with sharp teeth and snarl. We can see the holes for his peg leg in the deck, but even more—rather than a smooth, shiny peg leg, Ahab's is flesh-colored and jagged with humps.

Will Eisner, with a long and distinguished career in comic books, produced, at eighty years of age, his own graphic novel version of *Moby-Dick*. He takes liberties, as he must, with the novel. His opening page has illustrations of a whaling ship and then of a great whale upending a whaleboat. The words on the page are: "It was a time when mighty whales swam the great oceans. They were valued for their oil and bone. So men in tall sailing ships roamed the seas to hunt them. But the whales were a fierce foe. And from the struggle between man and whale came stories of great adventure."

What follows, of course, is one of them, but it does not begin with Melville's famous opening words, "Call Me Ishmael." That is of little matter. Eisner's Ahab is a tall but stooped, commanding, animated presence, whose eyes shine with madness as he contemplates sweet revenge against the White Whale.

Neither comic book appreciates Melville's blasphemy. Kids will encounter that only in the full print version of the novel.

For those too young to read, there is the Japanese anime version of *Hakugei: Legend of the Moby Dick*. Shown first on Japanese television between 1997 and 1999, these programs are available on DVD, in Dolby stereo with English subtitles. They are enticing. Ahab is captain of a spaceship roaming the universe after Moby Dick, a beast that terrorizes a planet. Lucky is the name of the lad who, like Ishmael, signs on board for adventure with the intergalactic whale hunters. Even if the story only barely touches upon themes from the original *Moby-Dick*, the vibrant colors, captivating graphics and soundtrack will entrance. Perhaps too, in time, viewers of it will turn to Eisner and company before taking on Melville's volume.

More is in the offing, at the time of writing. Timor Bekmambetov is planning to direct a film adaptation of *Moby-Dick*, with screenplay by Adam Cooper and Ben Collage, for Universal Pictures. This film promises to bring the sensibility of a graphic novel to the large screen. The writers plan to depict Ahab as heroic rather than obsessed; Bekmambetov will apply his "frenetic" directing style to capture the chase and demise of the *Pequod* with a realism that is sure to both fascinate and disgust.

Writer Cooper sums up the essentials of this new production which desires to bring a new generation to the novel. "Our vision isn't your grandfather's Moby Dick. . . . This is an opportunity to take a timeless classic and capitalize on the advances in visual effects to tell what at its core is an action-adventure story."

Even if their film sinks, it attests to the immortality of the original.

CHAPTER 118

The Quadrant

AHAB CURSES SCIENCE AND TOSSES HIS QUADRANT OVERBOARD

Robert Pirsig's *Zen and the Art of Motorcycle Maintenance* (1974) is a modern version of *Moby-Dick*. Rather than taking to sea, Pirsig and Chris, his eleven-year-old son, ride a motorcycle across the United States. Each is hammered by fears, some of which will be realized on the journey into the expanse of the country and the crooked roads within their souls. Pirsig is both Ishmael, the teller of the tale, and Ahab, the fanatic in search of meaning. In this case, however, Pirsig's quest is for that all-important, symbolically laden, yet elusive thing that he calls "quality."

Pirsig is desperate to communicate his "metaphysics of quality" thesis—about meaning and value, about a foundation for the universe. It is a form of philosophical monism with a capital M. By dint of it, Pirsig once stated, "We gain a far better way of organizing our understanding of everything, from physics to religion. That gain is its own justification."

The value of this metaphysics goes well beyond philosophical explanation. Pirsig finds meaning everywhere. He is disdainful of those airy academics that dismiss the beautiful logic behind and within a motorcycle. There is a practical Zen in understanding the mechanism of the bike, in becoming masterful in keeping it humming to perfection and in becoming one with the machine. To gain such understanding and skill is to travel along the road of the "metaphysics of quality."

Alas, a ghost lurks in the machine of Pirsig's soul, one that pursues him vigorously. "Modern man has his ghosts and spirits, too, you know." Years before this motorcycle journey with his son, Pirsig had suffered a severe breakdown, which confined him by court order to a mental hospital. Phaedrus is his ghost, named after a figure in Plato; it is his former self, his earlier ideal of a classical, rationalist mind. This "evil spirit" sought to turn all the wonders of the world into a rational, limiting straitjacket. The Zen-oriented Pirsig now realizes that the romantic and the rational are but two parts that must be one, that are united as part of the "metaphysics of quality."

Ahab as "madness maddened" tosses into the ocean his quadrant, binding his fate to his feelings. It is a rash move, a rejection of scientific knowledge. Pirsig would, in his hard-won knowledge, scoff at this decision. Vision and mind, rationality and romance, are one; they serve and seek the identical end—quality. This is the sharp edge of Pirsig's harpoon of thought and being. But hovering on the horizon, forever frightening him—and his son who sees its manifestations in his dad's demeanor—is the ghost of the past, of the White Whale of rationality that almost chopped off his sanity years ago.

Pirsig has, perhaps, learned the lesson that eluded Ahab and that led to his demise. Speaking of his earlier self, Pirsig tells his son: "I knew a fellow once who spent all his whole life doing nothing but hunting for a ghost, and it was just a waste of time. So go to sleep."

Pleasant dreams?

CHAPTER 119

The Candles

DURING A TYPHOON, THE PHENOMENON OF "ST. ELMO'S FIRE" OCCURS

Hart Crane was besotted with drink and despair throughout the 1920s. Friends referred to him as "the Roaring Boy," laughing, crying, and drinking excessively. In the midst of a party, he would grow silent then rush to his room. A rumba would suddenly erupt from his phonograph, perhaps followed by Ravel's *Bolero*. Then Crane could be heard typing manically, stomping around. His "face brick-red, his eyes burning," Crane would explode out of his room and demand that someone read his just-composed lines. He would then exclaim to anyone nearby: "Isn't that the greatest poem ever written?"

During these years, he was achingly moving forward with his most important work, *The Bridge*, finally published in 1930. Like Melville's novel, Crane wanted his extended poem to swallow America whole—to capture its founding, to chronicle its settlement, to narrate its ravaging of Native Americans, to embrace its technology without materialism, and to build a bridge between the past and future, from pessimism to hope. Crane sought to write a love poem, mythical and symbolic, anchored in the hard ground of American reality yet reaching to the mythic heights of transcendent possibility.

The presence of *Moby-Dick* in *The Bridge* is powerful. In the first poem, "Ave Maria," Christopher Columbus is at sea. Crane's Columbus is an intrepid mariner like Ahab, wanting to conquer "space, chaos." But if Melville's Ahab is a man questing for knowledge, anxious to the point of madness to discover what lies behind the nature of things, Crane's Columbus is a man of powerful faith, assured in his religious affections. He imagines receiving a "greeting by the corposant," or holy body, "flamed it in a cloud / Urging through night our passage to the Chan."

Chapter 119 introduces the frightening corposants. Stubb remarks that he hopes "the corpusants [sic] have mercy on us all," as he witnesses amazing things on board the *Pequod* during the typhoon. Ahab is suddenly transfigured by the "white flame" or corposant of the phenomenon known as St. Elmo's fire. In this supernatural moment, he exclaims to the crew: "Look at it; mark it well; the white flame but lights the way to the White Whale."

Ahab stands, triumphant for the moment, "before the lofty tri-pointed trinity of flames." This is for Ahab a "sacramental" act. He is marked in various ways by the fire—by his earlier scar, his madness, and his soul. In effect, Ahab has made a pact with the Devil.

In contrast, Columbus's viewing of the "corposant" is a mark of direction and of the bright future of America. Crane's vision is about a richness of the spirit, a sense of redemption and unity. Although he has suffered greatly, Crane's Columbus is not monomaniacal like Ahab; he is not blind to all that does not fit into his own field of vision.

Section three of the poem, "Cutty Sark," takes the form of a self-described "fugue" devoted to Melville. Crane signals this by opening with a quote from Melville's Civil War poems *Battle Pieces* (1866): "O, the navies old and oaken / O, the Temeraire no more!" Here, Crane refers back to his take on Melville in "At Melville's Tomb." The French word *temeraire* means a reckless or foolhardy person, such as Ahab, or Melville when he was in his manic mode. The "Cutty Sark" section plays with the line uttered early by Ishmael in *Moby-Dick* about how "meditation and water are forever wedded." Thus, "Murmurs of Leviathan he spoke, / and rum was Plato in our heads."

The Melville encountered on these dream-like pages was once a whaling man, and he remains a "Democrat" to the core of his "bony hands." Crane's poem respects the tragic air that defined Melville but makes a leap into the arms of Whitman, his fellow singer of the promise of America and the potential for democracy in male love.

Crane was buoyed briefly when he received a Guggenheim Fellowship in 1931. Friends suggested that he consider spending his fellowship year in Mexico—writer Katherine Ann Porter was already living there, enjoying the culture and living well on a small budget. Crane had traveled throughout the 1920s, living briefly in Paris, vacationing and working in the Cayman Islands and on the Isle of Pines, off the coast of Cuba. During his sojourns in these places, Crane kept *Moby-Dick* and his "beloved Melville" near to hand. In 1927, during a particularly trying time, besieged by mosquitoes and the smoke of "a smudge fire going all the time," Crane found refuge in the text of *Moby-Dick*—"which I think saved my mind."

Melville and *Moby-Dick* could not save Hart Crane. During nearly two years in Mexico, Crane was battered by the harsh reviews of his poems, still embroiled in problematic relations with his mother, drowning himself in alcohol, undertaking new routes in his sexuality, and fearful of his declining poetic powers. Writing of Crane in 1931, Porter described him as knowingly "destroying himself." Crane "talked of suicide almost every day." Sometimes, he did more than talk about it. In April 1932, while living in Mexico, in the midst of a drinking spree, he consumed a bottle of mercurochrome in a frenzied attempt at suicide. His life at this time was complicated, to put it mildly. He was in love with Peggy Baird Cowley, estranged wife of his old friend, writer Malcolm Cowley. He and Peggy had been boon companions for over twelve years and their relationship, much to the surprise of both of them, had evolved into romance. Crane pronounced that he was "happy" in the relationship, but it was punctuated with bitter arguments and drinking binges. For a host of reasons, Crane and Peggy decided soon after his suicide attempt to return to the United States aboard the ship *Oriziba*.

After an argument with Peggy about a mixed-up rendezvous, a temper tantrum, and heavier drinking, Crane, in pajamas and coat, sauntered towards a railing on the ship. The *Oriziba* was then about ten miles off the coast of Florida, bound for New York City. At a few minutes before noon, witnesses described Crane taking his coat off and then carefully dropping himself overboard, rather than leaping. His body was never recovered.

There are Melvillean undertones to Crane's suicide. We know that Crane had read Melville's *White-Jacket* in 1926, finding it "delightful." Perhaps, also, in the back of his mind was the powerful description therein of the main character, White-Jacket, falling from the main top of the ship. For White-Jacket, and maybe for Crane, "Time seemed to stand still, and all the worlds seemed poised on their poles, as I fell, soul-becalmed, through the eddying whirl and swirl of the maelstrom air." When White-Jacket hits the water, he feels his death, but miraculously, a magical current "some fashionless form brushed my side" and he feels alive anew, soon to be "bounded up like a buoy" and rescued. The language in *White-Jacket* is strikingly similar to the way that Crane had described the sea in his "Voyages" poems. But there was to be no rescue or surcease for Crane.

Indeed, irony abounds in the very manner of Crane's violent demise. Upon hitting the water, one of two things happened to him. According to the captain of the ship—who in twenty-six years of command had never been inconvenienced by a suicide—either sharks got Crane or he was made into "mincemeat" by the ship's propellers. He was, in all probability sucked back under the ship because he was swallowed by the vortex—the vortex that had claimed Ahab and his crew now devoured Crane. Perhaps like Melville, in his own death, "the sea keeps" now Crane's "fabulous shadow."

CHAPTER 120

The Deck Towards the End of the First Night Watch

ANTICIPATION OF A STORM

The second shortest chapter in the novel.

A television actor and adman, John Moschitta Jr., in *Ten Classics in Ten Minutes*, fast-talks his way through the outlines of *Moby-Dick* in one minute. He ends, "And everybody dies . . . but the fish . . . and Ish."

For the shortest chapter, go to Chapter 122.

CHAPTER 121

Midnight—The Forecastle Bulwarks

ON A VERY NASTY NIGHT, STUBB AND FLASK TRY TO MAKE SENSE OF THINGS

"I wonder," Stubb inquires of Flask, "whether the world is anchored anywhere" A good question.

Perhaps, as Wittgenstein would have it, the world is anchored in language, but if so, then the world is hardly secure (see chapter 99).

Melville created a world of symbols in *Moby-Dick*, and into this world we voyage. No less than Ahab, we attempt to harpoon meaning, to attach ourselves to this great bulk of a volume, its white pages teeming with signifiers of something.

Frank Lentricchia, a well-known literary critic at Duke University, has spent a lifetime deciphering texts. A mercurial presence in the profession, he is known for his machismo persona (on the back cover of one book he is pictured with his beefy arms akimbo) and for his rejection of certain critical practices. In the evening of his career, he drifted away from criticism (at least in its traditional form) towards fiction. Fiction is now the ship that carries his critical insights.

Thomas Lucchesi, the protagonist of Lentricchia's novel *Lucchesi and the Whale*, is a novelist, of sorts. He has published in his career one five-page story in *The Salvador Dali Bulletin*. He employs there the names of his parents in what is to them an embarrassing tale of sexual intimacy and the eroticization of various work tools! In contrast with Melville, whose rat's hole of a writer's den was "cushioned with thousands of pages," Lucchesi's is strewn with blank pages. At best, Lucchesi is an "obscure American novelist," and so he will remain.

He teaches an occasional course at the local college, his last being a seminar on *Moby-Dick*. One day, Lucchesi tells his class that, "I was, and continue to be, terminally sick of myself. Nevertheless, while at home, I managed to bulldoze my way joyfully through a seventh draft of my experimental novel." He next holds up the "fat text of *Moby-Dick*," which "he waved high overhead, and screamed, 'I have no idea what this is. Do you? Answer me! I AM AFRAID! I AM AFRAID OF THIS COCKSUCKER!!'" This tirade results in his being dropped from the ranks of teachers at Central College.

But Lucchesi, or Lentricchia, is then freed to chase after the meaning of *Moby-Dick*. It is a wild journey into an unanchored world.

Lucchesi reflects on the life of Herman Melville, on the utter significance of his being cast adrift in the world at the age of twelve with the death of his father. He is—like Ishmael—the "abandoned son" of an "immortally problematic father." Add to this an "emotionally remote mother" and you have the potential for an artist, attempting in fiction to make a hard and secure foundation for his own life.

We can, through Lucchesi, hear Lentricchia's voice, as the esteemed professor of literature, working through the possible meanings of *Moby-Dick*. At one point, thirty-six possible meanings for the White Whale are offered, ranging from "the Devil" to "phallic aggressor" to "pastoral ideal: pulled out in buckets, his oil bubbles 'like a dairy-maid's pail of new milk'" to "God" to "the nothing beneath everything" to "a thing of countless names" to a "dead, blind wall." Not a bad list from Mr. Lucchesi.

Modifications are in order, as the White Whale's meaning begins to solidify (in a manner of speaking):

> "So: The White Whale is"
> "a loss of depth;
> a gain of a world of infinite surfaces, captured in
>   verbal reflections: ultimate superficiality;
> end of theology and metaphysics;
> beginning of a new kind of literature;
> despair of nihilism;
> vitality of affirmation;
> the vital yes of literary passion;
> incidentally, the destroyer of the Pequod and all her crew
>   but one. (The mere White Whale of the story.)"

Lucchesi jumps into the nature of things and Melville's novel. *Moby-Dick* is an "Antistory," a vehicle for Melville's torrents of creativity. The truth is not in the narrative, as such, but in the riffs. It is a monument to "the joy of the analogical leap itself." It is about Melville's art, his upholding of "The mortal yes of metaphor against the metaphysics of nihilism."

Thus, the book's "antistory" is its essence, its creative core without end, since "Analogical writing, in the hands of this infidel, unlike story, can have no ends."

We are, again, in an unanchored world—and we are the better for it, at least according to Mr. Lucchesi.

CHAPTER 122

Midnight Aloft—Thunder and Lightning

TASHTEGO, THE NATIVE-AMERICAN HARPOONER, LABORS HIGH UP ON THE TOP MAST WHILE THUNDER RESOUNDS AROUND HIM

The shortest chapter in the novel. From the London *Telegraph* tweet contest (140 characters or less): "Bloke goes bonkers pursuing large white whale across oceans and ends up harpooned to its side. Moral: don't become a fisherman."

CHAPTER 123

The Musket

IN AHAB'S CABIN, STARBUCK HOLDS A MUSKET

No character frustrates more than Starbuck. We know that he is "an honest, upright man," someone ready to do battle with any impediments that cross his path when they interfere with his livelihood. But he realizes that Ahab is mad and that "if Ahab have his way" then "deadly harm" will befall him and the entire crew.

He stands in Ahab's cabin with the "death-tube" musket in his hands while Ahab sleeps. Starbuck imagines surviving this voyage, returning home to "hug his wife and child again.—Oh Mary! Mary!—boy! boy!" Aim and pull the trigger, Mr. Starbuck—this is your only opportunity to have that reunion.

Yet Starbuck places the musket back in the rack and returns to the deck; his fate is now entwined with that of Ahab.

Why does the stalwart Starbuck fail at this task? In the 1956 film version, the correctness of his revolt is strongly suggested. According to the contract under which the *Pequod* sails, when the captain is either indisposed (in this case insanity) or when the captain fails in his task (to hunt whales for profit), then it is proper to unseat him. Mutiny, alas, leaves a bad taste in Starbuck's mouth. Better to die than to mutiny?

Melville was, in no small manner, a social psychologist of the highest order. He understood that Ahab's rule rested on more than simply the power of his office, strong though that be. Ahab periodically reinforces his anointed status as leader with triumphant orations and monetary bribes. This works to bind most of the crew to him. Ahab's siren songs are, however, ill pitched to Starbuck's ears.

Perhaps we are too hard on poor Starbuck. Mutiny is serious business. But at the core of his plight is a lesson that has come to light in the last half century with a bloodcurdling scream. People follow orders; they crave authority. Social psychologist Erich Fromm, writing with the hot breath of Nazism near to him, concluded that most people want an "escape from freedom," for freedom is difficult. Responsibility for one's own actions is too heavy a burden to bear. In part, this is what makes totalitarian leaders—Hitler, Stalin, and Ahab—appealing. They provide symbolic opponents and join isolated individuals in a heroic quest, even if that voyage leads to failure and death.

Consider, as well, the famous Milgram experiments in the early 1960s. A social psychologist at Yale University, Stanley Milgram devised a clever set of tests to gauge whether or not subjects would follow orders. Subjects, none with any previous proclivity to violence, were asked to administer shocks, in escalating intensity (up to 450 volts), to a person in a room, whenever that person failed to properly answer a question. Note, the person in the room, in point of fact, was an actor but the screams of anguish sounded genuine. The subjects believed, then, that they were causing harm, perhaps even death. But when the authority figure intoned that the experiment must continue, that the subject was not responsible, over sixty percent of them went on with the experiment.

Starbuck is our modern Milgram subject, bowing to authority, even when he knows better. Melville comprehended the power of authority, and it made him queasy, both on sea and on land.

Figure 27.
Commander Charles Wilkes, a possible model for Captain Ahab. Frontispiece from *Narrative of the U.S. Exploring Expedition* (1845).

CHAPTER 124

The Needle

AHAB PREPARES FOR HIS ACCOUNTING WITH THE WHITE WHALE

Ahab, we are told, stands apart, a man of "magnetic energy" and "fatal pride." The question returns: from whence did this larger-than-life figure spring in Melville's mind? Is he pure invention or might he be based upon some contemporary of Melville's?

Speculation abounds. While many answers have been tendered, David Jaffé's explanation is compelling. He argues that Ahab is modeled upon Lieutenant Charles Wilkes, commander of the U.S. Exploring Expedition. The expedition grew out of America's increasing confidence in itself as a maritime power in the early nineteenth century. The charge to the expedition was monumental in its scope: to crisscross the Pacific, to explore the Antarctic regions, to draw up charts and maps, and to collect specimens of all types for further study. And, of course, to plant the American flag in hitherto unexplored regions.

Despite grave challenges, the expedition was a huge success. Composed of a squadron of six vessels, with 346 men, and nine artists and scientists (some quite distinguished), they left Norfolk Navy Yard on August 19, 1838, not to return to New York until June 1842. During the long voyage, the group traversed over 87,000 miles of sea, surveyed 280 Pacific Islands, braved icebergs to explore Antarctica, and did much more. A 1,900-mile section of the Antarctic coast is still named for the expedition's captain, Wilkes Land.

Wilkes was a man unhinged. He drove his men relentlessly, often summoning the whip to keep them in line. Officers were summarily dismissed and humiliated. A rather inexperienced sailor, Wilkes made many mistakes and was unwilling to rely on the judgments of better mariners. He also ordered the destruction of villages and the unnecessary killing of Pacific Islanders. The list of his problems piled up during the cruise and upon his return, many of his officers, present and past, brought charges against him. He was found guilty of unnecessary punishment of crewmen.

As ordered by Congressional mandate, Wilkes prepared an account of his travels. Published initially in six volumes in 1844 (with another nineteen to come until completed in 1875), the *Narrative of the U.S. Exploring Expedition, 1838–1842* has much fascinating material in its 2,500 pages.

We know, as Jaffé points out, that while composing *Moby-Dick*, Melville had the initial volumes near to hand.

A glance at a frontispiece engraving of Wilkes contained in one of the volumes initiates the line of comparisons between him and Ahab. Ahab's visage is marred by a scar that begins on his face, extending down the length of his body. It is described by Melville as akin to a mark of "crucifixion." While Wilkes had no such defining mark upon his face, the engraving of him that Melville viewed does show what looks to be a scar extending from his forehead down to near his chin. Jaffé thus hypothesizes that Melville might have hit upon at least one aspect of Ahab's mien through Wilkes's portrait.

By all accounts, Wilkes was a tragically flawed individual. Brilliant and energetic, he was also petty and fanatical. He earned the nickname "the Stormy Petrel." In his willingness to risk the life and limb of his crew, to destroy his ships by navigating through treacherous waters and icebergs in order to gain his place in the annals of discovery, Wilkes's affinity with Ahab's monomania with the whale is palpable. Of course, it must be noted, Wilkes's dash to claim the white-capped Antarctic summons forth images of the White Whale, with its "snowy dome."

Both Ahab and Wilkes as young children lost their mothers, each of them was married for twelve years at the time of their respective voyages, and each of them left behind a young child. Melville's connection with Wilkes, Jaffé further relates, is that both men had fathers who were New York City businessmen, their families lived in the same neighborhood, and they also had relatives in Albany.

Does this pin the tail on the donkey of Ahab's identity? No, but it does tantalize us with a precursor figure who shared Ahab's monomania. Except in the case of Wilkes, he lived to tell his own tale.

CHAPTER 125

The Log and Line

AHAB REMAINS FIXED IN HIS GOALS AND MADNESS

Ahab is a man with a mission, and neither the pleas of Starbuck nor the frustrations of the chase can deter him from it. One of the only times that he exhibits a hint of humanity comes in this chapter, when he takes mad

Pip to his cabin. This wave of emotional connection soon breaks, leaving nothing of note in its wake.

Ahab says to Pip, "Come! I feel prouder leading thee by thy black hand, than though I grasped an Emperor's!" This is quite an admission, one that can be said to show Melville's essential democratic sentiments, his willingness to see the humanity of others. It is also more. The line is a reworking of what King Lear says to the Fool in act 3, scene 4, in the midst of a frightening storm: "In, boy; go first. You houseless poverty / Nay, get thee in."

Both Ahab and Lear have their madness, yet they can be humane towards the fool. But what is the connection between Melville and Shakespeare? We know that Melville in 1847 procured a copy of Shakespeare, *The Dramatic Works of William Shakespeare*, published in seven volumes. The work astonished him, "I have been passing my time very pleasurably here, But chiefly lounging on a sofa . . . & reading Shakespeare." He found the Bard "inspired," and he exulted over every page. Shakespeare's works were certainly known to him prior to this excited reading; indeed, the plays were a staple in the American consciousness of the nineteenth century. In printed form, with large type, Melville could read the plays more easily, and they engaged him with irresistible vigor.

The first person to make central the importance of Melville's reading of Shakespeare to his work, *Moby-Dick* in particular, was Charles Olson. We have already come upon the energetic Mr. Olson (see chapter 76). The first piece that he published on the subject appeared in the avant-garde journal *Twice-a-Year* in 1938, and it was titled simply "Lear and Moby-Dick."

In this path-breaking article, Olson claimed that Melville's reading of Shakespeare's plays in general, and in particular of *King Lear*, had "precipitated" or been a "catalytic agent" for *Moby-Dick*. In fact, "Melville and Shakespeare melted together . . . and *Moby-Dick* was the result." It was a case of one genius reading another.

Olson scouted down Melville's copies of Shakespeare's plays, and he carefully deciphered and read the cramped handwriting of Melville's marginalia. The first fruits of Melville's encounter resulted in his essay "Hawthorne and His Mosses" (1850), where he praised Shakespeare as one of the great truthtellers and "profoundest of thinkers," specifically referring to *King Lear* as a work in which "Lear the frantic King tears off the mask, and speaks the same madness of vital truth." Within a year, Melville was presenting Ahab, his mad King of the Sea, who is seeking "the same madness of vital truth."

In the 1938 piece, Olson focused on the impact of *Lear* on Melville and *Moby-Dick*. He remarked that Melville's copy of the play was marked with more notations than any other play, except for *Antony and Cleopatra*. *Lear* is a tragedy that surrounds its themes of madness, evil, treachery, and human relations. It is, of course, about the aged, mad King Lear, who conjures up a world of illusion. How different is Lear, in Olson's estimation, than Ahab who "conjures up his own evil world. He himself uses black magic to achieve his vengeful ends. With the very words 'in nomine diaboli' he believes he utters a Spell and performs a Rite of such magic."

The illusions of both men numb their feelings and focus their madness. Such illusions, in the end, result in their humbling and death.

CHAPTER 126

The Life-Buoy

THE *PEQUOD* FINDS ITSELF IN NEED OF A LIFE BUOY

The name Coffin pops up occasionally in *Moby-Dick*. The proprietor of the Spouter-Inn, where Ishmael spends his first evening in New Bedford, is one Peter Coffin. The name, as Ishmael remarks, is rather "ominous in that particular connection." Indeed it is, as he reasons correctly, a name quite common in Nantucket, and he pays it little mind.

Ships that sail in dangerous waters, either in times of war or pursuit of perilous adventures, are called floating coffins. The designation applied most powerfully to slave ships that traversed the Atlantic with horrible conditions and passengers chained together in the hold.

Artist Zineb Sedira has a video-art installation called *Floating Coffins*. The video opens with a rusty tanker ship. The angle of vision makes it impossible to determine if the ship is rotting away on land or anchored nearby. Subsequent images detail the waste and pollution that the artist associates with these whales of a vessel, decaying monuments to avaricious consumerism and world trade.

You may recall in chapter 110, "Queequeg in His Coffin," that aboard the *Pequod* a coffin is built, which Queequeg intended to hold him. But he rallies from his sickness and the highly decorated coffin is forgotten. At least until this chapter. The *Pequod*, in its chase after Moby Dick, has lost its life-buoy, along with a man who "was swallowed up in the deep." Starbuck is directed to get a replacement for the buoy. He is stopped by Queequeg who, with "certain strange signs and innuendoes" gives a hint that his own coffin might serve such a purpose.

"'A life-buoy of a coffin!' cried Starbuck, starting." Stubb agrees, announcing it "Rather queer."

As a thrifty New Englander, Starbuck warms to the idea and, thanks to the help of the ship's carpenter, the coffin is transformed into a buoy. You can be certain that on this ship destined for hell, it will be employed.

CHAPTER 127

The Deck

AHAB ASKS THE CARPENTER, "FAITH? WHAT'S THAT?"

An intriguing religious analysis of *Moby-Dick* came from poet W. H. Auden. Ahab represented for Auden a tragic hero, of the Christian type. Both Ahab and Ishmael take to the sea, which for Auden captured "that state of barbaric vagueness and disorder out of which civilisation has emerged." It is the space of the primitive into which modern civilization is always on the verge of relapsing.

Auden had been interested in Melville since the 1930s. In a poem, "Herman Melville" (1939), which evokes Crane's earlier poetic vision of Melville at rest at the end of his life, Auden spoke directly to his dangerous age. "Evil is unspectacular and always human," he wrote while war began to rage in Europe. Melville had seen evil, and he had also experienced the good. He understood this universe and its duality, and he presented it in *Billy Budd* with Captain Vere's imposing the death sentence on the stammering sailor. "Even the punishment was human and a form of love." Entrenched in his experiences and bearing his burdens, Melville chose to produce art, "And sat down at his desk and wrote a story."

Auden considered *Moby-Dick* at length in the years immediately after the Second World War. He was obviously engorged with the horrors that had just occurred. At the same time, he had moved away from his earlier Communist commitments to a Christian belief system, one heavily inflected with Kierkegaardian despair. As with everything that Auden touched, his own particular sensibilities penetrated to the core of the matter. Ahab was not mistaken so much in viewing the whale as a symbol of what was wrong in the world, even as a stand-in for the deity. In fact, this ability to universalize is what constituted Ahab's greatness. He erred, however, when he began to narrow his vision, to rest behind the view that "all suffering is personal malevolence." Ahab chooses his own death.

Auden gets to his key reversal after a less than successful comparison of Ishmael with Don Quixote as fellow romantic heroes, because they are both solitary, wandering men, rejected by the world, and unhappy failures in love. Ishmael is a hero because he is alone on a voyage of discovery. Most of the men sign up simply for wages. Ahab is intent on revenge, or on finding and killing the whale of his fevered imagination. Thus, there is no discovery for Ahab, only a reflection of his own maddened consciousness. In contrast, Ishmael is the "recording consciousness," the man who is tested in various ways early in the novel.

We do not normally think of Ishmael as being tested. But Auden asserts that when Ishmael accepts Queequeg, once a cannibal, he passes his first test. He is able to accept others without fitting them into simplistic categories. By his love for Queequeg, he "proves himself worthy of the voyage." Another test arises from Ishmael's relation to Father Mapple's sermon. Auden sees the sermon, revolving around the story of Jonah, as in large part about a man who flees from God and society, or who believes that he can do so. To a degree, Ishmael is doing the same by taking to the sea.

For Auden, the sea voyage traditionally "signifies the exploration of the self and the world, of potential essences." What our hero Ishmael finds is "neither evil nor good but simply numinous, a declaration of the power and majesty of God which transcends any human standards of ethics." Here Auden is transposing Kierkegaard's take on Abraham's willingness to sacrifice his only son Isaac at God's behest. That he is willing to do so, even if it flaunts every traditional and rational law, is a testament to the necessary absurdity of faith. Abraham is rewarded and Isaac is saved. By coming to accept God's mysterious power, in Auden's interpretation, Ishmael "the spectator" survives to become "a baby reborn."

CHAPTER 128

The *Pequod* Meets the *Rachel*

THE *RACHEL* REQUESTS AHAB'S HELP. HE REFUSES

The next to last ship the *Pequod* meets is the *Rachel*. The *Rachel* has no interest in a pleasant gam. Her captain's son, along with several other seamen, has been lost at sea. His request to Ahab is simple: join him in his search for the boy. Noticing how "icily" Ahab had "received his petition," he seeks to charter the *Pequod* and its crew to aid in the search. These are plaintive and reasonable requests, ones that any captain would be bound by duty and humanity to honor.

Yet, Ahab "stood like an anvil, receiving every shock, but without the least quivering of his own."

The captain of the *Rachel* is incredulous, swearing that he will not leave until Ahab helps him. He knows that Ahab has a son "nestling safely at home." How could Ahab fail to understand the plight of a father? Ahab, alas, is beyond the heartstrings of humanity and fellowship. His internal gyroscope refuses to waver from its purpose. He must drive on after the White Whale to exact his recompense and meaning. He orders Starbuck to allow the *Pequod* to "sail as before." As the *Pequod* distances itself from the *Rachel*, the latter ship, sprayed by the sea, appears to be "weeping for her children."

Melville illustrates in this chapter the depths of his monomania and distance from common humanity. But he is also, in effect, raising a key question in moral philosophy. When is it proper for someone to refuse to help another in distress? How wide is the circle of our fellowship when it comes to such aid?

Clearly, Ahab is drawing that circle in the narrowest of ways. Are we ever justified in allowing someone else to perish because of our own narrow bonds of fellowship and connection? Interestingly enough, this vexing philosophical problem is often presented by way of a story about drowning.

One fine day, a vigorous man walks the countryside. He hears screams coming from a deep pond nearby. He sees two lads drowning, and he knows that he can save only one of them. He dives in and swims toward one of the boys, pulling him to the shore. The other boy drowns. The lad that he has saved is his child, and the conclusion to this story is clear: we draw the lines of our circle of compassion most strongly around those to whom we are closest. This is neither surprising nor morally problematic.

The upshot of this moral tale is simple, too. While we begin to draw the circle narrowly, to be fully moral and responsive to the world at large we need to draw its lines more expansively. It would have been immoral for that father, if he could have accomplished it, not to have saved the other child.

Part of the tragedy of Ahab is that he has cordoned himself off from others. This allows him to chew the cud of his mania—it will rob his shipmates, with but one exception, of their lives. For all of his heroism and desire to grasp the meaning that he associates with the White Whale, Ahab is a moral monster of the highest order.

CHAPTER 129

The Cabin

THE BOND BETWEEN AHAB AND PIP IS TIED BY THEIR MADNESS

Recall that Pip has gone mad. Abandoned by Stubb's whaling boat, bobbing in the ocean, descending at one point to its greater depths, he has apparently seen things that have shocked him silly. He refers to his "drowned bones [that] now show white, for all the blackness of his living skin."

Pip and Ahab are linked by their madness, a bond that Ahab recognizes and that tugs at his heart. Pip's experience of abandonment in the sea has bequeathed him a gentle madness. Ahab's madness is fierce and unyielding. They are two sides of a similar coin—one needing to find meaning, the other having found it.

Charles Johnson, an immensely talented and philosophically erudite novelist, is but one of the many writers who have been inspired by Melville. In *Middle Passage* (1990), he plays on themes in both *Moby-Dick* and "Benito Cereno." It is a complex story about one Rutherford Calhoun, a free black who finds himself unable to avoid various forms of enslavement. He ends up on a ship that is carrying African slaves, along with a more mysterious and valuable cargo. Like the journey of the *Pequod*, his ship, the *Republic*, is doomed—its sailors mutiny against Captain Falcon (a dwarf with a massive, well-earned paranoia) while the slaves rebel against both the captain and his crew. Freedom, however, does not bring salvation, for the ship is in dire circumstances, the survivors are forced into cannibalism, and the boat finally sinks. Rutherford and a few others survive to tell the tale.

One of the most powerfully drawn episodes mimics the experience of Pip. A mysterious cargo crate has been brought onto the ship. The mad captain has big plans for "the thing" that lives in the crate, and he alone feeds it. The crew of the *Republic* speculates about the contents of the crate, much as the crew of the *Pequod* had ventured opinions about the meaning of the images on the gold doubloon that Ahab hammered to the mast. One thinks it "the Missing Link between man and monkey"; another contends that "it was most probably a nearly extinct lizard, maybe intelligent." One suggests that it is something "fallen from the sky" centuries ago.

Whatever it is, the crew's curiosity has been stoked to a fevered pitch. They draw lots to choose which of them will be lowered down to open up the crate and peer inside it to determine its content. Tommy O'Toole, the white cabin boy, draws the short lot, with dire consequences.

The rope around his waist breaks, and Tommy spends ten minutes in the crate. When he finally emerges, he is with "only half his mind." Listen to the echoes of Melville as Johnson describes Tommy: "His skin was cold, all one bluish color as if he had been baptized in the Deep. . . . His eyes glowed like deck lights, less solid orbs of color, if you saw them up close, than splinters of luciferin indigo that, like an emulsion, had caught the camphor of a blaze once before them."

And what is it he has seen? As best as the first mate can discern from Tommy's maddened mind, he had confronted something "which did not so much occupy a place as it bent space and time around itself like a greatcoat." The "creature's defecation" was all about, in "dark coils . . . slithering with insects, worms, and sluglike beings that apparently lived inside its bowels." The creature "scritching its nails on the walls, muttering to itself like a devil chained inside a mountain for a thousand years, its voice gently syllabled and honeyed, as sacramental as a siren's, or peradventure its very breathing was a chant so full of love and werelight, vatic lament and Vedic sorrow."

Tommy can barely breath in its presence, he cannot even recall his purpose in being in the crate. But the experience has transformed him, even if he cannot put his trembling finger upon its meaning. The crew are unenlightened by his attempt at explanation. As one sailor remarks, "It eats people, that's what it eats." Another sailor says, "Saints preserve us." But, "[a]ll could see the ship's boy would never come about. He was lost to us."

The meaning of the mystery remains huddled with madness. Pip and Tommy, each in his own manner, have discerned what Ahab desperately desires—entry into the mystery of the nature of things. The riddle, alas, is that while one can come face to face with that meaning, its mastery remains—it renders its viewer mad, without language to communicate its essentials.

Perhaps that is the tragedy of Ahab. He hungers not just for revenge about a lost limb but for a deeper penetration of the meaning of life, to return—via the whale—to the Garden of Eden, before the Fall, before the intimate relationship between man and things was ripped asunder; before language became our ship taking us both towards and away from the objects of the world and its meaning. Or, perhaps, the meaning of such confrontations with the abyss—as Pip and Tommy O'Toole have both learned—is that there is nothing there, other than the horror of nothingness. The Whiteness of the Whale blinds us to the blackness of being.

CHAPTER 130

The Hat

AHAB REMAINS ON DECK SEARCHING FOR MOBY DICK

We saw that Melville modeled some aspects of Ahab upon Lieutenant Charles Wilkes, who was also, in equal parts, blessed with "magnetic energy" and damned by "fatal pride" (see chapter 124).

Other figures from the hyperventilated politics of mid-nineteenth-century America might also have served as models for Ahab. For example, William Lloyd Garrison.

Garrison emerged in the 1830s as one of the nation's leading abolitionists. He was uncompromising in his antislavery sentiments, rejecting politics—the art of compromise and negotiation—as trafficking with evil. He burned the United States Constitution because it sanctioned slavery, calling it in 1844 "a Covenant with Death, an Agreement with Hell." He refused to bow to religious authority; it had cozied up to the evil forces of slavery. Everywhere he looked, he found examples of the slave power conspiracy working to defend its evil institution and to spread its influence further.

He famously intoned in his journal, *The Liberator*, "I am aware that many object to the severity of my language; but is there not cause for severity? I will be as harsh as truth, and as uncompromising as justice. On this subject, I do not wish to think, or speak, or write, with moderation. No! No! Tell a man whose house is on fire to give a moderate alarm; tell him to moderately rescue his wife from the hands of the ravisher; tell the mother to gradually extricate her babe from the fire into which it has fallen;—but urge me not to use moderation in a cause like the present! I am in earnest—I will not equivocate—I will not excuse—I will not retreat a single inch—AND I WILL BE HEARD."

Better to bring on the apocalypse of the Civil War than to continue to compromise with the evil of slavery. Yes, Garrison does have affinities with the character of Ahab.

Might Ahab's monomaniacal desire to strike the harpoon into the pure white body and symbolism of Moby Dick signal a further connection with Garrison? Might Ahab/Garrison be attempting to strike at the whale as symbolic of the slave power conspiracy? Might the killing of this White Whale further suggest the freeing of blacks from their inhumane chains of oppression? The *Pequod*, after all, carries a crew of various nationalities (thirty "isolatoes" who are "federated along one keel"), and Ahab/Garrison's solicitude is greatest for that poor boy Pip, who had been abandoned.

Or might Melville, despite his democratic sentiments, be wary of the fanaticism of Ahab/Garrison? His single-minded devotion to killing the White Whale promises disaster—the sinking of the American ship of state in a vortex of violence that was realized in the Civil War.

Some scholars have nominated John C. Calhoun, the proslavery senator from South Carolina, as a likely model for Ahab. Calhoun's physical description certainly resembles that of Ahab. In the words of English visitor Harriet Martineau, Calhoun was "the cast-iron man, who looks as if he had never been born, and could never be extinguished." Henry Clay described Calhoun as "Tall, careworn, with furrowed brow, haggard, and intensely gazing." His eyes were "magnetic" and mesmerizing. He was also prone to being "deeply gullied by intense thought." He was, like Ahab, regarded as blessed, or damned, with an "indomitable will."

Calhoun directed that "indomitable will" to defend slavery. With pride, paranoia, and monomania, he railed against all hints that slavery must be ended or contained. He supported American imperial plans and manifest destiny, seeing them as extending the reach of slavery and furthering the ends of American greatness.

Whether Ahab be akin to the abolitionist Garrison or the slavery-intoxicated Calhoun, the upshot of the tale, if read as political allegory, is clear: the American ship of state is headed into dangerous waters, and fate seems to have decreed its end, thanks to its uncompromising relationship to the purity of its whiteness.

CHAPTER 131

The *Pequod* Meets the *Delight*

PREMONITIONS OF THE ACCOUNTING SOON TO COME WITH MOBY DICK

On a clear but terrible September morning in 2001, two passenger planes hijacked by terrorists reduced the buildings of the World Trade Center to rubble and robbed nearly 3,000 people of their lives. While embers from the massive destruction continued to burn, rhetoric about the attack increasingly grew inflamed.

Edward Said, a well-known professor of comparative literature at Columbia University, about three miles north of the site of many deaths, and an impassioned advocate for the Palestinian cause, turned to the text of *Moby-Dick* to illumine this dark passage in American history. President George W. Bush and much of the American population in the wake of this tragedy, according to Said, were allowing their "collective passions" to drive them in a manic and dangerous quest for revenge, quite in the fashion that had driven Ahab to his demise.

Furthermore, Said remarked that the architect of the attack, Osama bin Laden, had emerged as the White Whale of the American consciousness, endowed with evil and symbolism. While Said never condoned the terrorist attack upon civilian targets, he desperately sought to convince Americans to view it as an understandable, if wrong-headed, response to American imperialism and policies in the Middle East over the last half-century. He focused on the destruction in the offing for Afghanistan and the Muslim world at the hands of the American military leviathan.

If one reads *Moby-Dick* as a tale of monomaniacal Ahab out for revenge (against an innocent enemy) and the *Pequod* as representative of America in the years prior to the conflagration of the Civil War, then additional meanings for the novel emerge. The American post-9/11 tendency to see the complexities of the world in manichaean simplicity, with the forces of good versus evil arrayed, foretells, as it had in the novel, the sinking of the American leviathan. Thus America would become a victim of its self-righteousness, its belief in its mission, and its unwillingness to examine itself critically. In "this hand," America seemed to "hold death."

Almost precisely 150 years after their birth in November 1851, Captain Ahab and Moby Dick were not only deemed relevant but critical as analogical devices to better comprehend the new world inaugurated from the flames of 9/11.

Do not think that references to the characters in *Moby-Dick* were limited only to this horror or to the public imagination of a Columbia professor of literature. Anthony Lewis, in the *New York Times* had years earlier likened President Ronald Reagan to "a political Ahab" in his quest to destroy the Moby Dick of the Sandinista government in Nicaragua. The distinguished American scholar Arthur M. Schlesinger, also writing in the *Times*, described prosecutor Kenneth Starr as driven by "Ahab's monomaniacal 'quenchless feud' with the White Whale." Except that in this case, Ahab/Starr's sights were set on bringing down the presidency of Bill Clinton. One final example: Karl Rove, the mastermind behind many of George W. Bush's political victories, referred to himself as Moby Dick because a handful of Democratic-Ahab members of congress were out for revenge against him.

CHAPTER 132
The Symphony

AHAB AND STARBUCK ESTABLISH SOME HUMAN CONTACT WITH ONE ANOTHER

Ahab, for the only time in the voyage, reflects about his marriage. "I widowed that poor girl when I married her," he says. A few moments later, Ahab imagines home, "I see my wife and my child in thine eye." This moment of weakness is quickly squelched; Ahab must pursue his final accounting with the whale.

As we saw earlier (chapter 114), it is exciting to imagine who Ahab had married—for novelist Sena Jeter Naslund it is a young woman who is fully his equal in intellect and adventurous spirit.

But what of Ahab's son—what are we to make of him?

Christian novelist Louise M. Gouge has written three volumes about Ahab's wife and son. Hannah Rose is an independent-minded young woman. She and Ahab fall for one another instantly; she finds him "the most magnificent man." Her liberal religion is sufficiently expansive to accept his godlessness. He worries that "such a delicate rose [might] cease to bloom in my savage garden." No, opines Hannah Rose, "mighty Caesar will find his equal in Cleopatra."

You can imagine much of the rest. Their lovefest is interrupted when Ahab returns home from a whaling voyage, "dismasted and transformed." With revenge-soaked mind, Ahab goes off again to the sea, with results that are tragic and familiar.

Hannah Rose is soon a widow, left with a young son named Timothy, who has his father's dark eyes. The young boy is mocked by his fellows because the Ahab name is infamous. The mother changes the family name to Jacobs. She seeks a conventional life but is, after much soul-searching and circumstance, drawn into helping runaway slaves evade enforcement of the Fugitive Slave Act.

Let's forget about the story of the mother and look at the son, for he possesses more than his father's eyes. Will he realize his mother's nightmare and take to the sea that claimed his father? The boy, she realizes, also has his father's pride and "dark Ahab brow."

Actually, things grow complicated. Although he is haunted a bit by his father, Timothy is an upright, honest, and caring young man. He does, however, have a sworn enemy—Isaiah Starbuck. Yes, the son of Ahab's first mate. Young Starbuck believes that the sins of the father are heaped upon the son, and his hatred for Timothy is immense. They end up midshipmen at the Naval Academy at Annapolis in the years before the Civil War. Isaiah, for a host of reasons, gets in trouble but unbeknown to him, Timothy bails him out. Finally, Isaiah learns that his benefactor all along, behind the scenes, has been Timothy, the son of Ahab. This shock of recognition occurs while they are aboard ship together, fighting for the Union in the Civil War. Isaiah goes up to the deck to beg Timothy's forgiveness.

Alas, before he can do so, Timothy realizes that Isaiah is in mortal danger and pushes him to safety away from an incoming shell. Guess what? Timothy loses his right leg and his face is scarred, just like his father's had been! Isaiah now cares for the recovering Timothy, but his pleas for forgiveness are spurned, for Timothy's heart has grown cold and mean. He breaks off his engagement with Jemima Starbuck—yes, the sister of Isaiah. He must get as far inland, away from the curse of the father and the dangers of the sea as he can.

Let's rush to the conclusion of this tale. As you might imagine, it has a happy ending, one bathed in redemption. Once recovered, Timothy flees to the farm of relatives in Indiana, where he had spent some happy days as a child. But the past is never far away. Starbuck comes anew to try to reconcile. Timothy rejects him once more. He finally, after years of refusal, reads Ishmael's book, *Moby-Dick* and realizes that his father was mad with arrogance and pride against God. This is where he went wrong. Timothy acknowledges that he need not reenact the sins of his father; he now understands that God is love and forgiveness. In no time, he returns to Boston, marries Jemima, and becomes a loving husband, father, and a valued citizen.

Moby-Dick, for the son of Ahab, is a tale of redemption and love.

CHAPTER 133

The Chase—First Day

AHAB ENCOUNTERS THE WHITE WHALE, WITH LESS THAN SUCCESSFUL RESULTS

Ahab finally gets his rematch with Moby Dick. The first round goes poorly for him. Noticing Moby coming up from the depths of the ocean, Ahab rapidly maneuvers his small boat. Sensing this, the whale with his "malicious intelligence" manages to recalibrate and emerges, with jaw agape and teeth flashing, mowing through the boat. Ahab survives but clearly the victory that day belongs to the White Whale.

On September 21, 1955, Archie Moore and Rocky Marciano faced off for the Heavyweight Championship of the World at Yankee Stadium. Moore, known as "the Old Mongoose" for his wily style of fighting, was forty-two years old, rather advanced for a professional fighter. But he was not over the hill. Marciano, then thirty-one years old, was the undefeated champion, a force of nature with a fighting style that was relentlessly straightforward. He possessed devastating power, especially in his right hand.

A. J. Liebling covered the fight for the popular magazine, the *New Yorker*. A gourmand and fan of boxing and horseracing, Liebling was also a prose stylist of the highest order. He titled his account of the match "Ahab and Nemesis," with Marciano as the White Whale and Moore as Ahab. To a degree, the references were apt. Marciano's raw power was mighty; he had up to that point vanquished forty-eight opponents, almost all of them by knockout. He was born in Brockton, Massachusetts, less than forty miles from New Bedford. And he was a white man: in fact, the first white heavyweight champion in fifteen years. Moore was Ahab-like in his advanced age and, one imagines, as Ahab was a sailor of immense skills, so was Moore a craftsman in the ring. Moore reminded Liebling of Ahab "honing his harpoon for the White Whale." But there was nothing mysterious about Marciano, and he was hardly a giant of a man. In fact, Moore slightly outweighed Marciano for their fight that night.

Moore managed to strike at Marciano in the second round. Marciano had landed a good left then missed with his right. Moore countered with a right hand that knocked Marciano down. But not out. He survived and opened up the next round with his usual aggressive onslaught. By the end of the eighth round, he had knocked Moore down four times. He put Moore down for the count in the ninth round, retaining his championship. The White Whale, for Liebling, had vanquished Ahab.

Marciano retired undefeated not long after the fight. Unlike Ahab, Moore lived to fight again. In fact, he soldiered on, thanks to his ring smarts, for another eight years, retiring at the rather advanced age of fifty. He had fought 220 matches, winning 185 of them—in a remarkable career. In contrast to Ahab, he passed away at the age of eighty-four.

CHAPTER 134

The Chase—Second Day

INITIAL AND FEARLESS BATTLING AGAINST MOBY DICK

"Ahab is for ever Ahab." Without doubt, but the face that we associate with him changes over time. For one generation, the face of Ahab was John Barrymore's. Since 1956, most have identified Ahab with Gregory Peck, although some may think of Patrick Stewart when they summon up a visage for Ahab.

We need an Ahab for the twenty-first century. Who should play the role? Many actors come to mind immediately. There is no lack of leading men capable of performing adventurous feats, walking and talking with authority, mimicking obsession, and thirsting after revenge. But will they falter when asked to ponder the muddy waters of metaphysics and the muck of meaning?

No one could do a better job starring as Ahab and directing the film than the German-born director, occasional actor, and writer Werner Herzog.

Now that you have recovered from the shock of this recommendation, let me make my case.

Herzog is an Ahab-like figure. He is a man driven by obsessions, willing to take enormous risks, and visionary to the core of his being.

As a younger man, he learned that the dean of German film historians, Lotte Eisner, was deathly ill in Paris. Herzog got the news in Munich, and he determined that she could not die until after he had arrived at her bedside. A reasonable enough hope, but he decided that he must go from Munich to Paris by foot, beginning his trek on November 23. Through snow and sleet, slush and stink, he wends his way. He rarely stays at a hotel, preferring to smash in windows of summer homes and seek refuge for the night. Driven forward by some inner voice that he dare not ignore, lest his respected friend perish, Herzog continues his trek until he arrives at Eisner's bedside on 14 December. She lived for another nine years.

In some ways, Herzog has already made film versions of *Moby-Dick*. *Aguirre, Wrath of God* (1972). Aguirre is an officer in Pizarro's bloody expedition against the Incas. Things go awry and supplies are desperately needed. Aguirre accompanies a superior officer and an odd lot of individuals (the wife of the officer and Aguirre's daughter come along) to scout downriver for necessities. Aguirre quickly usurps power, driven to discover El Dorado. His monomania about the fabled city pushes him forward; his comrades slowly die all around him, from starvation, disease, and hostile natives. It is a futile, absurd, grueling quest, akin to sailing a lone ship across the oceans in search of a single whale. Aguirre remains, seemingly unconquered, and sheltered by his madness.

A similar theme is present in his film *Fitzcarraldo* (1982) about a man with a dream—he wants to open an opera house on the edge of the Peruvian jungle, celebrating civilization and satisfying his yen for the art. But to make it happen, he must first brave the Amazon and the elements, taking his beat-up old steamer boat up a mountain, with a forty-degree incline, in order to navigate a new route so that unclaimed areas where rubber trees grow can become cultivated. Fitzcarraldo succeeds and the opera house opens, to his great pride. In the story upon which the film is loosely based, the aftermath of that opening is less than splendid, as a majority of those performing the opera come down with jungle ailments and die.

Isn't the dialogue from that film pure Ahabian? Here is Fitzcarraldo on his dream:

> As truly as I stand here before you, someday I shall bring Grand Opera to the jungle! I will outnumber you! I will outbillion you! I am the grand spectacle in the forest! I am the inventor of rubber! Only through me will rubber become a word!

Herzog has taken his camera and concerns to the ends of the earth. In the documentary *Encounters at the End of the World* (2007), he trains his lens on Antarctica, filming men and women as they perform their daily chores in the most chilling of environments. He even follows scientists as they dive into the icy waters to film various sea creatures. In another documentary, *Grizzly Man* (2005), Herzog pieces together the life of Timothy Treadwell, a visionary and monomaniac, if ever there was one. Treadwell is the self-proclaimed protector and friend of grizzly bears in the Alaskan wilderness. Treadwell sleeps in a tent, wanders around while bears are near, and films them. But his status as an alien in this environment eventually catches up to him, as one bear kills him and a friend. Treadwell can be with but not of the grizzlies.

At the heart of Herzog's filmography, and the list of his films is lengthy, is a common theme—men who are guided by a vision, with intensity, passion, and monomania. They will go into the most ferocious climes; indeed, that is in part what makes their quest both precarious and positive. They are Ahabs, following their own marching orders, pursuing a fate that seems to have been "immutably decreed."

Herzog is the man for the role as actor and director. No one blazes with his inner intensity and fixed vision. No one would be more willing to leap upon the back of a giant whale if a scene is to succeed. And no one has as much experience, as Herzog, in occupying a mind like Ahab's.

What of Herzog's heavily German-inflected English? No one will notice it in the face of his intense dive into the depths of the character and the environment.

Figure 28.
Gregory Peck as Ahab, bound up for eternity with the White Whale, in John Huston's 1956 film of *Moby-Dick*.

CHAPTER 135

The Chase—Third Day

THE FINAL, FATAL BATTLE WITH MOBY DICK

In this chapter we bid adieu to the White Whale. His presence, symbolic and real, has been central to the novel. But what do we really know of the White Whale? We never hear his voice.

What if Moby Dick were to have a voice? Jack London, in his novel *White Fang* (1906), allowed a dog (mostly wolf) to speak. Has anyone given Moby Dick similar potential?

Moby Dick, known by his whale name Whitewave, is the main character in Alison Baird's novel for young readers, *White as the Waves* (1999). It is a curious and winning conceit.

We learn that Moby, born to a whale called Seaspray, has always been a bit of an outsider, given his shockingly white skin. He dreams of adventure, has an inquiring mind, appreciates the history of his species, and comes into contact with those strange creatures—human beings.

"Killer-men" aboard ships, he learns, are hunting him and his brethren. They kill Moontail, his wife who is heavy with child. He is horrified at how the whalers hack away at the bodies of dead whales like Moontail. Enraged, Whitewave vows revenge. He also comes to realize that if these "killer-men" are not stopped, then whales are doomed to extinction.

When he comes into contact with whalers he attacks. His huge jaw snaps their small ships to bits. In the battles, Whitewave is riddled with harpoons and wounds but he survives. He becomes convinced that there is a oneness to the universe, a meaning that is secure, and this thought buoys him. He fights now not for revenge but for survival.

Whitewave encounters Ahab and whaling men, who are towing a wounded young bull whale. In the ensuing fight with the whalers, White-wave destroys the boat, although he is hit with a harpoon from another boat and then another. But Whitewave manages to upend the boat with the sweep of his tail. Despite his terrible wounds, he inspects the damage and comes upon the harpooner who has wounded him flailing away in the sea. He examines this man, who has such piercing eyes. But this man, who we know to be Ahab, is a foe of immense proportions. He lunges with a knife, aiming at Whitewave's eye. In defense, he strikes at Ahab, using his lower jaw, clipping off his attacker's leg. Whitewave assumes that Ahab is "doomed"—his blood stains the water and sharks are nearby.

Ahab survives, however, picked up by a ship. His desire for revenge against Whitewave begins to boil.

We also know how the final battle between Ahab and Whitewave will be decided. But the whale cannot savor his victory over a maddened foe, for the horrible wounds inflicted upon Whitewave will soon prove fatal.

For every fanatical Ahab, there are a hundred Starbucks, men who hunt for profit. Even if the demand for whale oil plummeted in the nineteenth century, whale's meat and other byproducts still enthuse commercial hunters, now armed with exploding harpoons and sonar devices. According to Richard Ellis, the preeminent chronicler and illustrator of whales and whaling, the slaughter of sperm whales continues, despite various regulations. Under the name of "research," Japanese whaling ships kill thousands of whales, and the government has worked to end any moratorium on whale-hunting.

But the sperm whale—thanks to international whaling regulations and declining need for them as a food source—will survive man as a hunter. Whether the sperm whale will be able to survive man as ecological terrorist, with global warming, remains to be decided.

Figure 29.
Queequeg's coffin transformed into a life buoy for Ishmael, from John Huston's 1956 film of *Moby-Dick*.

Epilogue

"And I only am escaped alone to tell thee."

Job

ISHMAEL SURVIVES THE SINKING OF *PEQUOD*, RESCUED BY THE *RACHEL*

Born Robert Zimmerman in Duluth, Minnesota, he has long been known as Bob Dylan. We call him by that name, just as we accept the enigmatic and sometime absent narrator of *Moby-Dick* by his chosen moniker, Ishmael. Dylan and Ishmael are survivors, fellow troubadours. Both of them, each in his own manner, are self-created, fictions of authenticity, bearers of meandering meaning. Each of them dwells in the folds of the great American imagination. Dylan has gargled for close to fifty years about the American experiment, its pitfalls and potential. He is the Ishmael of our era.

In February 1964, along with a few friends, Dylan traveled in a station wagon across the United States, beginning in New York, ending in California, with stops along the way in New Orleans for Mardi Gras and to breathe in the Rocky Mountain air. It was a tumultuous moment in Dylan's life and in the rhythms of rock and roll. Dylan was an institution of folk music, having sung "Blowin' in the Wind," his classic ballad for equal rights for African-Americans. But the winds, as Dylan recognized, were blowing in a new direction on the music scene. As he traveled across the country, he heard on radio stations everywhere the music of the Beatles—a combination of blues roots, romantic love ballads, and energy electrified. Rather than be left behind, Dylan forged ahead, experimenting with electric guitar (a sin in the eyes of some folk purists) and continuing with his forays into surrealistic and poetic songs.

Out of this moment, Dylan composed and recorded "Bob Dylan's 115th Dream," which appeared on his fourth album, *Bringing It All Back Home* (1965). In this song, Captain Ahab, referred to as Captain Arab, is the central figure, along with Bob Dylan adopting the persona of Ishmael. The song is, in effect, not unlike *Moby-Dick*, a surreal meditation about the failed promise of America. In a waterfall of mixed historical references and absurdities, Captain Arab commands the Mayflower—he espies a new land, and announces to his crew, "Boys, forget the whale." Ishmael, who is in the business of naming, says: "I think I'll call it America."

No sooner has Arab touched land than he is greedily engaged in "Writing up some deeds," buying land with beads, and building forts. Arab and most of the crew somehow end up in jail, for crimes imagined or in the offing. Dylan/Ishmael manages to extricate himself from his own problems with the "paranoid" authorities. In the last stanza of the song, he announces that "Well, the last I heard of Arab / He was stuck on a whale." Dylan/Ishmael then sees "three ships a-sailin'" in his direction. "I asked the captain what his name was / And how come he didn't drive a truck / He said his name was Columbus / I just said, 'Good luck.'"

From Ahab, with the Mayflower and Nina, Pinta, and Santa Maria thrown in, this hallucinatory, comic, and symbolic Dylan song is a fitting destination point for our voyage with Moby Dick, Ahab, and company. Like Melville, Dylan is riffing about the lost promise of America, about how monomaniacal devotion to hunting the white whale and profits leads to ruin. But upon the shards of utopian dreams, the artist, be it Melville or Dylan, constructs a new vision, an artistic voice that beguiles us, that demands that we see with new eyes or hear with pricked ears. In the best of these creations, the onus is upon us to dive into the mysteries of meaning, into the storms of existence, and into the depths of our souls. Melville's *Moby-Dick*, as Dylan and so many others have recognized, is America's novel, the text upon which the American artistic imagination is built and upon which it rises and falls.

ACKNOWLEDGMENTS

The well-known line about how we stand on the shoulders of giants applies with particular force to anyone going to sea with *Moby-Dick*. I have profited greatly from the work of many Melville scholars, in particular, Hershel Parker, Howard P. Vincent, Andrew Delbanco, John Bryant, Robert Wallace, Philip Hoare, Charles Olson, Michael Paul Rogin, Nathaniel Philbrick, Clare L. Spark, Richard Ellis, Harrison Hayford, Leon Howard, Newton Arvin, Richard Chase, James Creech, Samuel Otter, and Melton M. Sealts Jr., and many others. Elizabeth Schultz has been exemplary, not only for her scholarship on *Moby-Dick* and art, but for her encouragement for this book. Jay Parini has supported and inspired me in numerous ways, especially by example. David Dowling's reader's report for Oxford University Press was a model of insight, twenty-two double-spaced typed pages worth!

As the dedication to this book indicates, friends have played a central role in my life and scholarship. Without being able to bounce ideas and drafts off them, I would have floundered even more. In addition to those named in the dedication, I especially thank Kendra Boileau, Melody Herr, Michael McCormick, James Cushing, Kyle Cuordileone, Steven Marx, Larry Inchausti, Maria Quintana, Ralph Leck, Richard Shaffer, Michael Hannon, Nancy Dahl, Leslie Sutcliffe, Heidi Harmon, Joan Rubin, Martin Woessner, David A. Hollinger, John Thomas, Cindy Green, Jeffrey Ward Larsen, Russell Bunge, and Christina Firpo. D. Graham Burnett, Matt Kish, Hershel Parker, Dan Beachy-Quick, Robert Wallace, and Elizabeth Schultz each glanced at a chapter. For helpful tips and information, thank you to John Bryant, Alton Chase, and Samuel Otter. Charles Capper put me in touch with the folks at Oxford.

John Thornton, my agent, has been unflagging in his support for this project. Oxford University Press editor Shannon McLachlan's enthusiasm for the project has been appreciated from day one. Brendan O'Neill, who took over from Shannon, has been most expert in handling all matters. Marc Schneider has been excellent in overseeing of production, Marian John Paul has patiently and expertly dealt with proofs and Michael

Durnin copy-edited with a sure hand. With two brief sentences, Paul Elie made me realize that a change of direction for the book was in order. I owe much to Julian Barnes's *Flaubert's Parrot* and Charles Simic's *Dime-Store Alchemy: The Art of Joseph Cornell* for stylistic inspiration.

Janice Stone and Linda Hauck, from Cal Poly's Interlibrary Loan, helped me secure research materials for this book. Linda Halisky, dean of the College of Liberal Arts, and Andrew Morris, chair of the department of history, have been supportive, along with my wonderful colleagues in the department and administrative staff, Kim Barton, Linda Eaton, and Sherrie Miller.

All of my work depends fiercely on the love and support from my wife, Marta Peluso, and my dad, Morris Cotkin.

CREDITS

The author and publisher gratefully acknowledge the permission granted to reproduce the copyright material in this book. Every effort has been made to trace copyright holders and to obtain their permission for the use of copyright material. The publisher apologizes for any errors or omissions in the above list and would be grateful if notified of any corrections that should be incorporated in future reprints or editions of this book.

Fig. 1:
Photograph by Scott Krafft, Charles Deering McCormick Library of Special Collections, Northwestern University Library.   13

Fig. 2:
Andrea Bryant, design, "From a Whale's Point of View." Illustration by Andrea Bryant. 2008.   14

Fig. 3:
"Moby Dick Inn," Chad Perry (January, 2010), New Bedford, MA.   19

Fig. 4:
Rockwell Kent, courtesy of the Rockwell Kent Legacies and Plattsburgh State Art Museum.   21

Fig. 5:
Kim Weston, "Moby Dick Meets Mr. and Mrs. Avocado," Weston Photography, Carmel Highlands. Copy from collection of Elizabeth Schultz, courtesy of the artist.   24

Fig. 6:
Photograph by Bob Penn; from *Moby Dick* (1956), courtesy Warner Bros. Pictures. Photofest.   29

Fig. 7:
Ko-Towatowa, from *Narrative of the U.S. Exploring Expedition* (Philadelphia: Lea and Blanchard, 1845), vol. 2, p. 396.   44

Fig. 22:
Matt Kish, *Moby-Dick in Pictures: One Drawing for Every Page* (Portland, OR: Tin House Books, 2011), p. 109; colored pencil, ink, and marker on found paper; 11 inches by 7.75 inches. Courtesy of the artist. 197

Fig. 23:
Artwork by Catherine Roach. 202

Fig. 24:
© 1998 USA Networks, Photofest. 205

Fig. 25 and 26:
"Ahab 2" shirt designed by Kristin Walko; courtesy Kristin Walko. Yellow shirt with whale and Ahab, designed by Mat Hudson, Moby-Dick Tee Shirt Design, courtesy of Mat Hudson and Threadless Tees. 209

Fig. 27:
Charles Wilkes, frontispiece from *Narrative of the U.S. Exploring Expedition* (Philadelphia: Lea and Blanchard, 1845). 232

Fig. 28:
Still from *Moby Dick* (1956), courtesy Warner Bros. Pictures. Photofest. 251

Fig. 29:
Still from *Moby Dick* (1956), courtesy Warner Bros. Pictures. Photofest. 253

Excerpts from *Call Me Ishmael* by Anne Finger, reprinted by permission of the publisher, University of Nebraska Press.

Excerpts from *A Whaler's Dictionary* by Dan Beachy-Quick by permission of Milkweed Editions. Excerpts from *Spell* by Dan Beachy-Quick reprinted by permission of the publisher, Ahsahta Press, Boise State University.

Excerpts from "Genoa" by Paul Metcalf in *Paul Metcalf: Collected Works, 1956–1976* reprinted by permission of publisher, Coffee House Press, Minneapolis.

Excerpts from Damion Searls, ed., *; or The Whale* from *Review of Contemporary Fiction* 29. Copyright © 2009 Dalkey Archive Press.

Excerpt from "The Quaker Graveyard in Nantucket" from *Lord Weary's Castle* by Robert Lowell. Copyright 1946 by Robert Lowell. Copyright © renewed 1974 by Robert Lowell. Used by permission of Houghton Mifflin Harcourt Publishing Company. All rights reserved.

NOTES

CHAPTER 1

Albert Camus, "Herman Melville," *Lyrical and Critical Essays*, trans. Philip Thody (1952; London: Hamish Hamilton, 1967), pp. 205–9. Elizabeth Hawes, *Camus: A Romance* (New York: Grove Press, 2009). Excellent full accounts of Melville and *Moby-Dick* are Hershel Parker, *Herman Melville: A Biography*, 2 vols. (Baltimore and London: Johns Hopkins University Press, 1996, 2002), Andrew Delbanco, *Melville: His World and Work* (New York: Knopf, 2005), Philip Hoare, *Leviathan: or, The Whale* (London: Fourth Estate, 2008). On whaling in general, see Eric Jay Dolin, *Leviathan: The History of Whaling in America* (New York and London: Norton, 2007); on whales in general, see Richard Ellis, *Men and Whales* (New York: Knopf, 1991); on sperm whales in particular, see Richard Ellis, *The Great Sperm Whale: A Natural History of the Ocean's Most Magnificent and Mysterious Creature* (Lawrence: University of Kansas Press, 2011). Also wonderful, see D. Graham Burnett, *The Sounding of the Whale: Science and Cetaceans in the Twentieth Century* (Chicago and London: University of Chicago Press, 2012). Nathaniel Philbrick's *Why Read Moby-Dick?* (New York: Viking, 2011), is a lively and insightful rumination about the book. A good introduction to the surfacing of the novel and its characters in American culture can be obtained by listening to Kurt Andersen's 2004 National Public Radio program *American Icons* (http://www.studio360.org/2011/dec/30/). Newcomers to *Moby-Dick* would be well served by looking at *Herman Melville: Moby-Dick*, ed. Nick Selby (New York: Columbia University Press, 1999). On the popular reaction, see M. Thomas Inge, "Melville in Popular Culture," in *A Companion to Melville Studies*, ed. John Bryant (New York: Greenwood Press, 1986), pp. 695–739, and Elizabeth Schultz, "Melville in Visual Media and Popular Culture," in *A Companion to Herman Melville*, ed. Wyn Kelley (Malden, MA: Blackwell, 2006), pp. 532–52.

CHAPTER 2

James McCune Smith, "Our Leaders," *The Works of James McCune Smith: Black Intellectual and Abolitionist*, ed. John Stauffer (Oxford and New York: Oxford University Press, 2006), pp. 123–7; also the introduction by John Stauffer, pp. xiii–xl; Smith, "Horoscope," *Works*, pp. 143–8, 179 n. 3. Robert S. Levine and Samuel Otter, eds., *Frederick Douglass and Herman Melville: Essays in Relation* (Chapel Hill: University of North Carolina Press, 2008); Robert K. Wallace, *Douglass and Melville: Anchored Together in Neighborly Style* (New

Bedford, MA: Spinner Publications, 2005); John Stauffer, *The Black Hearts of Men: Radical Abolitionists and the Transformation of Race* (Cambridge: Harvard University Press, 2001); William S. McFeely, *Frederick Douglass* (New York and London: Norton, 1991), pp. 74–85. Frederick Douglass, *My Bondage and My Freedom* (Salem, NH: Ayer, 1984), pp. 341–56. On the "oscillating" aspects of Melville's politics, throughout his life, see Dennis Berthold, "Democracy and its Discontents," in *A Companion to Herman Melville*, pp. 149–164.

CHAPTER 3

David Dowling, *Chasing the White Whale: The Moby-Dick Marathon; or, What Melville Means Today* (Iowa City: University of Iowa Press, 2010), pp. 43–69.

CHAPTER 4

Barry Werth, *The Scarlet Professor: Newton Arvin, A Literary Life Shattered by Scandal* (New York: Talese/Doubleday, 2001), pp. 58–63, 73; Gerald Clarke, *Capote: A Biography* (New York: Simon & Schuster, 1988), p. 129; Phoebe Piece Vreeland and Daniel Aaron, quoted in George Plimpton, *Truman Capote: In Which Various Friends, Enemies, Acquaintances, and Detractors Recall His Turbulent Career* (New York: Talese/Doubleday, 1997), pp. 63–5; John Malcolm Brinnin, *Truman Capote: Dear Heart, Old Buddy* (New York: Delacorte Press, 1986), 20; Lawrence Grobel, *Conversations with Capote* (New York and Scarborough, Ontario: New American Library, 1985), p. 105; K. A. Cuordileone, "'Politics in an Age of Anxiety': Cold War Political Culture and the Crisis in American Masculinity, 1949–1960," *Journal of American History* 87 (September, 2000), pp. 515–45; David K. Johnson, *The Lavender Scare: The Cold War Prosecution of Gays and Lesbians in the Federal Government* (Chicago and London: University of Chicago Press, 2004). On the Kinsey Report, see Miriam G. Reumann, *American Sexual Character: Sex, Gender, and National Identity in the Kinsey Reports* (Berkeley: University of California Press, 2005), pp. 54–85; John D'Emilio and Estelle B. Freedman, *Intimate Matters: A History of Sexuality in America* (New York: Harper & Row, 1988), pp. 285–6; Chris Castiglia, "'A Democratic and Fraternal Humanism,' The Cant of Pessimism and Newton Arvin's Queer Socialism," *American Literary History* 21 (Spring, 2009), pp. 159–182; Newton Arvin, "The House of Pain: Emerson and the Tragic Sense," in *American Pantheon*, ed. Daniel Aaron and Sylvan Schneider (New York: Delacorte Press, 1966), pp. 16–38.

CHAPTER 5

Edward H. Rosenberry, *Melville and the Comic Spirit* (Cambridge, MA: Harvard University Press, 1955); Richard Boyd Hauck, *A Cheerful Nihilism: Confidence and the "Absurd" in American Humorous Fiction* (Bloomington: Indiana University Press, 1971), pp. 77–111; Jane Mushabec, *Melville's Humor: A Critical Study* (Hamden, CT: Archon, 1981), pp. 79–110; Constance Rourke, *American Humor: A Study in the National Character* (New York: Harcourt, Brace, & Co., 1931), p. 196; John Bryant, *Melville and Repose: The Rhetoric of Humor in the American Renaissance* (Oxford: Oxford University Press, 1993), esp. pp. 186–233.

CHAPTER 6

Rory Nugent, *Down at the Docks* (New York: Pantheon, 2009).

CHAPTER 7

Hart Crane, "At Melville's Tomb," *The Complete Poems of Hart Crane*, ed. Marc Simon (New York and London: Liveright, 1986), p. 33. Helpful analyses of "At Melville's Tomb" are Sherman Paul, *Hart's Bridge* (Urbana: University of Illinois Press, 1972), pp. 134–142; Paul Mariani, *The Broken Tower: A Life of Hart Crane* (New York: Norton, 1999), pp. 190–191; Cleanth Brooks and Robert Penn Warren, *Understanding Poetry* (1938; New York: Holt, Rinehart, & Winston, 1960), pp. 320–22; Vincent Quinn, *Hart Crane* (New York: Twayne, 1963), pp. 41–2; R. W. Butterfield, *Broken Arc: A Study of Hart Crane* (Edinburgh: Oliver & Boyd, 1969), pp. 115–117. Also, Langdon Hammer and Bram Weber, eds., *O My Land, My Friends: The Selected Letters of Hart Crane* (New York: Four Walls Eight Windows, 1997), pp. 276–8, 286; On Harriet Monroe, see Joan Shelley Rubin, *Songs of Ourselves: The Uses of Poetry in America* (Cambridge and London: Harvard University Press, 2007), pp. 336–7.

CHAPTER 8

Gilbert Haven and Thomas Russell, *Incidents and Anecdotes of Rev. Edward T. Taylor* (Boston: Russell, 1872); Robert Collyer, *Father Taylor* (Boston: American Unitarian Association, 1906); Dickens quoted in Michael Kammen, *Salvages & Biases: The Fabric of History in American Culture* (Ithaca, NY: Cornell University Press, 1987), pp. 194–5.

CHAPTER 9

Giorgio Mariani, "'Chiefly Known by His Rod': The Book of Jonah, Mapple's Sermon, and Scapegoating," in *"Ungraspable Phantom": Essays on Moby-Dick*, ed. John Bryant, Mary K. Bercaw Edwards, and Timothy Marr (Kent, OH: Kent State University Press, 2006), pp. 37–57; Nathalia Wright, *Melville's Use of the Bible* (1949; New York: Octagon Books, 1969); T. Walter Herbert, Jr., "Calvinist Earthquake: *Moby-Dick* and Religious Tradition," *New Essays on Moby-Dick* (Cambridge: Cambridge University Press, 1986), pp. 109–140; Howard P. Vincent, *The Trying-Out of Moby-Dick* (Boston: Houghton Mifflin, 1949), pp. 65–75.

CHAPTER 10

On the play, see Henry Jenkins, "The Whiteness of the Whale (Revisited)," *http://www.henryjenkins.org/2007/05/moby_dick.html*, May 16, 2007; the first act of the play can be viewed online at *http://techtv.mit.edu/videos/111-moby-dick-then-and-now-full-play—act-i*, accessed December 26, 2011; for a brief summary of the play by *Moby-Dick* scholar Wyn Kelley, see *http://techtv.mit.edu/videos/557-plot-of-moby-dick-then-and-now*, accessed December 26, 2011.

CHAPTER 11

Herman Melville, "Hawthorne and His Mosses" in *The American Intellectual Tradition: A Sourcebook*, ed. David A. Hollinger and Charles Capper (New York: Oxford University Press), vol. 1, pp. 374–85. Brenda Wineapple, *Hawthorne: A Life* (New York: Knopf, 2003), p. 378.

CHAPTER 12

Almost all information about Melville is contained in Hershel Parker's two-volume biography.

CHAPTER 13

Clifford Geertz, *The Interpretation of Cultures* (New York: Basic Books, 1973), p. 5.

CHAPTER 14

Vincent, *The Trying-Out of Moby-Dick*, pp. 81–8; Hector St. John Crevecoeur, *Letters from an American Farmer* (1782; Garden City, NY: Doubleday, n.d.), pp. 99, 150–155; Obed Macy, *The History of Nantucket* (Boston: Hilliard, Gray, 1835); Joseph C. Hart, *Miriam Coffin, or The Whale-Fisherman* (New York: Harper, 1835); Nathaniel Philbrick, *Away Off Shore: Nantucket Island and Its People, 1602–1890* (New York: Penguin, 2011); Lisa Ann Norling, *Captain Ahab Had a Wife: New England Women & the Whalefishery, 1720–1870* (Chapel Hill: University of North Carolina Press, 2000).

CHAPTER 15

Perry Miller, *The Raven and the Whale: The War of Words and Wits in the Era of Poe and Melville* (New York: Harcourt, Brace & World, 1956); Sheila Post-Lauria, *Correspondent Colorings: Melville in the Marketplace* (Amherst: University of Massachusetts Press, 1996); Donald Yanella, "Writing the 'Other Way': Melville, the Duyckinck Crowd, and Literature for the Masses," in *A Companion to Melville Studies*, ed. John Bryant (New York, Greenwood Press, 1986), pp. 64–81. For a subtle examination of Melville and Duyckinck, see David Dowling, *Literary Partnerships and the Marketplace: Writers and Mentors in Nineteenth-Century America* (Baton Rouge: Louisiana State University Press, 2012), pp. 37–60.

CHAPTER 16

Richard Drinnon, *Facing West: Indian Hating and Empire Building* (New York: Schocken Books, 1980), pp. 35–45, 355–62. For a classic account that lays blame upon the Pequots for the war, see Alden T. Vaughan, "Pequots and Puritans: The Causes of the War of 1637," *William and Mary Quarterly* Third Series, 21 (April, 1964), pp. 256–69. For more, Steven T. Katz, "The Pequot War Reconsidered," *New England Quarterly* 64 (June, 1991), pp. 206–224; Michael Freeman, "Puritans and Pequots: The Question of Genocide," *New England Quarterly* 68 (June, 1995), pp. 278–93; Stephen Katz, "Pequots and the Question of Genocide: A Reply to Michael Freeman," *New England Quarterly* 68 (December, 1995), pp. 641–9; Ronald Dale Karr, "'Why Should You Be So Furious?': The Violence of the Pequot War," *Journal of American History* 85 (December, 1998), pp. 876–909.

CHAPTER 17

David Jaffé, *Stormy Petrel and the Whale: Some Origins of Moby-Dick* (Baltimore, MD: Port City Press, 1976), pp. 41–56. Another possible source for Queequeg can be found in George Lillie Craik, *The New Zealanders* (1830), cited in Dowling, *Chasing the White Whale*, p. 49. On Friedrich Ledebur, see Lawrence Grobel, *The Hustons* (New York: Scribners, 1989), p. 426.

CHAPTER 18

Available through *http://itunes.apple.com/us/album/whos-on-first/id344792722*.

CHAPTER 19

Sacvan Bercovitch, *The American Jeremiad* (Madison: University of Wisconsin Press, 1978); Wright, *Melville's Use of the Bible*, pp. 60–72.

CHAPTER 20

Hart, *Miriam Coffin*; Norling, *Captain Ahab Had a Wife*.

CHAPTER 21

Raymond Chandler, "The Simple Art of Murder" (1950), *http://www.en.utexas.edu/ amlit/amlitprivate/scans/chandlerart.html*, accessed December 26, 2011.

CHAPTER 23

Harrison Hayford, "Unnecessary Duplicates: A Key to the Writing of *Moby-Dick*," in *New Perspectives on Melville*, ed. Faith Pullin (Kent, OH: Kent State University Press, 1978), pp. 128–161; George R. Stewart, "The Two Moby-Dicks," *American Literature* 25 (January, 1954), pp. 417–48; James Barbour, "The Composition of *Moby-Dick*," *American Literature* 47 (November, 1975), pp. 343–60; Leon N. Howard, "'Ungainly Gambols' and Circumnavigating the Truth: Breaking the Narrative of *Moby-Dick*," in *Ungraspable Phantom*: pp. 27–8; Richard Chase, *Herman Melville; A Critical Study* (New York: Macmillan, 1949), pp. 30–41, passim.

CHAPTER 24

Eric Jay Dolin, *Leviathan*, pp. 17–29; Richard Ellis, *Men and Whales*, pp. 141–3; John Smith, *A Description of New England* (London: Humfrey Lownes, 1616), pp. 17, 46. Also, Granville Allen Mawer, *Ahab's Trade: The Saga of South Seas Whaling* (New York: St. Martin's Press, 1999); Lance E. Davis, Robert E. Gallman, and Karin Gleiter, *In Pursuit of Leviathan: Technology, Institutions, Productivity and Profits in American Whaling, 1816–1906* (Chicago and London: University of Chicago Press, 1997).

CHAPTER 25

Mick Wall, *When Giants Walked the Earth: A Biography of Led Zeppelin* (New York: St. Martin's Press, 2009).

CHAPTER 26

F. O. Matthiessen, *American Renaissance: Art and Expression in the Age of Emerson and Whitman* (New York: Oxford University Press, 1941), p. 444. On the work, see Giles Gunn, *F. O. Matthiessen: The Critical Achievement* (Seattle: University of Washington Press, 1975), pp. 68–104; Jonathan Arac, "F. O. Matthiessen: Authorizing an American Renaissance," in *The American Renaissance Reconsidered*, ed. Walter Benn Michaels and Donald E. Pease (Baltimore, MD: Johns Hopkins University Press, 1985), pp. 126–7. Arthur Kinoy, who revered Matthiessen, is the source for Matthiessen's appreciation of this material from Melville: Arthur Kinoy, *Rights on Trial: The Odyssey of a People's Lawyer* (Cambridge and London: Harvard University Press, 1983), pp. 40, 264. Also, Matthiessen, *From the Heart of Europe* (New York: Oxford University Press, 1948), p. 36. Matthiessen, "The Making of a Socialist" and Paul M. Sweezy, "Labor and Political Activities," both in *F. O. Matthiessen: A Collective Portrait*, ed. Paul M. Sweezy and Leo Huberman (New York; Henry Schuman,

1950), pp. 3–20, 61–75. Michael Cadden, "Engendering F.O.M.: The Private Life of *American Renaissance*," in *Engendering Men: The Question of Male Feminist Criticism*, ed. Joseph A. Boone and Michael Cadden (New York and London: Routledge, 1990), pp. 27–8. Louis Hyde, ed., *Rat & the Devil: Journal Letters of F. O. Matthiessen and Russell Cheney* (Hamden, CT.: Archon Books, 1978), pp. 29, 124, 200. For strong interpretations of Matthiessen and many other Melville scholars, see Clare L. Spark, *Hunting Captain Ahab: Psychological Warfare and the Melville Revival* (Kent, OH, and London: Kent State University Press, 2001).

CHAPTER 27

C. L. R. James, *Mariners, Renegades, and Castaways: The Story of Herman Melville and the World We Live In* (1953; Hanover, NH, and London: University Press of New England, 2001), pp. 9–10, 29, 40–42, 50, 62–5. James to Constance Webb, July 28, 1944, in *Special Delivery: The Letters of C. L. R. James to Constance Webb, 1939–1948*, ed. Anna Grimshaw (Oxford, and Cambridge, MA: Blackwell, 1996), p. 167; On James, see Anna Grimshaw, "Notes on the Life and Work of C. L. R. James," in *C. L. R. James: His Life and Work*, ed. Paul Buhle (London and New York: Allen & Busby, 1986), pp. 9–21; Constance Webb, *Not Without Love: Memoirs* (Hanover, NH, and London: University Press of New England, 2003); Stuart Hall, "C. L. R. James: A Portrait," in *C. L. R. James's Caribbean*, ed. Paget Henry and Paul Buhle (Durham, NC: Duke University Press, 1992), pp. 3–16. C. L. R. James, *The Black Jacobins: Toussaint L'Ouverture and the San Domingo Revolution* (1938: New York: Vintage Books, 1989).

CHAPTER 28

See account in Rockwell Kent, *N by E* (New York: Literary Guild, 1930); Kent, *Wilderness: A Journal of a Quiet Adventure in Alaska* (New York and London: Putnam's, 1920); David Traxel, *An American Saga: Life and Times of Rockwell Kent* (New York: Harper & Row, 1980), pp. 17, 47; Kent to William Kittredge, November 11, 1926, quoted in Jake Wien, *Rockwell Kent: The Mythic and the Modern* (New York: Hudson Hills, 2005), p. 134; Fridolf Johnson, "Introduction," *Rockwell Kent: An Anthology of His Works*, ed. Fridolf Johnson (New York: Knopf, 1982), pp. 44, 49; Kent, *It's Me O Lord: The Autobiography of Rockwell Kent* (New York: Dodd, Mead & Co., 1955), p. 438. Good on background for Kent and his artwork is Constance Martin, *Distant Shores: The Odyssey of Rockwell Kent* (Berkeley: University of California Press, Chameleon Books, in association with the Norman Rockwell Museum, 2000). Perhaps the strongest set of illustrations, done after Kent's, is by Barry Moser, for an edition from the Arion Press, published in 1979.

CHAPTER 29

Delbanco, *Melville*, pp. 59–60, 114–115.

CHAPTER 30

Walter Benjamin, "Theses on the Philosophy of History," in *Illuminations: Essays and Reflections*, ed. Hannah Arendt (New York: Schocken Books, 1968), p. 256.

CHAPTER 31

Edward F. Edinger, *Melville's Moby-Dick: A Jungian Commentary, "an American Nekyia"* (New York: New Directions, 1978), pp. 66–73.

CHAPTER 32

D. Graham Burnett, *Trying Leviathan: The Nineteenth-Century New York Court Case That Put the Whale on Trial and Challenged the Natural Order* (Princeton and Oxford: Princeton University Press, 2007), pp. 95, 20, 171.

CHAPTER 33

Norman Mailer, "Evaluations: Quick and Expensive Comments on the Talent in the Room," *Advertisements for Myself* (1959; Cambridge and London: Harvard University Press, 1992), pp. 463–73; Harvey Breit, "Talks with Norman Mailer," in *Conversations with Norman Mailer*, ed. J. Michael Lennon (Jackson and London: University of Mississippi Press, 1988), p. 15; Bernard Horn, "Ahab and Ishmael at War: The Presence of *Moby-Dick* in *The Naked and the Dead*," *American Quarterly* 34 (Autumn, 1982), pp. 379–95; George Cotkin, *Existential America* (Baltimore and London: Johns Hopkins University Press, 2003), pp. 184–192.

CHAPTER 34

Carolyn L. Karcher, *Shadow Over the Promised Land: Slavery, Race, and Violence in Melville's America* (Baton Rouge and London: Louisiana State University Press, 1980); Samuel Otter, *Melville's Anatomies* (Berkeley: University of California Press, 1999), pp. 101–171.

CHAPTER 35

Melville to Evert Duyckinck, March 3, 1849, in Merrell R. Davis and William H. Gilman, eds., *The Letters of Herman Melville* (New Haven: Yale University Press, 1960), p. 79; Ralph Waldo Emerson, "The American Scholar," *Nature, Addresses, and Lectures* (New York: AMS Press, 1979), pp. 56–7.

CHAPTER 37

Susan Jacoby, *Wild Justice: The Evolution of Revenge* (New York: Harper & Row, 1983); William Ian Miller, *Eye for an Eye* (Cambridge, UK: Cambridge University Press, 2006).

CHAPTER 38

As with much information on Melville, turn to Parker's two-volume biography. On various characters, see Wendy Stallard Flory, "Melville, *Moby-Dick* and the Depressive Mind: Queequeg, Starbuck, Stubb, and Flask as Symbolic Characters," in Bryant et al., eds., *"Ungraspable Phantom"*, pp. 81–99.

CHAPTER 39

Alan Dagovitz, "*Moby-Dick*'s Hidden Philosopher: A Second Look at Stubb," *Philosophy and Literature* 32 (October, 2008), pp. 330–46.

CHAPTER 40

Sterling Stuckey, *African Culture and Melville's Art: The Creative Process in Benito Cereno and Moby-Dick* (New York: Oxford University Press, 2009); Lawrence Levine, *Black Culture and Black Consciousness: Afro-American Folk Thought from Freedom to Slavery* (New York: Oxford University Press, 1977), pp. 21–4, 38, 165–6.

CHAPTER 41

Fred V. Bernard, "The Question of Race in *Moby-Dick*," *Massachusetts Review* 43, no. 3 (Autumn, 2002), pp. 384–404; W. Jeffrey Bolster, *Black Jacks: African American Seamen in the Age of Sail* (Cambridge: Harvard University Press, 1977); Toni Morrison, "Unspeakable Things Unspoken: The Afro-American Presence in American Literature," *Michigan Quarterly Review* 28, no. 1 (Winter, 1989), esp. pp. 15–18. For the complexities of pinning down a meaning to Melville's presentation of race and slavery—and in terms of the survival of the union—see Michael Paul Rogin, *Subversive Genealogy: The Politics and Art of Herman Melville* (New York: Knopf, 1983), pp. 140–151.

CHAPTER 42

William Gass, *On Being Blue: A Philosophical Inquiry* (Manchester, UK: Carcanet New Press, 1979), p. 75; Albert Murray, *The Blue Devils of Nada: A Contemporary Approach to Aesthetic Statement* (New York: Pantheon, 1996).

CHAPTER 43

Tony Kushner, *Angels in America: A Gay Fantasia on National Themes* (New York: Theatre Communications Group, 2003), pp. 114, 159, 214, 280; Kushner, *The Art of Maurice Sendak: 1980 to the Present* (New York: Abrams, 2003), pp. 64–5; Atushi Fujita, "Queer Politics to Fabulous Politics in *Angels in America*: Pinklisting and Forgiving Roy Cohn," in *Tony Kushner: New Essays on the Art and Politics of the Plays*, ed. James Fisher (Jefferson, NC: McFarland, 2006), pp. 112–126; Michael Cadden, "Strange Angel: The Pinklisting of Roy Cohn," in *Approaching the Millennium: Essays on Angels in America*, ed. Deborah R. Geis and Steven F. Kruger (Ann Arbor: University of Michigan Press, 1997), pp. 78–89.

CHAPTER 44

Lawrence Buell, "The Unkillable Dream of the Great American Novel: *Moby-Dick* as Test Case," *American Literary History* 20 (Spring–Summer, 2006), pp. 132–159; J. W. De Forest, "The Great American Novel," *The Nation* (January 9, 1868), pp. 27–9; A. O. Scott, "In Search of the Best," *New York Times* (May 21, 2006), sec. G17.

CHAPTER 45

Nathaniel Philbrick, *In the Heart of the Sea: The Tragedy of the Whaleship Essex* (New York: Viking, 2000), pp. 80–83, 89, 118.

CHAPTER 46

Anne Finger, "Moby Dick, or, The Leg," *Call Me Ahab* (Lincoln and London: University of Nebraska Press, 2009), pp. 181, 182, 186, 191, 192.

CHAPTER 47

Stacy Kors, "Call Me Laurie," *Salon*, October 5, 1999, *http://www.salon.com/ent/ feature/1999/10/05/moby*; Bernard Holland, "The Water, The Whale, and a Bold Bass Guitar," *New York Times* (October 7, 1999), sec. E1; Roselee Goldberg, "Hitching a Ride on the Great White Whale," *New York Times* (October 3, 1999), sec. AR29; Jon Pareles, "The Same Old Song? Homages as Updates," *New York Times* (October 16, 1999), sec. B13; Scott Saul, "Mysteries of the Postmodern Deep," *Theater* 30 n.2. (2000), pp. 160–163. On Herrmann, see Steven C. Smith, *The Life and Music of Bernard Herrmann* (Berkeley: University of California Press, 1991), pp. 53, 62; Bernard Herrmann, "On Composing a Setting of 'Moby Dick,'"

New York Times (April 7, 1940), p. 129. Barber's quote is in Michael S. Sherry, *Gay Artists in Modern American Culture: An Imagined Conspiracy* (Chapel Hill: University of North Carolina Press, 2007), p. 175.

CHAPTER 48

See Hershel Parker, "Historical Note," in *Moby-Dick, or The Whale*, ed. Harrison Hayford, Hershel Parker, and G. Thomas Tanselle (Evanston and Chicago: Northwestern University Press and The Newberry Library, 1988), pp. 686–9; Henry David Thoreau, *Journal* (November 14, 1851); *New York Daily Times* (November 15, 1851), p. 4; William S. Ament, "Bowdler and the Whale: Some Notes on the First English and American Editions of *Moby-Dick*," *American Literature* 4 (March, 1932), pp. 39–46. An invaluable compendium of these reviews is Hershel Parker and Harrison Hayford, eds., *Moby-Dick As Doubloon: Essays and Extracts, 1851–1970* (New York: Norton, 1970). Also, Hugh H. Hetherington, *Melville's Reviewers: British and American, 1846–1891* (Chapel Hill: University of North Carolina Press, 1961); David Potter, "Reviews of Moby-Dick," *Rutgers University Library Journal* 3 (1940), pp. 62–5. On the literary expectations and how *Moby-Dick* confounded them, see James Cesarano Jr., "The Emergence of *Moby-Dick*: An Archaeology of Its Critical Value," Ph.D. dissertation, State University of New York at Binghamton, 1984. Also, G. Thomas Tanselle, "The Sales of Melville's Books," *Harvard Library Bulletin* (April 18, 1969), pp. 195–215.

CHAPTER 49

Walter E. Bezanson, "Moby-Dick: Work of Art," in *Moby-Dick Centennial Essays*, ed. Tyrus Hillway and Luther S. Mansfield (Dallas: Southern Methodist University Press, 1953), pp. 36ff. Alfred Kazin, "Introduction to *Moby-Dick*," reprinted in *Contemporaries* (Boston and Toronto: Atlantic Monthly Press, 1962), pp. 30–33. Donald E. Pease, "*Moby-Dick* and the Cold War," and Jonathan Arac, "F.O. Matthiessen: Authorizing an American Renaissance," in *The American Renaissance Reconsidered: Selected Papers from the English Institute, 1982–1983*, ed. Walter Benn Michaels and Donald E. Pease (Baltimore and London: Johns Hopkins University Press, 1985), pp. 113–155, 90–112; Eric Cheyfitz, "Matthiessen's *American Renaissance*: Circumscribing the Revolution," *American Quarterly* 41 (June, 1989), pp. 341–61.

CHAPTER 50

Lawrance Thompson, *Melville's Quarrel with God* (Princeton: Princeton University Press, 1952), pp. 197–203; Robert L. Gale, *A Herman Melville Encyclopedia* (Westport, CT: Greenwood Press, 1995), p. 136.

CHAPTER 51

MC Lars, *The Graduate* (Horris Records, 2006); Henry Jenkins, "Teaching 'Ahab': An Interview with MC Lars," *http://henryjenkins.org/2008/09/teaching_ahab_an_interview_wit.html*, accessed December 26, 2011; for the lyrics, go to *http://www.lyricsmania.com/ahab_lyrics_mc_lars.html*, accessed December 26, 2011.

CHAPTER 52

"Mr. Barrymore on Props and Pictures," *New York Times* (May 6, 1928), p. 111; John Kobler, *Damned in Paradise: The Life of John Barrymore* (New York: Athenaeum, 1977), pp. 216–17.

CHAPTER 53

Steve Chandler and Terrence N. Hill, *Two Guys Read Moby-Dick: Musings on Melville's Whale and Other Strange Topics* (Bandon, OR: Robert D. Reed, 2006).

CHAPTER 54

Karcher, *Shadow Over the Promised Land*, pp. 55–61; Don Geiger, "Melville's Black God: Contrary Evidence in the 'Town-Ho's Story'" *American Literature* 25, no. 4 (January, 1954), pp. 464–71.

CHAPTER 55

Harold Rosenberg, "The American Action Painters," *The Tradition of the New* (Chicago: University of Chicago Press, 1960), pp. 23–39; Evan R. Firestone, "Herman Melville's 'Moby-Dick' and the Abstract Expressionists," *Arts Magazine* 54 (1980), pp. 120–124; Deborah Solomon, *Jackson Pollock: A Biography* (New York: Simon and Schuster, 1987), pp. 138–9.

CHAPTER 56

Arthur C. Danto, Timothy Hyman, and Marco Livingstone, eds., *Red Grooms* (New York: Rizzoli, 2004); Michael Mills, "Whale's Tale," *Broward Palm Beach New Times*, December 10, 1998, *http://www.browardpalmbeach.com/1998-12-10/culture/whale-s-tale*.

CHAPTER 57

Frank Stella, *Working Space: The Charles Eliot Norton Lectures, 1983–84* (Cambridge and London: Harvard University Press, 1986); Robert K. Wallace, *Frank Stella's Moby-Dick: Works & Shapes* (Ann Arbor: University of Michigan Press, 2000); Elizabeth A. Schultz, *Unpainted to the Last: Moby-Dick and Twentieth-Century American Art* (Lawrence: University Press of Kansas, 1995), esp. pp. 148–160; Jane Kinsman, "*The Fountain*: A Print Epic: Frank Stella and Ken Tyler," National Gallery of Australia, *http://nga.gov.au/InternationalPrints/Tyler/Default.cfm?MnuID=6&Essay=artonview19*, accessed December 26, 2011; "1989 Previews from 36 Creative Artists," *New York Times* (January 1, 1989), sec. H1.

CHAPTER 58

Thomas Farber, *On Water* (Hopewell, NJ: Ecco Press, 1994), pp. 6–7, 24–25.

CHAPTER 59

Tim Severin, *In Search of Moby Dick: Quest for the White Whale* (London: Little Brown, 1999), pp. 158, 180–182, 188.

CHAPTER 60

George Cotkin, *Existential America*.

CHAPTER 61

Dan McCall, *The Silence of Bartleby* (Ithaca and London: Cornell University Press, 1989).

CHAPTER 62

Ellis, *Men and Whales*, p. 259; Peter Matthiessen, *Blue Meridian: The Search for the Great White Shark* (New York: Penguin, 1971), pp. 8–14. Roys quoted in Frederick P. Schmitt, Cornelius de Jong, and Frank H. Winter, *Thomas Welcome*

Roys: *America's Pioneer of Modern Whaling* (Charlottesville: University Press of Virginia, 1980), p. 71.

CHAPTER 63

Many of the quotes from letters about the project are in the Harrison Hayford Papers, Northwestern University Archives. Also, "Harrison Hayford (1916–2001): His Students Recollect," *Leviathan* 5 (March, 2003), pp. 7–86; Hershel Parker, "Foreword," to Harrison Hayford, *Melville's Prisoners* (Evanston, IL: Northwestern University Press, 2003), pp. xvii–xi; G. Thomas Tanselle, "Melville and the World of Books," in *A Comparison to Melville Studies*, ed. John Bryant (New York: Greenwood Press, 1986), esp. pp. 814–17. On criticism of the standard edition, see Julian Markels, "The Moby-Dick White Elephant," *American Literature* 66 (March, 1994), pp. 105–122. On "fluid texts," see John Bryant, "Witness and Access: The Uses of the Fluid Text," *Textual Cultures* 2 (Spring, 2007), pp. 16–42.

CHAPTER 64

Stefan Aust, *Baader–Meinhof: The Inside Story of the R.A.F.*, trans. Anthea Bell (New York: Oxford University Press, 2008), pp. 193–6, 313.

CHAPTER 65

Nancy Shoemaker, "Whale Meat in American History," *Environmental History* 10, no. 2 (April, 2005), pp. 269–94.

CHAPTER 66

Rebecca Newberger Goldstein, *36 Arguments for the Existence of God: A Work of Fiction* (New York: Pantheon, 2010), pp. 351–5; Thompson, *Melville's Quarrel with God*.

CHAPTER 67

Herman Melville, *Moby Dick*, abridged by A. E. W. Blake (New York: Alfred A. Knopf, 1926), 9.

CHAPTER 68

John T. Irwin, *American Hieroglyphics: The Symbol of the Egyptian Hieroglyphics in the American Renaissance* (New Haven and London: Yale University Press, 1980). Ralph Waldo Emerson, "Nature," *Nature, Addresses, and Lectures*, ed. Robert E. Spiller and Alfred R. Ferguson (Cambridge and London: Harvard University Press, 1971), p. 18.

CHAPTER 69

Edwin Haviland Miller, *Melville* (New York: Venture/Braziller, 1975), pp. 315–16; Hershel Parker, *Herman Melville: A Biography, 1851–1891*, vol 2, pp. 920–21; Parker, *Melville: The Making of the Poet* (Evanston, IL: Northwestern University Press, 2007); "Literary Fame," *New York Times* (November 12, 1890), p. 7. On September 29, 1891, that paper's obituary for Melville gave the title of his great work as "Mobie Dick." Keats is quoted in Stanley Plumly, *Posthumous Keats: A Personal Biography* (New York: Norton, 2008), p. 77.

CHAPTER 70

Dan Beachy-Quick, *A Whaler's Dictionary* (Minneapolis, MN: Milkweed Editions, 2008), pp. 32, xiii, xi, 45, 106, 179, 315, 317; poetry lines from *Spell* (Boise: Ahsahta Press, 2004), p. 104.

CHAPTER 71

Henry David Thoreau, *The Journal of Henry David Thoreau*, ed. Bradford Torrey and Francis H. Allen (Salt Lake City, UT: Peregrine Smith Books, 1984), vol. 3, p. 115 [November 14, 1851]; *New York Daily Times* (November 15, 1851), p. 2.

CHAPTER 72

Elizabeth Renker, *Strike through the Mask: Herman Melville and the Scene of Writing* (Baltimore and London: Johns Hopkins University Press, 1996), pp. 49f.

CHAPTER 73

Sanford E. Morrison, "More Chartless Voyaging: Melville and Adler at Sea," *Studies in the American Renaissance* (1986), pp. 373–84.

CHAPTER 74

Discussions with Hershel Parker, Morro Bay, 2009.

CHAPTER 75

Ned Rozell, "Bowhead Whales May Be the World's Oldest Mammals," *Alaska Science Forum*, February 15, 2001, *http://www.gi.alaska.edu/ScienceForum/ ASF15/1529.html*.

CHAPTER 76

Charles Olson, *The Maximus Poems* (New York: Jargon/Corinth Books, 1960), p. 32; Olson, *Call Me Ishmael* (Baltimore and London: Johns Hopkins University Press, 1967), pp. 69, 71, 39, 47–51, 61–2, 13–15. Tom Clark, *Charles Olson: The Allegory of a Poet's Life* (New York: Norton, 1991), pp. 22–3, 30–33, 67–8 70–72, 77–8. Ralph Maud, ed., *Selected Letters: Charles Olson* (Berkeley: University of California Press, 2000), pp. 10, 17; Ralph Maud, *Charles Olson's Reading: A Biography* (Carbondale: Southern Illinois University Press, 1996), pp. 25–7, 35, 49; Merton M. Sealts Jr., "A Correspondence with Charles Olson," *Pursuing Melville, 1940–1980* (Madison and London: University of Wisconsin Press, 1982), p. 94. Also, Lewis Mumford, "Baptized in the Name of the Devil," *New York Times* (April 6, 1947), sec. BR4; Edward Dahlberg, "Moby-Dick, A Hamitic Dream," in *The Edward Dahlberg Reader*, ed. Paul Carroll (New York: New Directions, 1967), pp. 171, 175, 178, 180. Also, Paul Christensen, ed., *In Love, In Sorrow: The Complete Correspondence of Charles Olson and Edward Dahlberg* (New York: Paragon House, 1990), pp. 3–30. Ann Charters, *Olson/Melville: A Study in Affinity* (Berkeley, CA: Oyez, 1968), p. 15; Olson, "Equal That Is, To the Real Itself," in *Human Universe and Other Essays*, ed. Donald Allen (New York: Grove Press, 1967), pp. 52, 60, 120–122.

CHAPTER 77

Los Angeles Times: (November 19, 1937), sec. A6; (April 24, 1938), sec. E3; (January 25, 1931), sec. F1; (August 24, 1938), p. 5; *New York Times* (March 4, 1963), p. 20; *Los Angeles Times* (December 4, 1964), sec. D14; "Advertisement," *New York Times* (June 22, 2009), sec. D10; Carolyn Kellogg, "Jacket Copy," *Los Angeles Times*, March 6, 2009, *http://articles.latimes.com/2009/mar/06/ entertainment/et-kindle6*

CHAPTER 78

John Barrymore, *Confessions of an Actor* (Indianapolis: Bobbs-Merrill, 1926), [unpaginated] last page. Also, "'Sea Beast' Now in Last Week at Figueroa," *Los Angeles Times* (April 17, 1926), sec. A6. On Barrymore, see Kobler, *Damned in Paradise*, p. 213; Gene Fowler, *Good Night, Sweet Prince: The Life and Times of John Barrymore* (Philadelphia: Blakiston, 1944), p. 235. In 1930, Barrymore reprised his role in an early talking film, *The White Whale*. The essential story remained much the same as *The Sea Beast*, bearing but dim relation to the novel. In the new version, however, the dastardly half-brother is reduced to a weakling, without threat to Ahab. And, of course, the movie ends with Ahab getting the girl and the whale! William Dean Howells quoted in Geoffrey Wheatcroft, "Horrors beyond Tragedy," *Times Literary Supplement*, no. 5071 (June 9, 2000), p. 10.

CHAPTER 79

Sam Ita, *Moby-Dick: A Pop-Up Book* (New York: Sterling, 2007).

CHAPTER 80

Donald L. Miller, *Lewis Mumford: A Life* (Pittsburgh and London: University of Pittsburgh Press, 1989), pp. 4–5, 263, 267, 271, 456; Lewis Mumford, *Sketches From Life: The Autobiography of Lewis Mumford, The Early Years* (Boston: Beacon Press, 1982), pp. 140, 163–8, 249–51, 456; The diving metaphor for Melville was a favorite of Mumford's. See Mumford, "The Writing of 'Moby-Dick'," *American Mercury* 15 (December, 1928), p. 490; Mumford to Weaver, May 21, 1928, Weaver Papers, Columbia University Archive; Casey Nelson Blake, "The Perils of Personality: Lewis Mumford and Politics After Liberalism," in *Lewis Mumford: Public Intellectual*, ed. Thomas P. Hughes and Agatha C. Hughes (New York: Oxford University Press, 1990), pp. 291ff.; Mumford, *Herman Melville* (New York: Harcourt, Brace & Co., 1929), p. 5–6.

CHAPTER 81

Bryant Simon, *Everything but the Coffee: Learning about America from Starbucks* (Berkeley: University of California Press, 2009), p. 28. On the corporate history, see Howard Schultz and Dori Jones Yang, *Pour Your Heart into It: How Starbucks Built a Company One Cup at a Time* (New York: Hyperion, 1997).

CHAPTER 82

Melville to Duyckinck, December 13, 1850, in Davis and Gilman, eds., *Letters of Herman Melville*, pp. 115–117.

CHAPTER 83

Thompson, *Melville's Quarrel With God*. Howard P. Vincent, in a review of the volume, marveled at Thompson's interpretive skill but wondered whether it had, in the end, "tripped" him into a failure to understand Melville's religious sentiments: Vincent, "The Real Melville?," *New York Times Book Review* (March 30, 1952), sec. BR6; for this view of Melville's intention, see Vincent, *The Trying-Out of Moby-Dick*, pp. 389–91. While Ahab is heroic, Vincent finds that he is "destructive" in his quest. Ishmael survives because he realizes the "great spiritual theme" of the book, "the metaphysics of resurrection." Thus, in the Epilogue, Melville returns the reader to "the memorable message of Father

Mapple." On Ishmael's openness leading to pantheism, see Charles Feidelson Jr., "Introduction," *Moby-Dick* (Indianapolis: Bobbs-Merrill, 1964), p. 15.

CHAPTER 84

Francis Steegmuller, ed., *The Letters of Gustave Flaubert, 1830–1857* (Cambridge: Belknap Press, 1980); Julian Barnes, *Flaubert's Parrot* (New York: Vintage International, 1990).

CHAPTER 85

Paul Metcalf, ed., *Enter Isabel: The Herman Melville Correspondence of Clare Spark and Paul Metcalf* (Albuquerque: University of New Mexico Press, 1991), pp. 16, 55, 57, 97; Metcalf, "Genoa: A Telling of Wonders," *Paul Metcalf: Collected Works, 1956–1976* (Minneapolis: Coffee House Press, 1996), pp. 79, 136, 179, 185.

CHAPTER 86

G. Thomas Tanselle, "Historical Note VI," *Moby-Dick*, ed. Hayford, Parker, and Tanselle, pp. 679–681. Ray Bradbury to John Huston, August 29, 1954, John Huston Papers. On Breen and censorship, see Thomas Doherty, *Hollywood's Censor: Joseph I. Breen and the Production Code Administration* (New York: Columbia University Press, 2007). Breen to Marvin Mirisch, May 17, 1954; Mirisch to Breen, May 19, 1954, John Huston Papers, Production Code File; "Analysis of Film Content," July 13, 1956; "Film Cleared Form," John Huston Papers, Production Code File.

CHAPTER 87

Harold Bloom, *How to Read and Why* (New York: Scribner, 2000), pp. 235–8, 254–63; Dennis Sansom, "Learning from Art: Cormac McCarthy's *Blood Meridian* as a Critique of Divine Determinism," *Journal of Aesthetic Education* 41 (Spring, 2007), pp. 1–19; Petra Mundik, "'Striking the Fire Out of the Rock': Gnostic Theology in Cormac McCarthy's *Blood Meridian*," *South Central Review* 26 (Fall, 2009), pp. 72–97.

CHAPTER 88

New York Times (May 15, 1949), sec. BR18; (July 3, 1950), p. 23; (July 9, 1950), sec. BR5; (July 23, 1950), sec. BR2; (November 6, 1960), sec. E9; (May 10, 1959), sec. BRA3; (May 19, 1946), p. 18; (November 27, 1960), sec. E7; (December 12, 1954), p. 130; (October 28, 1962), p. 272; *Moby-Dick* (New York: Classics Illustrated, 1956), pp. 1, 47.

CHAPTER 89

Star Trek II: The Wrath of Khan, directed by Nicholas Meyer (Paramount Pictures, 1982). In *Star Trek: First Contact*, directed by Jonathan Frakes (Paramount Pictures, 1996), Captain Jean-Luc Picard is Ahab-like in his search for revenge against the Borgs. He quotes from *Moby-Dick* but thanks to his limits, he does not destroy the good ship *Enterprise*. On *Star Trek* and the novel, see Elizabeth Jane Wall Hinds, "The Wrath of Ahab; or, Herman Melville Meets Gene Roddenberry," *Journal of American Culture* 20, no.1 (Spring, 1997), pp. 43–6.

CHAPTER 90

F. O. Matthiessen, "New Standards in American Criticism," (1929), *The Responsibilities of the Critic* (New York: Oxford University Press, 1952), p. 181; Vernon Louis Parrington, *Main Currents in American Thought*, vol. 2, *The Romantic*

Revolution in America, 1800–1860 (1927; New York: Harcourt Brace, 1954), pp. 249–59. V. F. Calverton, *The Liberation of American Literature* (New York: Charles Scribner's Sons, 1932), pp. xii, 271–2; Granville Hicks, *The Great Tradition: An Interpretation of American Literature since the Civil War* (New York: Macmillan, 1935), pp. 7–8; Larzer Ziff, *Literary Democracy: The Declaration of Cultural Independence in America* (New York: Penguin, 1982), pp. 171–2; Jane Tompkins, *Sensational Designs: The Cultural Work of American Fiction, 1790–1860* (New York and Oxford: Oxford University Press, 1985), pp. 124, 126–8. Obviously, *Uncle Tom's Cabin* was an icon for its time. But does its literary power remain, or is that power consigned to its historical moment? In 1868, J. W. De Forest wondered why America had not produced a great work of fiction. He listed a host of reasons, including that America was too young in culture and experience. The only novel that he felt came close to the prize was *Uncle Tom's Cabin*.

CHAPTER 91

Damion Searls, ed., "Herman Melville's; or The Whale," *Review of Contemporary Fiction* 29 (Summer, 2009), pp. 16–344; Scott Esposito, "The Other Half of Moby-Dick: The Damion Searls Interview," *Quarterly Conversation*, http://quarterlyconversation.com/half-of-half, accessed December 26, 2011.

CHAPTER 92

Jay B. Hubbell, *Who Are the Major American Writers? A Study of the Changing Literary Canon* (Durham, NC: Duke University Press, 1972), p. 335. On Carl Van Doren, see his *Three Worlds* (New York and London: Harper & Bros., 1936); note from Raymond Weaver, attached to letter from Carl Van Doren, July 1, 1919, Weaver Papers, Columbia University Archive, Box 1. Also, Raymond Weaver, "The Centennial of Herman Melville," *The Nation* 109 (August 2, 1919), pp. 145–6; Weaver, "Pierrot Philosophique," unpublished manuscript, Weaver Papers, Columbia University Archive, Box 2, pp. 4–8; On Weaver, see Joseph Freeman, *An American Testament* (London: Victor Gollancz, 1938), pp. 110–115; Cerf, "The Reminiscences of Bennett Cerf," oral history interview, Columbia University Oral History Collection, Butler Library, pp 53–60. Also, Charles Simmons, "Mark Van Doren at Columbia," *New York Times* (December 31, 1972), sec. BR23; Mark Van Doren, *The Autobiography of Mark Van Doren* (New York: Harcourt, Brace, 1958), pp. 301–2; Weaver, *Black Valley* (New York: Viking, 1926); Weaver, *Herman Melville: Mariner and Mystic* (1921; New York: Pageant Books, 1961), pp. 16–18. Also, "Review of Weaver," *Catholic World* 114 (February, 1922), pp. 686–7. On this theme, see Fred Lewis Pattee, "Herman Melville," *The American Mercury* 10 (January, 1927), pp. 33–43.

CHAPTER 93

Toni Morrison, "Unspeakable Things Unspoken: The Afro-American Presence in American Literature," *Michigan Quarterly Review* 28 (Winter, 1989), pp. 1–34; Morrison, *Playing in the Dark: Whiteness and the Literary Imagination* (Cambridge and London: Harvard University Press, 1990), p. 94.

CHAPTER 94

Mark Twain, *Adventures of Huckleberry Finn: Mississippi Writings* (New York: Library of America, 1982), pp. 714, 835; Leslie Fiedler, *An End to Innocence: Essays on Culture and Politics* (Boston: Beacon Press, 1955), pp. 146–7; Fiedler,

Love and Death in the American Novel (New York: Criterion Books, 1960), pp. 209, 344–5.

CHAPTER 95

James Creech, *Closet Writing/Gay Reading: The Case of Melville's "Pierre"* (Chicago and London: University of Chicago Press, 2002).

CHAPTER 96

On Robinson, see Albert Christ-Janer, *Boardman Robinson* (Chicago: University of Chicago Press, 1946). Also, "Obituary, Boardman Robinson," *New York Times* (September 7, 1952), p. 84; Schultz, *Unpainted to the Last*, pp. 64–71; Michael Leja, *Reframing Abstract Expressionism: Subjectivity and Painting in the 1940s* (New Haven and London: Yale University Press, 1993); Clifton Fadiman, "Introduction," *Moby-Dick* (Norwalk, CT: Easton Press, 1977), p. vi; Fadiman stresses that the story is above all mythic and "a book about Evil"; Willard Thorp, *Herman Melville: Representative Selections* (New York: American Book Co., 1938), p. xcix. In his introduction, Thorp presents Melville as a social progressive; Mumford, quoted in Christ-Janer, *Boardman Robinson*, p. 66.

CHAPTER 97

Matthew Moore, "Emoji Dick: Moby Dick to be Translated into Japanese Emoticons," *Telegraph*, September 15, 2011, *http://www.telegraph.co.uk/news/worldnews/asia/japan/6218705/Emoji-Dick-Moby-Dick-to-be-translated-into-Japanese-emoticons.html*; Chris Matyszczyk, "'Moby-Dick' to be Rewritten in Emoticons," *CNET News*, October 17, 2009, *http://news.cnet.com/8301-17852_3-10377272-71.html*. On Mike Keith's Anagram, see *http://www.anagrammy.com/literary/mkeith/poems-dom21.html*, accessed December 26, 2011.

CHAPTER 98

Carl Van Doren, "Lucifer from Nantucket: An Introduction to 'Moby Dick,'" *The Century* 110 (August, 1925), pp. 494–501. Also, "Mr. Melville's 'Moby Dick," *The Bookman* 59 (1924), pp. 154–7. On *White-Jacket* and Melville's condemnation of flogging, see Van Doren, "Melville Before the Mast," *The Century* 108 (June, 1924), pp. 272–7; All stories in this paragraph come from the *New York Times*: (March 4, 1923), sec. XX8; (May 31, 1923), p. 32; (November 1, 1925), sec. BR16; (December 27, 1925), sec. E1; (March 22, 1926), p. 23; (March 16, 1930), sec. N3; (July 11, 1930), p. 1; (April 24, 1931), p. 33; (July 15, 1934), sec. S9. See reviews of Florence Bennett Anderson, *Through the Hawse-Hole: The True Story of a Nantucket Whaling Captain*, and Peter Freuchen, *The Sea Captain*, *New York Times* (July 31, 1932), sec. BR5, and (September 18, 1932), sec. BR8. Also, Helen Morgan, "Off the Whaling Quest: Journey of the Ulysses to Antarctic Revives the Glamour of Fictional Moby Dick," *New York Times* (October 30, 1938), sec. XX3; John Chamberlain, "Books of the Times," *New York Times* (June 25, 1934), p. 13; On the various editions, see G. Thomas Tanselle, *A Checklist of Editions of Moby-Dick, 1851–1976* (Chicago: Northwestern University Press and The Newberry Library, 1976), pp. 13–19; Claire Badaracco, *American Culture and the Marketplace: R. R. Donnelley's Four American Books Campaign* (Washington, DC: Library of Congress, 1992). The best analysis of the drawings in various editions is Schultz, *Unpainted to the Last*, pp. 18–75. On Kent's edition, see Jake Milgram Wien, *Rockwell Kent*, p. 134; Traxel, *An American Saga*, p. 166; All editions are discussed in articles or advertisements from the *New York Times*: (September 11, 1921), p. 48; (November 12, 1922), p. 15; (December 3, 1922), p. 50; (June 27, 1926), sec. BR24. Herman Melville, *Moby Dick*, abridged by Sylvia Chatfield Bates (New York: Charles Scribner's Sons, 1928), p. 117.

CHAPTER 99

K. L. Evans, *Whale* (Minneapolis and London: University of Minnesota Press, 2003), p. 1.

CHAPTER 100

Martha Minow, *Between Vengeance and Forgiveness: Facing History after Genocide and Mass Violence* (Boston: Beacon Press, 1998); Jeffrie G. Murphy and Jean Hampton, *Forgiveness and Mercy* (Cambridge and New York: Cambridge University Press, 1988).

CHAPTER 101

W. Clark Russell, "Sea Stories," and H. S. Salt, "Herman Melville," both reprinted in Parker and Hayford, eds., *Moby-Dick as Doubloon*, pp. 105, 109; Archibald MacMechan, "The Best Sea Story Ever Written," *Queen's Quarterly* 7 (October, 1889), pp. 120–130; for the Masefield poems, go to *http://www.archive.org/details/PoemsAndPlaysOfJohnMasefieldPoems*.

CHAPTER 102

D. H. Lawrence, *Studies in Classic American Literature* (New York: Penguin, 1977), pp. 153–170. Also, H. I. Brock, "D. H. Lawrence Strings Some American Literary Pearls," *New York Times* (September 26, 1923), sec. BR9. On Lawrence, America, and *Moby-Dick*, see Armin Arnold, *D. H. Lawrence and America* (New York: Philosophical Library, 1959), p. 44; Richard Foster, "Criticism as Rage," in *D. H. Lawrence: A Collection of Critical Essays*, ed. Mark Spilka (Englewood Cliffs, NJ: Prentice-Hall, 1964), pp. 151–161; Richard Swigg, *Lawrence, Hardy, and American Literature* (London: Oxford University Press, 1972); David Cavitch, *D. H. Lawrence and the New World* (New York: Oxford University Press, 1969).

CHAPTER 103

In book form, Matt Kish, *Moby-Dick in Pictures: One Drawing for Every Page* (Portland, OR: Tin House Books, 2011).

CHAPTER 104

Michael Chabon, "A Life in Books," *Newsweek* (April 6, 2009), p. 12; Jack Kerouac, *On the Road* (New York: Penguin Books, 2007), p. 234, and John Leland, *Why Kerouac Matters* (New York: Viking, 2007), p. 13; Christopher Lyden, "Interview with Amitav Ghosh," Radio Open Source, November 20, 2008, *http://www.radioopensource.org/amitav-ghosh-and-his-sea-of-poppies*; Marcela Valdes, "Alone Among the Ghosts," *The Nation* (December 8, 2008), p. 17; Augusten Burroughs, "A Life in Books," *Newsweek* (December 8, 2007); E. L. Doctorow, "Composing Moby-Dick: What Might Have Happened," in *"Unspeakable Phantom"*, pp. 15, 16, 22, 24; Jay Parini, *The Passages of H. M.: A Novel of Herman Melville* (New York: Doubleday, 2010); Joyce Carol Oates, "A Woman's Work," *New York Times Magazine* (April 12, 2009), p. 12. Also, John Updike, "Reflections: Melville's Withdrawal," *New Yorker* (May 10, 1982), pp. 120–147; Barbara Z. Thaden, "Charles Johnson's *Middle Passage* as Historiographical Metafiction," *College English* 59 (November, 1992), pp. 753–66; Elizabeth Schultz, "The Power of Blackness: Richard Wright Re-Writes *Moby-Dick*," *African-American Review* 33 (Winter, 1999), pp. 639–54. Chad Harbach, *The Art of Fielding: A Novel* (New York: Little, Brown and Company, 2011).

CHAPTER 105

Andrew Delbanco quoted in, Randy Kennedy, "The Ahab Parallax," *New York Times Week in Review* (June 13, 2010), pp. 1, 8. Paul Watson, as told to Warren Rogers, *Sea Shepherd: My Fight for Whales and Seals*, ed. Joseph Newman (New York and London: Norton, 1982); Paul Watson, *Ocean Warrior: My Battle to End the Illegal Slaughter on the High Seas* (Toronto, Canada: Key Porter, 1994); Watson, *Seal Wars: Twenty-Five Years on the Front Lines with the Harp Seals* (Buffalo, NY: Firefly, 2002). Also, Peter Heller, *The Whale Warriors: The Battle at the Bottom of the World to Save the Planet's Largest Mammals* (New York: Free Press, 2007).

CHAPTER 106

John Huston to Tyrus Hillway, October 13, 1953, John Huston Papers, Margaret Herrick Library, Department of Special Collections, Academy of Motion Picture Arts and Sciences, Los Angeles.

CHAPTER 107

Stewart quoted in Peter Marks, "From Mystic Novel to Manifest Spectacle," *New York Times* (March 15, 1998), sec. T4, T20, T21. Also, Lawrie Mifflin, "Melville Fans," *New York Times* (March 18, 1998), sec. E7.

CHAPTER 108

Fred V. Bernard, "The Question of Race in *Moby-Dick*," *Massachusetts Review* 43 (Autumn, 2002), pp. 387–91; Dowling, *Chasing Moby-Dick*, p. 108.

CHAPTER 109

Huston to Honorable Secretary, October 1, 1955, John Huston Papers, Margaret Herrick Library, Department of Special Collections, Academy of Motion Picture Arts and Sciences, Los Angeles; Bradbury to Huston, March 21, 1956, John Huston Papers, Bradbury File, Huston Papers. Robert Emmet Long, ed., *John Huston: Interviews* (Jackson: University Press of Mississippi, 2001), pp. 14–15. Sam Weller, *The Bradbury Chronicles* (New York: William Morrow, 2005), pp. 210–12, 216–17; "Ray Bradbury's Letters to Rupert Hart-Davis," *Missouri Review* 27, no. 3 (2004), p. 136 [September 9, 1954]. For a humorous and sometimes harrowing account of his time with Huston in Ireland, see Bradbury, *Green Shadows, White Whale: A Novel* (New York: Knopf, 1992), pp. 263–8. For a different account of the dispute between Bradbury and Huston, see Peter Viertel, *Dangerous Friends* (New York: Talese, 1992), p. 217.

CHAPTER 110

Otter, *Melville's Anatomies*, pp. 101–171.

CHAPTER 111

David Park Williams, "Hook and Ahab: Barrie's Strange Satire on Melville," *PMLA* 80 (December, 1965), pp. 483–8.

CHAPTER 112

Robert Lowell, "The Quaker Graveyard in Nantucket," *Selected Poems* (New York: Farrar, Straus & Giroux, 2006), pp. 6–10.

CHAPTER 113

Forrest G. Robinson, *Love's Story Told: A Life of Henry A. Murray* (Cambridge and London: Harvard University Press, 1992), pp. 1–6. Murray's barely concealed autobiography is "The Case of Murr," in *Endeavors in Psychology: Selections from the Personology of Henry A. Murray*, ed. Edwin S. Shneidman (New York: Harper & Row, 1980), 7–51; Henry A. Murray, "In Nomine Diaboli," *New England Quarterly* 24 (December, 1951), pp. 435–6. Alton Chase, *Harvard and the Unabomber: The Education of an American Terrorist* (New York and London: Norton, 2003), pp. 240–50, 280–85, 294.

CHAPTER 114

Sena Jeter Naslund, *Ahab's Wife: or, The Star-Gazer* (New York: William Morrow, 1999).

CHAPTER 115

On "Benito Cereno," see Stuckey, *African Culture and Melville's Art*, pp. 99–124.

CHAPTER 116

Richard Ellis, "Interview: Sea World Killer Whale Attack," *Washington Post*, February 25, 2010, *http://www.washingtonpost.com/wp-dyn/content/discussion/ 2010/02/25/DI2010022502321.html*.

CHAPTER 117

Herman Melville, *Moby-Dick*, adapted by Roy Thomas and Pascal Alixe (New York: Marvel Entertainment, 2008); Melville, *Moby-Dick*, retold by Will Eisner (New York: Nantier, Beall, Minoustchine, 1998); *Hakugei: Legend of Moby Dick*, 3 vols. (ADV films, 2005–2006); "Moby Dick 2.0" *Variety*, September 23, 2008. A German film version of *Moby-Dick* is in the works by Tele München, as a two-part television mini-series, see *http://www.tmg.de/tmg/index.php?StoryID=2 73&websiteLang=en*.

CHAPTER 118

Pirsig was a disciplined sailor. In *Lila: An Inquiry into Morals* (1991), his sequel to *Zen*, the journey takes place upon a ship. Julian Baggini, "An Interview with Robert Pirsig," *http://www.psybertron.org/wp-content/uploads/2006/01/ Pirsig-Baggini-Transcript.htm*, accessed December 26, 2011. In the boffo review that helped *Zen and the Art of Motorcycle Maintenance* gain critical attention (the book had been rejected by 121 publishers), critic George Steiner remarked that "the analogies with *Moby Dick* are patent": "Uneasy Rider," *New Yorker* (April 15, 1974), pp. 144.

CHAPTER 119

Matthew Josephson, *Life Among the Surrealists: A Memoir* (New York: Holt, Rinehart, and Winston), pp. 293, 305; Malcolm Cowley, *Exile's Return: A Literary Odyssey of the 1920s* (New York: Penguin, 1976), p. 228; Mariani, *Broken Tower*, pp. 313–14, 351–3, 419; R. W. B. Lewis, *The Poetry of Hart Crane: A Critical Study*

(Princeton: Princeton University Press, 1967), pp. 248ff; *O My Land*, pp. 131, 283, 314, 514–15; Crane quoted in Gorham Munson, *The Awakening Twenties: A Memoir-History of a Literary Period* (Baton Rouge: Louisiana State University Press, 1985), pp. 205, 230; Hammer and Weber, eds., *Letters of Hart Crane*, pp. 241, 307–308; Paul, *Hart's Bridge*, pp. 195, 232; Alan Trachtenberg, *Brooklyn Bridge: Fact and Symbol* (New York: Oxford University Press, 1965), pp. 161–2; Quinn, *Hart Crane*, p. 79; Tate and Winters quoted in Langdon Hammer, *Hart Crane & Allen Tate: Janus-Faced Modernism* (Princeton: Princeton University Press, 1993), pp. 175–6; John Unterecker, *Voyager: A Life of Hart Crane* (New York: Farrar, Straus & Giroux, 1969), pp. 659, 758; Melville, *White-Jacket* (New York: Library of America, 1983), pp. 763–4; Peggy Baird, "The Last Days of Hart Crane," in Susan Jenkins Brown, *Robber Rocks: Letters and Memories of Hart Crane, 1923–1932* (Middletown, CT: Wesleyan University Press, 1969), p. 173.

CHAPTER 120

http://en.wikipedia.org/wiki/John_Moschitta,_Jr., accessed December 26, 2011.

CHAPTER 121

Frank Lentricchia, *Lucchesi and the Whale* (Durham and London: Duke University Press, 2001), pp. 58, 13, 38, 39, 71, 73.

CHAPTER 122

The Telegraph, June 26, 2009, *http://www.telegraph.co.uk/comment/columnists/jimwhite/5653904/Twitter-literature-Bloke-goes-bonkers-pursuing-whale.html.*

CHAPTER 123

Stanley Milgram, *Obedience to Authority: An Experimental View* (New York: Harper and Row, 1973).

CHAPTER 124

Jaffé, *The Stormy Petrel*; Nathaniel Philbrick, *Sea of Glory: America's Voyage of Discovery: The U.S. Exploring Expedition, 1838–1842* (New York: Viking, 2003).

CHAPTER 125

Charles Olson, "Lear and Moby-Dick," *Twice-a-Year* 1 (Fall–Winter, 1938), pp. 165–189. On the *Lear* connection, see Denis Donoghue, "*Moby-Dick* after September 11th," *Law and Literature* 15 (Summer, 2003), p. 163. Melville, "Hawthorne and His Mosses," p. 378. On his excitement for Shakespeare, see Melville to Evert A. Duyckinck, in Davis and Gilman, eds., *Letters of Herman Melville*, p. 77 [February 24, 1849].

CHAPTER 126

To see the video, go to *http://www.artreview.com/video/video/show?id=1474022: Video:765168*, accessed December 26, 2011.

CHAPTER 127

W. H. Auden, *The Enchafed Flood or The Romantic Iconography of the Sea* (1950) in Auden, *The Complete Works of W. H. Auden: Prose, 1949–1955*, ed. Edward Mendelson (Princeton: Princeton University Press, 2008), vol. 3, pp. 10, 71–2. Auden, "Herman Melville" *Another Time: Poems* (New York: Random House,

1940), p. 20; Auden, "The Christian Tragic Hero," in *The Complete Works of W. H. Auden: Prose, 1949–1955*, ed. Edward Mendelson (Princeton: Princeton University Press, 2002), vol. 2, pp. 258–60.

CHAPTER 128

For an important discussion of the circle of "we," see David A. Hollinger, *Postethnic America: Beyond Multiculturalism* (New York: Basic Books, 1995).

CHAPTER 129

Charles Johnson, *Middle Passage: A Novel* (New York: Atheneum, 1990), pp. 67–70. Barbara Z. Thaden, "Charles Johnson's *Middle Passage* as Historiographic Metafiction," *College English* 59 (November, 1977), pp. 753–66.

CHAPTER 130

Among other candidates for Ahab are Andrew Jackson and Daniel Webster. See Willie T. Weathers, "Moby Dick and the Nineteenth-Century Scene," *Texas Studies in Literature and Language* 1 (Winter, 1960), pp. 477–501; Alan Heimert, "*Moby-Dick* and American Political Symbolism," *American Quarterly* 15 (Winter, 1963), pp. 498–534; Charles H. Foster, "Something In Emblems: A Reinterpretation of *Moby-Dick*," *New England Quarterly* 34 (March, 1961), pp. 3–35; Harry Slochower, "*Moby-Dick*: The Myth of Democratic Expectancy," *American Quarterly* 2 (Autumn, 1950), pp. 259–69. For an interpretation that finds the novel rich with political allegory and with Ahab as having "embodied the dangers facing America in 1850," see Rogin, *Subversive Genealogy*, pp. 124f.

CHAPTER 131

Edward Said, "There Are Many Islams," *Counterpunch*, September 16, 2001, *http://www.counterpunch.org/2001/09/16/there-are-many-islams*; Said, "Collective Passion," *Al-Ahram Weekly*, September 20, 2001, *http://weekly.ahram.org.eg/2001/552/op2.htm*; David Barasmian, "Interview with Edward Said," *The Progressive*, November 2001, *http://www.progressive.org/0901/intv1101.html*; Anthony Lewis, "By Hate Possessed: Reagan's Nicaragua Obsession," *New York Times* (March 24, 1986), sec. A19; Arthur M. Schlesinger Jr., "So Much for the Imperial Presidency," *New York Times* (August 3, 1988), sec. A19; Jake Tapper, "Rove: 'I'm Moby Dick,'" August 13, 2007, *http://abcnews.go.com/blogs/politics/2007/08/rove-im-moby-di*. Also, Donoghue, "*Moby-Dick* after September 11th," pp. 161–188. On Obama compared with Ishmael, see Hendrik Hertzberg, "Iraq's Cost," *New Yorker* (September 13, 2010), p. 22. In his book about eliminationist antisemitism on the part of Germans during the Second World War, Daniel Goldhagen summoned up the image of Ahab, comparing Ahab's zest to kill the White Whale with that of the Germans against the Jews, see Goldhagen, *Hitler's Willing Executioners: Ordinary Germans and the Holocaust* (New York: Knopf, 1996), pp. 398, 399.

CHAPTER 132

Louise M. Gouge, *Ahab's Bride: Book One of Ahab's Legacy* (2004), pp. 25, 53, 232; *Hannah Rose: Book Two of Ahab's Legacy* (2005), p. 67; *Son of Perdition: Book Three of Ahab's Legacy* (2006) (Colorado Springs, CO: River Oak Press).

CHAPTER 133

A. J. Liebling, "Ahab and Nemesis," *New Yorker* (October 8, 1955), *http://www. newyorker.com/archive/1955/10/08/1955_10_08_104_TNY_CARDS_000248048*, accessed December 26, 2011.

CHAPTER 134

Werner Herzog, *Of Walking on Ice: Munich-Paris, 23 November–December 14, 1974* trans. Marje Herzog and Alan Greenberg (New York: Free Association, 2007); Herzog, *Conquest of the Useless: Reflections on the Making of Fitzcarraldo* trans. Kristina Winston (New York: Ecco, 2009).

CHAPTER 135

Alison Baird, *White as the Waves: A Novel of Moby Dick* (St. John's Newfoundland: Tuckamore Books, 1999). Ellis, *The Great Sperm Whale*, pp. 291–300.

EPILOGUE

http://www.bobdylan.com/songs/bob-dylans-115th-dream. An excellent, little-known article that I found quite helpful is John Lardas Modern, "Walter Benjamin's 115th Dream," *Epoché: The University of California Journal for the Study of Religion* 24 (2006), pp. 113–160.

INDEX